ENGENDERING
LATIN AMERICA

VOLUME I

EDITORS:

DONNA J. GUY
UNIVERSITY OF ARIZONA

MARY KARASCH
OAKLAND UNIVERSITY

ASUNCIÓN LAVRIN
ARIZONA STATE UNIVERSITY

SEX &
DANGER

in Buenos Aires

Prostitution,
Family, and Nation
in Argentina

Donna J. Guy

UNIVERSITY OF NEBRASKA PRESS

LINCOLN & LONDON

Acknowledgments for the use
of copyrighted material appear on p. ix.
Copyright © 1990, 1991 by Donna J. Guy
All rights reserved
Manufactured in the United States of America
☯   The paper in this book meets the
minimum requirements of American National Standard
for Information Sciences – Permanence of
Paper for Printed Library Materials,
ANSI Z39.48-1984.
First paperback printing: 1995

Library of Congress Cataloging in Publication Data
Guy, Donna J.
Sex and danger in Buenos Aires : prostitution, family,
and nation in Argentina / Donna J. Guy.
p. cm. – (Engendering Latin America; v.1)
Includes bibliographical references and index.
ISBN 0-8032-2139-8
ISBN 0-8032-7048-8 (pbk.)
1. Prostitution – Argentina – Buenos Aires – History.
2. Women – Argentina – Social conditions.
I. Title.   II. Series.
HQ170.B8G89   1992   306.74'0982'12–dc20
91-8664   CIP

FOR GARY

Contents

Acknowledgments

This project began in 1981. It was financed in part by a Senior Fulbright Lectureship in Great Britain in 1982–83, a National Endowment for the Humanities Senior Summer Fellowship in 1984, and a University of Arizona Sabbatical Grant in 1985–86. Parts of chapters 2 and 3 appeared in an earlier version as "Prostitution and Female Criminality in Buenos Aires, 1875–1937," in *The Problem of Order in Changing Societies: Essays on Crime and Policing in Argentina and Uruguay, 1750–1940*, ed. Lyman Johnson (Albuquerque: University of New Mexico Press, 1990). Parts of chapters 1 and 3 appeared in an earlier version in "White Slavery, Public Health, and the Socialist Position on Legalized Prostitution in Argentina, 1913–1936," *Latin American Research Review* 23, 3 (1988).

Many library research specialists helped me. I particularly thank Georgette Dorn of the United States Library of Congress, Hispanic Division; Hugo A. Costa of the Biblioteca Tornquist; Estela Pagani, Marta Gigena de Molina, and María Victoria Alcaraz of the Archivo Histórico de la Municipalidad de Buenos Aires; and David Doan of the Fawcett Library of the London Polytechnic. Hugo Vainikoff's passion for the history of dubious women, and his generosity in sharing the results of his years of research, were essential to my work. Asunción Lavrin, K. Lynn Stoner, Karen Anderson, Ursula Lamb, Michael John, Hebe Clementi, Kevin Gosner, David Foster, Beatriz Sarlo, Felicity Nussbaum, Doris Sommer, Sheila Slaughter, Jorge Balán, and Julie Taylor helped me clarify fuzzy ideas. Angel Cal checked my notes. Responsibility for the contents is of course my own. Finally I thank my dear friend and husband, Gary Hearn, for putting up with my hectic work schedule and always being there to comfort, critique, and praise.

Introduction

This book is an attempt to integrate gender into Argentine political and economic history by examining the role and image of female prostitution in concepts of work, family, class, and citizenship. Such integration is essential because, as Joan W. Scott has commented, "politics constructs gender and gender constructs politics."[1] Furthermore, gender constructs, and in turn is shaped by, social, economic, and nationalist structures as well. The history of legalized prostitution in Argentina reaffirms this interaction.

Prostitution meant many things to many people. After all, what could a European rabbi, a British feminist, an Argentine doctor, a French-born tango singer, and an Argentine president have in common? The rabbi fretted over the unscrupulous ways Jewish men tempted poor women with marriage and a trip to South America. The feminist castigated men for sexual incontinence outside marriage. The doctor bemoaned the high incidence of syphilis in Buenos Aires. The tango singer lamented emotional betrayal by an unfaithful woman. And the president wanted to deter male homosexuality. Superficially it appeared that each was concerned with a different social or political issue, yet all were talking about the supposed consequences of female sexual commerce in the Argentine capital city, Buenos Aires.

Fears and anxieties about female sexual commerce in late nineteenth- and early twentieth-century Argentina were linked by a common concern about the relation of female sexual commerce to family, class, and nation. Concerns about the regulation of prostitution in Argentina preoccupied Europeans as well as local citizens. Argentina was a country newly reorganized in 1853, potentially attractive to European immigrants, and prostitution laws were among the first type of labor legislation to challenge the basic civil rights of working-class women. Medically supervised female prostitution ordinances were enacted in Buenos Aires and other Argentine cities before Congress finished formulating basic legal codes. In the meantime, the 1853 constitution was supposed to provide the basic ideological and legal underpinnings of the new nation.

According to the constitution, only native Argentine males, or naturalized foreign males, enjoyed political rights of citizenship, principally eligibility for public office and service in the army. Yet anyone born in Argentina was a citizen and thereby eligible to enjoy the non-political rights of citizens, as was any other inhabitant. Whether native-born or foreign, male or female, all had the right to earn a living, own property, practice religion, make a will, and get married.[2]

From the outset, regulations forcing female prostitutes to live in particular lodgings and submit to medical examinations before they could work violated basic constitutional precepts. Municipal officials were quite willing to curtail prostitutes because they believed that the family was the basic unit of their community, and women who did not remain sexually monogamous and who accepted cash for work that should have been performed at home violated family, social, and ultimately national norms.

Argentine politics confirms Benedict Anderson's assertion that family forms a critical link to national identity in most modern nations. He believes that the very definition of citizenship results from the conflation of family and nation into a form of "political love" that creates an imagined community: "Something of this political love can be deciphered from the ways in which languages describe its object: either in the vocabulary of kinship . . . or that of the home. . . . Both idioms denote something to which one is naturally tied. . . . The family has traditionally been conceived as the domain of disinterested love and solidarity."[3] Anderson is explicit about the role of the family in creating the imagined community, but he ascribes specific roles in this process only to men.

Nira Yuval-Davies and Flora Anthias have expanded the study of family and state processes to include women. To them, the family is one of several institutions constituting civil society, and within and outside the family women are key participants in national processes. Women reproduce collectivities and ethnic groups, they engage in ideological reproduction as transmitters of culture, and they participate in national, economic, political, and military struggles.[4]

If women's social and economic roles linked family and nation, then women who existed outside traditional family structures threatened the nation. Prostitution ordinances reaffirmed this view because they removed civil and hence patriotic rights from women who sold sexual favors in the public arena. And by linking inappropriate female labor with cash wages, politicians declared that lower-class women were as dangerous as prostitutes to the imagined Argentine national community. After all, according to the 1871 civil code, the role of good women was to marry and bear future generations. Mothers and children in turn were to obey the male patriarch who would select their occupations, thereby linking the family to class and ultimately, through birth, to the nation. Married women who engaged in reproduction or production outside the home for cash therefore had inheritance or business rights restricted.[5] Through prostitution ordinances councilmen were merely clarifying the parameters of family and citizenship.

Prostitution could not be separated from its relation to gender, reproduction, and capitalism. Hence the perceived need to control prostitutes forced Argentine political leaders to contemplate the threat presented by all women who worked outside the home. Using a combination of medical and class criteria, they realized that women who infected offspring with syphilis, as well as those who abandoned their men, families, or homeland for a life of sexual commerce or economic independence, were equally unacceptable. These women could all give birth to Argentines, and the prospects of a future generation riddled by disease and devoid of family life and economic stability concerned nationalists.

Politics of social control in modern Argentina thus rested upon the relation of gender and class to concepts of citizenship, and policies tended to change over time. Early efforts to control prostitution preceded the formation of a strong middle class with a clear set of bourgeois values. For this reason identifying individuals liable to be denied civil rights in Argentina was potentially much easier than defining the ideal family and citizen in theory and in practice. The application of moral and medical criteria, steeped in gendered definitions, made the task of defining the marginal simpler, and female prostitutes were among the first group examined, though they were not the only ones subjected to the scrutiny of public officials. National identity was central to this process, because Europeans claimed that their women in Buenos Aires bordellos were victims and implied that native-born women were not. In fact, the gendered construction of national identity affected all women, native-born and foreign.

The significance of marginal women to family and state is a critical issue often ignored in prostitution literature. Studies by Michel Foucault have confirmed the need to study the power structure that dominates marginals, one that emanates from multiple sources of authority.[6] Jacques Donzelot elaborated on Foucault's concepts of marginality by arguing that the family functions to create political marginals. It serves as the mechanism by which the modern state deprives the marginal individual of civil rights.[7] The history of legalized prostitution in Argentina shows how this process operates and how poor women shaped the political and social world in which they operated as much as they were forced to conform to regulations created by various political and medical officials.

The furor created by efforts to control prostitution provoked intense debate in Argentina. Most participants hoped they could find a way to make the problem disappear. Instead, all they managed to accomplish was to drive prostitutes into hiding from authorities. Even censorship could not prevent the male public from seeing, imagining, or seeking the services of female prostitutes. Thus efforts to cure Argentina of its prostitution problem turned a group of socially, politically, and economically marginal women into the subjects of a volatile discourse that infused Argentine politics, economics, and culture with gender.

I

On the Road to
Buenos Aires

At the end of the nineteenth century Buenos Aires had a terrible international reputation as the port of missing women, where kidnapped European virgins unwillingly sold their bodies and danced the tango. Some of its victims escaped from sexual bondage and later told horrendous stories of seduction and brutality; others created songs praising the city as their El Dorado.[1] The very name Buenos Aires caused many a European to shudder. Young girls, even those with no intention of migrating abroad, were advised not to walk unescorted at night in England or in European countries. They were discouraged from traveling by train to cities in search of work, lest they be kidnapped and sent abroad to end up in an Argentine bordello.

By the 1860s the Continental press reported frightening stories of women lured away by strangers with false promises of marriage or work, only to be trapped in some sordid house of ill repute. In 1867 a shortage of women in Argentina led two Hungarians, "Bohemian Dovidl" Auerbach and Lieb Hirshkovitz, to develop their entrepreneurial skills. According to a Budapest newspaper, they arranged transportation and promises of marriage for women, then sold them as prostitutes in Buenos Aires.[2] In 1875 Adolf Weissman was arrested in Hungary for escorting girls bound for South American bordellos. He was one of at least twenty-three male associates involved in the Buenos Aires–Montevideo (Uruguay) area.[3]

Alarming reports reached fever pitch. The *Bulletin Continental* claimed in 1889 that two hundred German or Austrian women were held against their will in Buenos Aires by Polish Jewish pimps.[4] In 1890 German authorities arrested Czezich Kantor, a known trafficker, at a Berlin train station. With him were two young Russian girls en route to a Buenos Aires bordello. According to the *Vigilance Record*, the magazine of the British National Vigilance Association, "The only odd thing about this case is that the offender was caught."[5] A letter to the *Arbeiter Zeitung* of Germany, read to the audience at an 1899 congress sponsored by the National Vigilance Association, proclaimed:

> There are hundreds of wretched parents in Europe who do not know whether their daughters are alive or dead, for they have suddenly vanished. . . . Well, we can tell where they have been brought to and what has become of them. They are in Buenos Ayres or Rio de Janeiro. . . . This trade is a very lucrative one, for the men in South America are of a very amorous disposition and "fair merchandise" from European lands easily finds buyers. If anybody wants to find out how the girls are treated they may simply take a walk along the Calle Juan and the Calle Lavalle, those two streets that have been nicknamed by the people "Calle Sangre y Lagrima" (the streets of tears and blood).[6]

Even though these journals occasionally apprised their readers that "there is no more danger in Buenos Ayres than in any large town," all too often the image of an immoral city filled with irresponsible men and victimized women left an indelible impression.[7]

These reports were cautionary tales for independent European females: the fortunate would be rescued; the others wound up in Near Eastern brothels or—horror of horrors—in Buenos Aires. Thus middle-class British and European women learned that the road to Buenos Aires led to white slavery, the international traffic in young women for sexual exploitation.[8]

How many confirmed cases proved the existence of an organized traffic? One? Five? Three thousand? Frequently one or two particularly nasty incidents were sufficient to persuade the European public that their women were endangered in foreign lands. In fact, verifiable cases of white slavery were infrequent, but they did involve a system of forced recruitment by lovers, fiancés, husbands, and professional procurers. Once inside a bordello, however, "white slaves" faced the same prospects as native-born recruits. They were inspected by doctors, monitored by house madams, and arrested by the police if their behavior was publicly offensive.

Contemporary European impressions of Buenos Aires were based partly on true incidents whose frequency was highly exaggerated. Although many European women ended up as prostitutes in foreign cities, few fit the stereotype of the middle-class virgin who had been seduced, drugged, or beaten into submission. Most had engaged in prostitution before arriving in the New World and were fully cognizant of what awaited them there. Despite the fears of the British, their women were rarely found in South American bawdy houses. The vast majority of Europeans came from eastern Europe, France, and Italy.

In many ways the reality of prostitution was less glamorous and more depressing than reflected in most white slavery stories. European prostitutes in Buenos Aires, for the most part, came from poverty-stricken families and worked out of desperation. Marginalized by the industrial revolution, driven from their homelands by hunger or by family, political, or religious persecution, they saw immigration to a new land or even a new continent as the key to survival. Cheap steamship fares and imbalanced sex ratios in rapidly growing port cities made it easier and more attractive for them to emigrate. Under these conditions, prostitution was more typically a self-conscious response to poverty than the result of trickery by an evil procurer. When deception led women into prostitution, family members often played key roles.

European women filled Buenos Aires bordellos during the years of peak European emigration between 1870 and World War I. Compared with the total number of immigrant women in the city, they constituted a small but extremely disturbing minority. Their nationality became an issue because municipal law allowed them to work if they registered, and they had to identify their country of birth. The compilation of statistics obtained from prostitute registries created the "facts" and "evidence" used to promote stories about white slavery.

Fears of white slavery in Buenos Aires were directly linked to European disapproval of female migration. Racism, nationalism, and religious bigotry fueled anxieties. Men could safely travel abroad, but unescorted women faced sexual danger. Women uncontrolled by family or nation could end up marrying unacceptable foreigners of any race and losing their nationality. Duped into sexual slavery, they brought shame to their homelands. In many ways the white slavery debate was the quintessential discourse on how presumed dangers of female immigration linked gender and family issues to national identity and international prejudice.

The international campaign to protect immigrant women began in the 1870s when Jewish groups, fearful of increased anti-Semitic violence in Europe, tried to rally support among moral reform groups. Their goal was to stop the sexual exploitation of Jewish women, most of whom came from Poland and Russia. Ironically, to control deviance within the international

Jewish community, reformers had to create a climate of religious concern. Their reports, however, encouraged the very thing they feared: anti-Semitism.[9]

Jewish men and women had become involved in prostitution rings after social structures collapsed in towns and refugee camps following outbreaks of religious persecution in Germany, Austria, Russia, and Poland. Efforts by the Russian government to deprive Jewish men of their livelihood exacerbated already desperate economic conditions. By the early twentieth century, according to German-Jewish sources, six million Jews in Russia were impoverished, and one-third of Galician (Polish) Jews lived on the brink of starvation.[10] Horrified as the European Jewish community might have been by the presence of Jewish women in foreign brothels, they understood the desperation experienced by many refugee families. As a rabbi noted grimly in 1899, "One must have seen the misery of the Polish Jewish cities . . . to understand that a trip to Buenos Aires is not frightening."[11]

Jewish laws further aggravated political conditions. Orthodox women abandoned by their husbands for any reason could not remarry. After pogroms and political upheaval, many found themselves separated from their husbands, unable to prove whether they were alive or dead. These abandoned women were considered outcasts by their own community and went into prostitution with little coaxing. Many contemporaries believed that such women had voluntarily opted for a life of vice. In fact, questions of volition were irrelevant. The choice was survival or death.[12]

Easily arranged fraudulent religious marriages forced other Jewish women into prostitution. Young girls were literally sold to pimps by poor families lured by large dowry payments. Nefarious traffickers arranged proxy weddings performed without benefit of a rabbi, then shipped the girls to their "husbands." Since a valid marriage made all women subordinate to their husbands, pimp-husbands rarely had trouble forcing wives to "work" to support the family.

Among religious Jews, weddings could be performed by two male witnesses who would sign a marriage certificate. The existence of the *ketubah*, or certificate, when used by traffickers, "made apprehension of the criminal impossible, because he could 'prove' he was the victim's husband."[13] Thus, often with the knowledge and consent of their parents, unmarried women were duped by false promises of marriage and by the belief that they had to obey their husbands. In most cases they too "willingly" took up the life. According to an American investigator who went to Europe in 1909:

A favorite trick of these dealers is to get their victims by a promise of good marriage. . . . The owner of a house of prostitution in South America sends his agents in Galicia a printed engagements blank in Hebrew Language, which is a recognized formula. . . . In these documents the name of the man . . . is already filled in who allegedly wants to marry. The name is usually the one of a procurer, the owner of a house of prostitution or one of his employees. Armed with such documents, the agents visit the poor Jews with large families depicting in the most alluring ways the future of their girls if they would get married in America.[14]

Accounts of Jewish white slavery were published with unnerving frequency in Europe. In 1889 the fourth annual report of the National Vigilance Association, the principal British anti-white slavery society, recounted:

In the course of the spring we were informed of the business details of an arrangement for taking girls to Buenos Ayres for immoral purposes. In the particular party of which we heard three were Jewesses, of whom only one could speak English. . . . The party were to go via Rotterdam, as Havre was not considered safe. All fares were to be paid by the agents, who would secure pleasant treatment for the girls until they arrived at Buenos Ayres. They would sell them there for £200 each, and after deducting the expenses of the passage, the proceeds would be shared by the partners in the business. . . . After . . . anxiously considering the course to be taken, the Committee most reluctantly found themselves unable to go farther and track this crime to its completion.[15]

This was the first of several incidents published in the report. Significantly, the religion and nationality of all other female victims were unmentioned.

The following year the National Vigilance Association veiled references to Jewish criminality in the cloak of national identity. Instead of emphasizing religion, the organization complained that British law was too lenient toward immoral foreigners. It cited the dilemma of three Polish (read Jewish) girls who had left Southampton on a steamer headed ultimately for Buenos Aires. An unnamed foreigner recruited them "professedly to find them good situations in Buenos Ayres, but really to sell them into profligacy there." When a British consul was asked to intervene at an unexpected stop at a "Continental" port, he replied that "as neither the man nor his victims were British subjects, he could not interfere."[16]

In 1903 the German National Committee to Combat White Slavery claimed that among thirty-five known traffickers in Buenos Aires, most were "Polish Jews." Sixty-five percent of registered prostitutes in that city were Polish, Russian, or Austro-Hungarian. "It assumed that most of the women from these three countries were Jewish (and this was probably correct)." Four years later, another report of the National Vigilance Society used surnames to identify victims and criminals as Jewish. Louis Gold and Harry Cohen, "Russian subjects," were accused of trying to force Jane Goldbloom and another woman to leave England for a life of debauchery. Gold decided to recruit women upon receiving a letter offering £100 for "good looking girls with long hair." During the early stages of the trial it became evident that Buenos Aires was the destination, and that Gold believed Goldbloom would not squeal on him: "Sara (aka Jane) won't say anything about me, and you can't prove how old she is. She was born in Russia."[17]

Jewish procurers, who in Argentina and Brazil were often called *caftens* because of the long coats worn by Orthodox Jews, became an organized international ring in major cities all over the world. They were particularly powerful in the Argentine port cities of Buenos Aires and Rosario. Officially ostracized by the local Jewish community, pimps as well as their prostitutes still practiced Judaism, and religious elders refused to modify marriage and divorce laws to deal with European and American immigration problems.

Jewish women from Poland, Russia, and Germany truly constituted the European group most likely to be ensnared by the international traffic in women. Lured into prostitution by inflexible religious laws, the economic desperation of entire families, and the belief that wives should obey their husbands, their survival options if they did not sell their bodies were limited at best. Equally important, Jewish populations were being marginalized and systematically attacked by the very European governments that so harshly criticized Latin American countries for allowing such women to survive as prostitutes.

Bertha Pappenheim, a German-Jewish feminist, clearly stated the special dilemma of the European Jewish prostitutes who ended up in foreign bordellos after other delegates suggested that such women be repatriated:

> Repatriation should be rejected for general reasons, not only because
> it visibly impresses the stigma of prostitution on women and girls . . .

but also because it does not afford sufficient protection from a technical point of view. . . .

In addition, however, it is also my duty as a Jewess to draw your attention to the fate of the Jewish girls, for whom an international binding convention with regard to repatriation would be a great disaster.

There are some European States where the Jewess is driven to vice through physical and mental distress. These Jewesses form a large contingent of the merchandise in the world's White Slave Traffic.

There is no consulate, no philanthropic society, no Home, no "friend" compelled to befriend this Eastern European Jewish girl if she is compulsorily sent back to the frontier of their native country . . . she would be an outlaw and at the mercy of the officials at the frontier and the agents of prostitution.[18]

Even though Pappenheim argued that Jewish women formed a large contingent in the white slave traffic, she did not mean that Jewish women engaged in prostitution more frequently than others, or that there were no other international trafficking rings. They simply were at greater risk to be recruited in this fashion, and that they were Jewish made them highly visible in a Christian world.

French men operated one of several other major organized prostitution rings. The 1889 National Vigilance Association report named the port of Havre as "the best port for a girl to go to, as so many American ships called there." Curiously, this statement implied that women voluntarily sought to migrate to France as well as to the Americas, a strong contrast to the accompanying stories about Jewish women.[19]

Information about organized groups of French pimps was less well reported than that on Jewish traffickers. A 1904 report from the French National Committee claimed that French girls were favored for harems, but the information was not considered reliable. Not until League of Nations investigations in the 1920s did Frenchmen appear to be so systematically involved. By then the Alliance Fraternelle (Fraternal Alliance), as one was known, claimed 250 members in Buenos Aires alone. Why was there such a discrepancy in information? As Edward Bristow succinctly noted: "We knew most about the Jewish sources of supply because Jewish philanthropy was at the forefront of the efforts against the traffic."[20]

British moral reform groups soon became the principal non-Jewish European opponents of white slavery. Protestant moral reform groups outraged by passage of the first of several British contagious diseases acts in 1864 mobilized to force their repeal just as Jewish reformers began to organize. Under 1864 and subsequent Contagious Diseases Acts, unescorted women in specified British port cities and garrison towns could be accused of soliciting, forced to have gynecological exams, and placed in a bordello. False accusations and medical exams with unsterilized specula often condemned women to the very diseases and life-style they sought to avoid. The charismatic feminist Josephine Butler led repeal efforts. She then extended the battle against legalized prostitution to Europe. In 1874 she went to Paris to oppose its prostitution ordinances. What began as an effort to combat the consequences of insatiable male sexuality, immoral procurers, government-regulated prostitution, and arbitrary police and medical powers on a local level soon took on the added dimensions of an international effort that promoted moral repression, nationalistic fears, and the stereotype of the immigrant prostitute as a passive victim.[21]

In 1875 the first international anti–white slavery congress was held in Liverpool. These meetings were convened with increasing regularity and gained support as nationalism competed with moral reform. It soon became evident that representatives were concerned principally with the fate of their own women. As Jewish anti–white slavery reformers contemplated future strategies at a special conference held in 1910, one of their members pointed out that "we are here to discuss [the subject] as a specifically Jewish one. What then was the Jewish differentia? . . . simply . . . an exceptional situation of persecution and lawlessness."[22] Yet non-Jewish groups identified the same problems when their women were found in foreign bordellos. What united national and religious organizations was their common fear and the possibility that goals such as an international treaty to rescue women in foreign bordellos might succor their own women.[23]

THE CATHOLIC-PROTESTANT DEBATE

During these anti–white slavery conferences, male sexual appetite seemed insufficient to explain the fate of immigrant women. Increased emphasis upon nationalistic or religious concerns was useful because it allowed moral reformers to blame others for the ills befalling their female nationals in foreign lands. Rather than recognize their own complicity, Europeans perceived the roots of the problem to be inherent female vulnerability and the immorality of host societies. That poor women were in colonial or postcolonial societies, in countries where the dominant race or religion was often distinct from that of their homeland or families, thus provided comforting political, racial, and religious explanations.

Argentina and Buenos Aires became ideal targets for vilification. A former Spanish colony with a Catholic heritage, the country had only recently ended years of dictatorship and antagonism toward Europe. By the 1860s Argentina reestablished trade links with Europe, particularly Great Britain. The country was attractive to Europeans looking for work or for land to farm, and women from all over Europe migrated alone or with family members. A few ended up in bordellos, and their plight outraged compatriots back at home. That prostitution was legal in Buenos Aires made it possible to blame Argentines without examining other possible causes. Religious differences reinforced nationalistic concern. Unlike the Protestant British and European Jews, few Argentines believed it was necessary or prudent to rid society of prostitution. Catholicism identified celibacy and devotion to God as the holiest of human aspirations, and only the few who attained them could enter religious orders. But for those who could not deny themselves sex, 1 Cor. 7:9 advised marriage. Nevertheless, Saint Augustine and Saint Thomas Aquinas had recognized that female prostitution, though repugnant, was necessary. Augustine, for example, believed that eliminating brothels would lead to pollution of everything with lust, "a lust at least equal to . . . fornication. . . . In his mind it was better to tolerate prostitution . . . than to risk the perils that would follow the successful elimination of the harlot from society."[24]

Thomas Aquinas perpetuated the Augustinian view and compared prostitution to a sewer whose removal would pollute the palace. Prohibiting prostitution might also lead to homosexual practices.[25] Unlike Augustine, he was more tolerant of sexual pleasure within marriage and more understanding of carnal sins. Neither Augustinian nor Thomist views on prostitution reflected official nineteenth-century Vatican policy that condemned licensed brothels; nevertheless Argentine Catholics and anti-clerics both referred to Aquinas and Augustine in their support of legalized prostitution.[26]

Protestants were more united in their stand that sexual self-control should be practiced by men and women outside marriage and that female prostitution must be suppressed. Like those of Catholics, Protestants' debates over extramarital sex, or even of sexual purity, were matters to be resolved by public vigilance, individual self-control, and religious dogma. Unlike Catholics, however, Protestants, particularly in England and the United States, believed it was necessary to abolish legal bordellos. It was claimed in Great Britain and many other Protestant societies after the repeal of the Contagious Diseases Act in 1885 that prostitution flourished only where there were immoral governments.[27] Jewish communities sided with this Protestant view. The few Protestant countries that did not prohibit or attempt to suppress prostitution tended to view licensed bordellos as part of a national work program. An example of this would be Sweden, which allowed legalized prostitution to function as part of a mandatory work and health program for poor women.[28]

In most Catholic societies pragmatic Augustinian and Thomist views still prevailed and encouraged anti-Catholic responses to legalized prostitution. When Protestants in England, Switzerland, Germany, and the United States examined the evidence of white slavery in Argentina, its Spanish Catholic tradition and tolerance of legal bordellos — added to its earlier history of political instability and its Indian-Spanish mestizo population — led many foreign reformers to perceive Argentina as inferior and immoral.

Buenos Aires' evil reputation began to develop as soon as Europeans, male and female, started emigrating to Argentina after 1860 in search of work and a new life. European prostitutes, however, had been plying their trade there for years. In 1797 sixty-six female convicts en route to a penal colony in Australia found themselves in the Río de la Plata after a mutiny took place on their prison ship, the *Lady Shore*. Subsequently some women continued to earn their living by selling their bodies in Buenos Aires. They were eventually joined by other foreign ladies of the night, and foreign prostitutes and pimps were already ensconced in Buenos Aires by the 1860s. White slavery (as defined by European reformers) thus predated legalized prostitution in Argentina, which began in 1875.[29]

The nationality of prostitutes, however, became an issue only after that date. Just three months after bordellos became legal enterprises, a Buenos Aires newspaper reported that a French court had ordered fines and imprisonment for a couple who had "corrupted the conscience of several young Frenchwomen and brought them to Buenos Aires to practice the disgusting vice of prostitution."[30] Within one year Hungarians were well entrenched in similar pursuits, earning a dubious reputation exceeded first by the French and then by Poles, principally Jews.[31] More stories of white slavery appeared. In 1877 another *porteño* (Buenos Aires) newspaper informed its readers that Italian *rufianes* (pimps) who specialized in exporting women to Buenos Aires and Egypt had been thwarted in Naples.[32]

The following April both porteño municipal officials and private citizens were scandalized by the appearance of *El Puente de los Suspiros* (the Bridge of Sighs), a newspaper that claimed to be devoted to the abolition of white slavery. Named after a bridge that provided access to a downtown neighborhood filled with houses of ill repute, one issue contained an open letter written by Elena Bezembajer and Gabriela Kick. They urged all bordello inmates to seek the help of the police:

> Our story is your story, the tale of all European women who, surprised and robbed of innocence, or because of misery, have been led to these shores ignorant of the truth and lured by unfulfilled promises. . . .
>
> Compañeras: Listen to the voice of friendship and affection. Your exploiters do not own you. If you want to abandon them, the police will protect you. . . . Stop being slaves and become ladies [*señoras*].
>
> Compañeras!
Long live liberty!
Long live independence!
End white slavery![33]

In the same issue editor Ramón Guerrero identified a number of men as pimps, including Abraham Robins (accused of selling the services of his own daughter), Jacobo Honig (engaged in pimping since his arrival in Buenos Aires in 1869), Carlos Rock, and Juan Hubler. Guerrero even provided drawings of pimps as well as one of prostitutes locked in cells by their madams.

Did the women actually write the article? Did prostitutes perceive themselves as victims of an international traffic in women? Had the police come to their aid? It is impossible to say. Municipal officials did not believe the stories. They considered the newspaper to be the act of one group of white slavers trying to expose and ultimately thwart another ring. *El Puente de los Suspiros* was quickly suppressed.[34]

Fears of involuntary female prostitution did not abate. In 1881 another porteño newspaper, *La Pampa*, reported several disturbing incidents. The first involved a fourteen-year-old girl reported missing by her mother. The adolescent had been offered live-in employment as a seamstress by one Margarita Charbanie. Instead of clothes to sew, the unnamed girl received the unwanted advances of a man who had paid five thousand pesos for the privilege. After she had been held against her will for twenty-six days and forced to accept the advances of any man who selected her, the police found her and arrested the Frenchwoman. Two months later Eduardo Giordino's brutal tale was told. An Italian immigrant, he forced his wife Rosa to support him through commercial sex. Even after she did everything he ordered and handed over all her money, he remained unsatisfied. Thereupon he went to the Catholic church, demanded a divorce, and then tried twice to murder Rosa. These stories, even though they involved European immigrants, did not fall into the stereotype of an organized group of strange men seducing innocent women. Nevertheless, they probably came closer to the typical causes of prostitution: economic need and family pressures led many women to sell themselves.[35]

The belief that Argentine bordellos were fed by the international white slave traffic grew as the proportion of foreign to native-born registered prostitutes increased. Between 1889 and 1901, there were 6,413 women registered in Buenos Aires, and only 25 percent were Argentine. In contrast, almost 19 percent were Russian, and combined with the Romanian, German, and Austro-Hungarian women they totaled 36 percent—far more than the proportion of those nationalities to the city's female population. The next largest groups came from Italy (13 percent) and France (9 percent). Only 65 English women registered during this time (1 percent). When the time period is extended to 1915, the percentage of registered Argentine women decreased, the proportion of Russian women remained the same, and the French increased to 15 percent. It was not until the 1920s that the percentage of registered Argentine prostitutes began to rise, and by 1934 they represented 43.9 percent of the total, while Polish and Russian women made up 48.6 percent.[36]

These statistics are accurate in that they correctly identify what prostitutes told registrars about their nationality. Despite the possibility that women might lie, as they often did, the data reliably indicated that foreign-born women registered in Buenos Aires more frequently than native-born prostitutes. The circumstances that led women to register, however, cannot be discerned from nationality statistics. Religious affiliation was also impossible to verify. Nevertheless, nationality statistics were used to document the international commerce in women and to identify Jews as key actors.

Other evidence was assembled to persuade the European public of white slavery in Buenos Aires. The existence of an organized pimping ring that benefited from legalized prostitution reinforced the image of an evil city. It was one thing to have occasional reports of isolated cases of so-called involuntary prostitution. It was quite another to allow a formal business association to promote sexual slavery.

The first highly publicized ring of local traffickers was formed in Buenos Aires in 1889 by Jewish pimps. Ostensibly a mutual aid association, El Club de los 40 (the Forty Club) was in the midst of the Jewish neighborhood and consisted of forty pimps who banded together to make the commerce in immigrant prostitutes more efficient. Revelations about their operations truly shocked the sensibilities of local residents, whether native-born or immigrant.[37]

It also terrified European moral reform groups. In 1890 the British Immigration Society was set up in Buenos Aires and the British Anglo-Jewish Association began to make serious inquiries about white slavery in Argentina. By 1901 it too had set up a committee in Buenos Aires to do rescue and prevention work. Meanwhile in Europe, the chief rabbis of major western European communities drafted a letter of warning to their counterparts in eastern Europe:

> Sad tidings have come to us that evil men and women go about in your countries from town to town and village to village and induce Jewish maidens, by false representations, to leave their native land and to go . . . to distant countries, telling them that they will find there good and remunerative situations in business houses.
>
> In some instances these wicked men add to their iniquity by going through the form of religious marriage with the girls. They then take them on board ship to India, Brazil, Argentine, or other countries in South America, and then sell them there to keepers of houses of ill repute. . . .
>
> It seems advisable that every Rabbi and Minister in his congregation should . . . warn parents . . . and tell them that it is their bounden duty to make strict enquiries as to the character of the man who wishes to marry their daughter and not to listen to those who would entice girls to leave their parental home, for their intentions are evil, and the life of their daughter is at stake.[38]

The Jewish Association for the Protection of Girls and Women (JAPGW), founded in London in 1885, made Buenos Aires its principal target in South America. With the help of the resident Jewish community and led first by Rabbi Henry Joseph and then by Rabbi Samuel Halphon, members questioned young Jewish women disembarking in Buenos Aires about who was meeting them and what type of work they sought.

In the first few years Jewish reformers faced a particularly difficult challenge. Every day boats docked at Buenos Aires. Who could protect these passengers from criminals waiting to pounce on unsuspecting people? An immigrant, Mordchai Alpersohn, arriving at Buenos Aires in 1891, recalled: "Near the gates of the immigration house we met a few dozen elegantly dressed women and fat men in top hats. Through the gates they were talking with our wives and gave children chocolates and candy." Alpersohn and his group were soon warned that these friendly people were "the uncleans," the Jewish white slavers, though not before procurers had lured some women away.[39]

Gradually, open attempts to recruit women at the immigration house declined, and in 1904 Joseph proudly wrote to the association, "I have a full list of arrivals and inscriptions of women as prostitutes during the past two months, and among them have been inscribed only eight Jewesses. . . . this is really a point for congratulations." Three years later the Buenos Aires committee boasted that an English-language newspaper had reported that "it is now possible to walk the principal streets of the City without meeting crowds of demi-mondaines," which was attributed to the Jewish committee there.[40]

Despite the JAPGW's progress in Buenos Aires, or perhaps because of it, organized prostitution was increasingly linked to Jewish immigrants residing in the city. Furthermore, the problem of Jewish prostitution in Buenos Aires was hard to ignore because until 1908 many bordellos, as well as El Club de los 40, were near the Plaza Lavalle in the midst of the Jewish business and religious center:

> The Plaza, between calles Lavalle, Viamonte, Libertad, and Talcahuano was the site of an informal labor exchange. In the late nineteenth and early twentieth centuries, new Jewish immigrants beat a path from the Immigrant Hotel to the Plaza. There they met coreligionists, acquainted themselves with their new surroundings, and sought work. . . . The plaza also housed . . . a synagogue at Libertad 785. Libertad rapidly became the Jewish community's main commercial street. . . . The mixed nature of the neighborhood is seen in its role as a center of prostitution, as well as of law, culture, and commerce.[41]

Religious Jews were forbidden to interact with the "uncleans" (*tenem*), but complete isolation was impossible. The precarious nature of commercial life in Buenos Aires often left immigrant Jews few financial alternatives to providing goods and services for the legal and clandestine prostitution businesses in their midst. Efforts to separate the uncleans from more respectable Jews were aided by a municipal ordinance in 1908 that banned bawdy houses near Libertad Street unless they were on small side streets. At the same time immigrant Jewish merchants and their families had already begun to gravitate to Plaza Once and there created a new barrio untainted by associations with prostitution.

The locus of Jewish commerce and bordellos changed, but trafficking continued to be identified as principally a Jewish activity. In 1910 Rabbi Halphon reported to the Jewish Colonization Association in London that "people often speak ill of the [Israelites], without anyone taking the time to demonstrate their good qualities."[42] The situation was considered so abnormal that for potential Jewish immigrants from Europe, Argentina was stained with the image of being a "contaminated land."[43]

Reports of the Jewish Association for the Protection of Girls and Women reinforced the unfavorable image of Jews in Argentina. The group claimed that in 1909 more than half of the 199 licensed houses were operated by Jewish madams and that half of all inmates were Jewish. Most Jewish prostitutes lived in establishments operated by Jewish madams. Furthermore, Jewish individuals represented most of those arrested in Buenos Aires between 1902 and 1908 for pimping, illegal brothel keeping, and sexual solicitation. These conclusions were based on the JAPGW's assumption that all Russian and Romanian prostitutes and pimps were Jewish.[44]

The astonishing proportion of women identified as Jewish in Buenos Aires brothels was a tremendous embarrassment to Jewish communities in Europe as well as in Argentina. But fears of anti-Semitism, rather than overt acts, helped fan the flames of the white slavery controversy. A turn of the century report of the Hamburg B'nai B'rith's Jewish Committee to Combat White Slavery concluded that most prostitutes in Buenos Aires were Jewish and that traffickers "dress with ostentatious elegance, wear huge diamonds, go to the theater or opera daily; they have their own clubs and organizations where wares are sorted, auctioned and sold. . . . They have their own secret wireless code, are well organized, and—heavens, in South America everything is possible!"[45]

In 1908 *Juventud*, an Argentine Jewish working-class organization, began a campaign to keep coreligionists from renting buildings to known Jewish traffickers. The following year the Chevrah Keducscha, the main Jewish mutual aid society in Buenos Aires, denied white slavers religious burials, and owners of Jewish theaters barred pimps and prostitutes from their establishments.[46]

Efforts by the Jewish community to keep men from pimping increased the visibility of Jewish prostitution. Anti–white slavery groups began street demonstrations in Buenos Aires. Traffickers were occasionally sighted and threatened with physical violence, but they protected themselves by organizing people to disrupt anti–white slavery meetings. More public meetings were scheduled after the publication of an anti–white slavery exposé in a local newspaper, *El Tiempo*. Manuel Gálvez, a young lawyer who had written his thesis on the white slave trade, was asked to serve on a committee organized by Jewish reformers. In his memoirs, Gálvez described how crowds hired by traffickers broke up the meeting by shouting insults in Yiddish and pelting the officers with a variety of objects. The reformers were forced to flee for their lives.[47]

Unfortunately, these events were viewed as proof of the immorality of all Jews in Buenos Aires. Presumed cases of white slavery involving Jewish people were immediately reported in the porteño press, often referring to them as Russians. The situation became so bad that in 1910 a Yiddish newspaper complained that "the word 'Russo' has become a shameful one among official elements, meaning a white slave dealer, a *cambalachero* (dealer in old stuffs), a person who has dark dealings."[48]

The continued links between prostitution and the Jewish community meant that at the same time the Buenos Aires chapter of the JAPGW boasted of progress, it still reported incidents of Jewish white slavery. The 1907 report included eight cases involving fifteen women, two of whom were Christians. All were rescued from bordellos.[49]

In 1912 the JAPGW recounted three terrible stories. The first dealt with a nineteen-year-old Jewish woman living in London. Approached by a *shadchan* (marriage broker) who tried to get her married in a secret ceremony, she refused, but he tricked her onto a boat that took her to Buenos Aires. She was kept in isolation in a bordello, but one day the door was left unlocked and she escaped to the street and found "a respectable old man." Eventually the girl was reunited with her mother, who had returned to Russia.

The second woman was less fortunate. The young Russian woman had been married in a fraudulent religious ceremony and taken to Buenos Aires by her husband, who unsuccessfully tried to force her into a brothel. She ended up in a hospital for her resistance. The last story involved a woman living in New York whose husband had left for Buenos Aires. When she joined him with their child, he tried to place her in a bawdy house, and she too was beaten for resisting. After her husband left with the child, the woman, unable to speak Spanish, finally found a benevolent Jewish man to assist her. She was ultimately repatriated to the United States.[50]

These stories are intriguing for a number of reasons. First of all, they all recount incidents where Jewish husbands abused their wives but other Jewish men rescued the unfortunates. Evidently women never turned to other women for help. Second, the tales deal with women who resisted immoral behavior, even when it was their husbands who told them to engage in prostitution. The combination of the dependent yet moral woman typified the ideal Jewish wife. Finally, these stories are significant because they were published in detail. Given the desire to report such horrifying tales when they occurred and the fact that later reports tended to give only lists of the number of boats met and people interviewed, it is most likely that all verifiable cases were printed.

In 1911 the Argentine committee of the Jewish Association for the Protection of Girls and Women expressed its frustrations. It could not stop white slavery in Buenos Aires because "a large amount of the evil is carried on secretly and cunningly. Traffickers no longer accompany their victims on their journeys, in a manner apparent to everybody. They resort to newer and more artful methods, and so are able to get into Buenos Ayres, and other places, with greater ease."[51] To comprehend the complexities of the issue, in 1913 Samuel Cohen, the international secretary, visited the Argentine capital and other South American cities.

Once Cohen reached Buenos Aires, he discovered that, to a certain extent, things were not as bad as he had imagined. Even though at that time moral reformers were not allowed to board ships to question young women, Cohen praised the efforts of the government-run immigrants' home to place "genuine" immigrants and the efforts of the local Jewish community to rescue young women. He also noted that Buenos Aires was a new, vigorous city with a large immigrant male population and that the demographic situation had made Argentina a haven for foreign prostitutes. Unfortunately, according to Cohen, residents of Buenos Aires, whether native-born or foreign, were all driven by the desire to make money, and Argentines had little interest in philanthropic activities. Nevertheless, Cohen reassured the association's members that "immorality is still bad, but it is not so flagrant, nor is it so much countenanced as it was formerly. Public opinion has been growing, the Argentineans have been travelling to Europe, they have become educated to the opinion held concerning their country and have resented it, and they are now trying to fall into line with Europe on this question." Rather than point to the circumstances that caused eastern Europeans to flee to the New World, he blamed the existence of licensed houses for perpetuating vice in the city, calling them "demoralizing and debasing to the lowest degree."[52]

Cohen went all around the city of Buenos Aires. He even entered a brothel:

> The rooms are generally of a large size, . . . always filled with men. . . . The girls walk about in this crowd of men, in various stages of undress, painted and powdered to a hideous degree. They soon disappear into other rooms, over which the "Madame" keeps guard. On coming out the girl hands to the "Madame" the money she had obtained, and receives in exchange a metal "tally" representing her share of the proceeds. With a room containing from 50 to 150 men, it can be imagined how many times in the course of a night the girl has to submit herself to immoral contact.[53]

One major flaw in Cohen's investigation was his failure to report the existence of a new Jewish pimps' organization, the Varsovia Society. Formed on May 7, 1906, in the Buenos Aires working-class suburb of Avellaneda, the group ostensibly functioned as a mutual aid society. Noé Trautman, a known pimp, led the group despite its formal mandate to accept only those of good reputation. In fact, the Varsovia consisted of pimps who wanted to maintain their business and still lead a religious life. Along with another society known as the Asquenasum, the Varsovia Society purchased land for a cemetery in Avellaneda, and there pimps and prostitutes were buried in religious ceremonies.[54]

The Varsovia and Asquenasum were responsible for the belief that Jews were well entrenched in prostitution, but since their operations were centered in the province, rather than the city, of Buenos Aires, reformers like Samuel Cohen may not have seen them in operation. The Varsovia Society soon extended its tentacles to other Argentine provinces. In Rosario, an important port city on the Paraná River in Santa Fe province, Varsovia associates established their own synagogue on Güemes Street in the midst of a traditional bordello district, as well as a cemetery in nearby Granadero Baigorria. In addition to these religious concerns, the Varsovia made business arrangements with local inhabitants, sometimes forming partnerships with native-born pimps.[55]

The existence of Jewish pimping organizations did not mean they controlled most prostitution. Nor did it mean they were the only groups operating. In 1928 Albert Londres, in his famous exposé *Le chemin au Buenos*

Ayres (The road to Buenos Aires) described Le Milieu (the Center), a Marseilles-based international prostitution ring:

> The "Center" is a body of men who deal in women, quite openly. . . .
> It is a corporation. It is more than that, it is a State! . . . These new
> men have turned our morals, our customs and our laws upside down.
> . . .
> They have broken with all public forces, except the Police. . . .
> They have also founded a league of the Rights of Man,—his rights
> over women. They have not only revived bigamy, they have sensibly
> improved it. . . .
> They work . . . among women who, for some reason, are in distress. . . . The best game is the inoffensive semi-professional, who
> does not know where to look for a bed. Having found the women,
> they send them off via Santander, Bilbao, La Carogne, Vigo and Lisbon. . . . That is the road to Buenos Ayres![56]

Despite Londres' account, or most likely because of its chauvinistic and sympathetic cast, the French role in white slavery was rarely vilified in the same way as that of Jewish traffickers. There can be little doubt that nationalism could work to rehabilitate the injury caused by fellow countrymen, whereas aspersions cast upon individuals of a particular religious faith or upon males of a different nationality were more indelible.

Other foreign communities in Buenos Aires were alarmed by the stories of white slavery among immigrant women. After years of trying to handle the problem of English immigrant women through their consulate and by local initiative, in 1912 the resident British community cooperated with another local anti–white slavery society and petitioned for a trained British rescue worker to be sent to Buenos Aires for one year. The British National Vigilance Association selected Rosalie Lighton Robinson, a seasoned caseworker, and she set out for Buenos Aires within a month. Her job was to meet incoming ships, and she stayed in Argentina for the rest of her life.[57]

The task confronting an anti–white slavery social worker was varied. Occasionally there might be verifiable incidents of forced sexual slavery, but most of Lighton Robinson's work had little to do with such matters. Meeting ships, talking with local reform societies, and corresponding with the London office of the National Vigilance Society constituted her principal duties.

Occasionally an interesting case might crop up. In 1917 a young pregnant Englishwoman was deserted by her husband in Brazil without money.

When she found out he was in Buenos Aires, she decided to accompany a group that was walking there! She made it to the northeastern province of Misiones, where she became ill. Befriended by the British consul there, she was taken by train to Buenos Aires, where she was hospitalized and gave birth to her child. After she had overcome such adversity, the *Vigilance Record* noted that she was in "such moral danger" that she was sent back to England to her parents. The report left the cause of her moral danger unresolved. It came either from her husband or from her presence in Buenos Aires, not from entrapment by white slavers.[58]

As Lighton Robinson began to work in Buenos Aires, the president of the National Vigilance Association, like Samuel Cohen, sailed there in search of truth. William Coote spoke to members of the Argentine government, the resident British community, and the local Argentine anti–white slavery committee. And though he too admitted that Buenos Aires was not the den of iniquity he had imagined and that the Argentine committee was doing an excellent job, much work remained, "owing to the absence of any public opinion on the moral question." Another factor he mentioned, often ignored by European reformers, was that the relatively high wages official and clandestine prostitutes earned made it difficult to keep poor women from selling their bodies.[59]

Coote's references to an absence of moral opinion and Cohen's denunciation of licensed bordellos revealed their cultural hostility toward Argentina and its Catholic acceptance of the inevitability of prostitution. It also emphasized the rage Europeans experienced when they found "their" women entrapped in such systems, though they evinced little sympathy for Argentine nationals caught in the same situation. Neither trusted immigrant women to select marriage partners or to seek work safely in the New World; hence their groups insisted on interrogating all newly arrived poor women while ignoring the plight of others.

European reformers, with few exceptions, saw only danger in female migration to countries like Argentina. And though Coote admitted few Englishwomen were registered and Argentine officials did nothing to prevent women from leaving bordellos, he still believed that "innocent girls of different nationalities are entrapped by false pretenses, taken to South America, and deliberately sold to houses of ill fame." It was not too alarmist to say that "South America today is one of the chief centres of the White Slave Traffic." For these reasons "the International Bureau suggests that in the interests of the girlhood of Europe and humanity at large, some definite action should at once be taken to bring South America, or at least Buenos

Aires and Rio, into line with the public opinion and national work of the European countries."[60]

Reformers could not even trust migrating women to marry suitably, because their husbands could become their pimps and consulates could not help. Before the Pan American Union and the League of Nations arranged treaties and conventions in the 1930s to guarantee nationality rights for married women, women who married foreigners lost their own nationality. The fate of women marginalized by marriage and economics thus linked the family and the nation in an international struggle. To keep women in their homelands and under the control of their families, reformers assured single women that they would be safe from sexual exploitation if they remained immobile and dependent upon other family members. To accomplish these goals, the strategy relied on racism to emphasize the immorality of forcing "white women" into sexual slavery.[61]

This comparison between black slavery and prostitution was first implied by Victor Hugo in 1870 and thereafter distinguished "voluntary" from "involuntary" prostitution. The term "white slavery" was calculated to enlist antislavery activists, many of whom were feminists, in a new moral campaign. The anti–white slavery campaign, in addition to its nationalistic concerns, was explicitly racist. It presumed that all white women found in foreign bordellos had been forced there against their will by immoral men. The possibility that white women chose to engage in sexual commerce with men of different races, even if starvation were the only other "choice," was inconceivable. Furthermore, the anti–white slavery movement offered no help to native-born prostitutes except the hope that "abolition" would liberate them.[62]

After 1889 a series of international congresses debated white slavery problems. By 1904 an international agreement, ratified in Paris, obliged contracting governments to create agencies to monitor the movements of people suspected of importing or exporting "women and girls destined for an immoral life." These women, within "legal limits," were to be repatriated if they so desired. Signatory countries were also asked to supervise companies that specialized in finding employment for women abroad.[63]

At the third international congress for the suppression of white slavery in 1906, a special study of Argentina and Brazil was included at the request of the German national committee. Based upon his travels to these countries, a Major Wagener concluded unhappily that German ships were being used to transport women involuntarily, but he was relieved that most of the women who spoke German were Polish, Russian, and Hungarian, and he objected to their being labeled "Germans."[64] That he downplayed the presence of European women in South American countries in order to defend German pride clearly identified his main concerns, which had little to do with protecting women from sexual victimization.

At the tenth International Abolitionist Federation meeting in September 1908, the Argentine situation was examined once again. Sir Percy W. Bunting, director of the *Contemporary Review*, accused the Buenos Aires licensed houses of promoting the white slave trade in Argentina. According to him, one only had to look at the nationality of registered women in Buenos Aires bordellos to realize that "prostitution is controlled by the international traffic and there [Buenos Aires] it is fed by the houses that receive these women and live off their sexual commerce."[65]

Moral reformers and public officials in Buenos Aires responded to these accusations with a mixture of outrage, embarrassment, and indifference. The official Argentine Catholic church did little to challenge the prevailing Augustinian view of prostitution. Nor did the Argentine national government. When the anti–white slavery treaty was being drawn up in 1902, Argentina was invited to send representatives, but national officials sent none.[66] Unable to name representatives to an international conference, Buenos Aires officials still made efforts to promote treaty goals and respond to local reformist demands. They periodically revised bordello statutes to improve sanitary conditions, control the number of women in each house, and protect women from unscrupulous traffickers. Nevertheless, all plans to end municipally authorized bordellos were thwarted until the 1930s, when political consensus in Buenos Aires allowed the ban to be implemented.

Several Argentine groups, however, remained firm in their resolve to end white slavery. Initially Buenos Aires society women, mostly foreign-born, founded local chapters of international organizations dedicated to the issue. In 1893 the Argentine chapter of the Swiss Union Internationale des Amies de la Jeune Fille (International Union of Friends of the Young Girl) set up a home for immigrant women subsidized by subscriptions from local consulates and the resident foreign commercial community.[67] Nine years later women affiliates of the Argentine and Italian chapters of the Swiss group founded the Asociación Nacional Argentina contra la Trata de Blancas (Argentine National Committee against White Slavery).

The new organization was taken over by prominent men: religious heads of the immigrant community and Argentine politicians and moral reformers. The first president elected was Dr. Arturo Condomí. With his leadership and the help of Vice President Ignacio L. Albarracín, the governing board proposed a law enabling the Argentine government to monitor immigration of unaccompanied or unauthorized female minors. These waifs would be placed in asylums or returned to their fathers. Traffickers would be subject to three years' imprisonment. A revised draft focusing more on trafficking than on the repatriation of minors was completed in June 1903 and sent to the Argentine Senate.[68]

It would take another ten years to get the Argentine Congress to approve an antitrafficking law, but the Asociación was determined to work at all levels to impede these nefarious male traffickers. Even before the national bill was presented, the group petitioned the Buenos Aires municipal council to raise the minimum age for prostitutes from eighteen to twenty-two. In response, city officials appointed a committee to study the problem. Thus within one year of its foundation, the Asociación Nacional Argentina contra la Trata de Blancas had outlined a definite plan of action to deal with immigration reform and prostitution laws. Members worked to keep minor women out of bordellos and to drum up support for a national antipimping law.[69]

The work of the Asociación continued in an aggressive fashion. In 1904 it received authorization to have an employee, a man who knew several languages, interview newly registered women. The same man also obtained permission to board incoming ships for similar purposes. Coordinated efforts by the Asociación and the National Vigilance Association stopped several traffickers from entering Argentina.[70]

By 1908, however, internal disputes indiscreetly blamed on the attempt of "Catholic" elements to force their religious views upon the committee led to a decline in membership. A new group called the Comité Argentino de Moralidad Pública (Argentine Committee on Public Morality) was organized and dedicated to a wider set of aims, including the "special task of prosecuting all those people who dedicate themselves to a suspicious and immoral life."[71]

The truth was that pimps quickly infiltrated the new Comité Argentino de Moralidad Pública, and until they were removed from positions of influence, the organization openly mocked its stated goals. As Samuel Cohen reported in 1913:

> This Society was started a few years ago by a gentleman who was a member of the Argentine National Committee, and who had left it. He meant very well, but . . . there gathered around him men who had

themselves engaged in the Traffic. . . . They advertised the Society
and got a very large number of subscribers, but many of these were of
doubtful respectabilities. They managed to obtain permission for
their inspectors to go on to the boats and to the Dispensario [prosti-
tutes' registry], but when the Authorities saw that some of them were
friends of the prostitutes, they quickly cancelled the permission. . . .
At last there appears to have been a Secretary, who himself ran away
with a woman, and this brought matters to a crisis. The Society has
now been reorganized.[72]

After the Comité Argentino de Moralidad Pública reorganized, relations
between it and the Asociación Nacional Argentina contra la Trata de Blancas improved.

The last, and eventually the most important, Argentine organization
dedicated to abolishing white slavery was the Socialist party, founded in
1890. By 1904 the party's first representative to the Argentine Congress,
Alfredo L. Palacios, had been elected. In 1907, with encouragement from
the Asociación Nacional Argentina contra la Trata de Blancas, Palacios introduced a bill to punish the activities of international pimps in Argentina,
but it was ignored by fellow legislators.[73]

Heartened by William Coote's visit, Palacios introduced another antipimping bill to the Argentine Congress on August 8, 1913. The new version broadened the definition of white slavery to encompass corruption of
minors, both male and female, and adult women under age twenty-two,
thereby differing from the 1903 plan advocated by the Asociación Nacional
Argentina contra la Trata de Biancas. Once again the guilty party faced a jail
sentence, and relatives, husbands, or tutors lost the right to exercise *patria
potestad* (parental authority) over the woman or minor. Foreign-born
pimps faced deportation and loss of citizenship if convicted of white slavery
more than once, but they would not have to pay repatriation costs.

The Palacios measure parted company with the goals of the Asociación
when it came to legalized prostitution. Whereas parents, guardians, and
white slavers would automatically be tried for the crime of corrupting minors, bordello madams would not. Only when they knowingly took in minors would madams be considered coauthors of the crime.[74]

In his accompanying message Palacios specifically mentioned how impressed he had been with the Coote visit and how embarrassed he was that
Buenos Aires was known in Europe as "the worst of all the centers of immoral commerce in women."[75] During his speech the Socialist legislator

emphasized that it was a matter of national shame that Argentina allowed the illegal traffic in young women to operate. To eliminate the scandal, female minors, even if they were prostitutes, had to have legal protection from pimps.

When the bill emerged from the Chamber of Deputies' legislative commission on which Palacios served, modifications included legal protection of adult females. According to the revision, if adult women were forced into prostitution because their consent had been given through deception or the threat of violence, the accused would face from one to three years of prison. With this provision, the projected law for the first time ensured that any woman forced into prostitution, whether by a stranger or a relative, could seek legal redress.[76]

In support of their bill, committee members pointed out that on February 26, 1904, the Argentine Ministry of Foreign Relations had promised to honor the recommendations of the 1902 Paris anti–white slavery conference. This included the decision to urge all nations to enact appropriate legislation to prevent the international traffic in women and children from operating in their own countries. Thus the legislation at hand was merely the fulfillment of the Argentine promise.[77] The only discordant note came from another Socialist deputy, Dr. Nicolás Repetto, who objected to the article that excluded madams who "simply admit women into licensed houses of prostitution" from being accused of corrupting women or children. From Repetto's perspective, no national law should dignify such a profession.

In contrast, Deputies Arturo Bas and Palacios, members of the commission, both defended the inclusion. As a staunch Catholic, Bas believed prostitution was a necessary evil that had to be controlled. Palacios agreed, but for different reasons. He justified legalized prostitution because municipalities had the right to license bordellos. He also believed it was unrealistic to suppose that a government could eliminate sexual commerce by closing the houses.[78]

Once Bas and Palacios began to discuss the value of prostitution laws, discord arose in the congressional debate. Most legislators refused to debate the merits of local ordinances. It was one thing to prosecute procurers and quite another to prohibit municipally regulated prostitution.

Locally and internationally, response to the legislation was favorable. European and Argentine moral reform groups were delighted, and according to the British *Vigilance Record*, "the effect [of the bill] was electrical;

according to the investigation department no less than 2,000 procurers . . . left the capital as if fleeing from an earthquake."[79]

The passage of the Ley Palacios, added to the outbreak of World War I the following year, should have put an end to Buenos Aires' evil reputation. If all the foreign pimps had left town and few returned because the war interrupted the migratory flow from Europe to the New World, the white slavery problem should have disappeared.

White slavery did not disappear, because the issue involved much more than verifiable incidents of sexual exploitation of immigrant women. Only occasionally would moral reformers try to restrain anti–white slavery histrionics and reflect on the campaign's hidden agenda. In an effort to reveal some of the underlying issues, feminist Teresa Billington-Grieg wrote an angry commentary in a 1913 issue of the *English Review*. There she criticized British feminists for supporting anti–white slavery campaigns that relied on false cases in Buenos Aires and other places to promote a vision of female helplessness. According to her, Assistant Commissioner F. S. Bullock, the Central Authority in England for the Repression of the White Slave Traffic could not recall "a single case of the forcible trapping of a girl or a woman by drugs, false message, or physical force during the last ten years that has been authenticated or proved."[80]

Billington-Grieg believed that white slavery accusations overemphasized the role of strangers, viewed women as only passive victims, and obscured internal family conflicts. She herself had left home after a dispute with her parents, but she did not end up a prostitute. To her it was "positively nauseating that we should have cases and statistics of girls missing from home quoted with solemn tone and finger pointing to the brothel, as though there and only there could they be." Most did not end up in bordellos, and those who did shared some of the responsibility for their actions.[81]

She concluded her critique by accusing all those who supported the new British laws to punish procurers (including feminists and female reformers, whom she called the mothers of the new church) of having given ammunition to "those who question the responsibility of women in public affairs . . . [and] women's emancipation." Defenders of the new laws presumed that unprotected women always end up as victims and are never responsible for their own decisions about sexuality. Although well intentioned, these people denied that women voluntarily worked as prostitutes. As she put it: "The Fathers of the old Church made a mess of the world by teaching the Adam story and classing women as unclean; the Mothers of the new

Church are threatening the future by the whitewashing of women and the doctrine of the uncleanness of men."[82]

Billington-Grieg's critique revealed yet another set of circumstances that might have led women to "disappear." It sidestepped the poverty and family coercion that led to prostitution and instead dwelled on the belief that women had control over and responsibility for their actions. European moral reformers ignored Billington-Grieg just as they sidestepped the issues of family conflict, racism, and nationalism. Instead they preferred to see the white slavery issue simply as a campaign to save innocent women, particularly in foreign lands. For them Buenos Aires was an appropriate target, and in the prewar years the task of keeping out evil men and dishonest women seemed overwhelming. As Samuel Cohen remarked:

> The work of any Society would be difficult in any case. Many boats come into Buenos Aires with very large numbers of immigrants and often two or three boats come in together. Then, too, those who wish to enter Buenos Aires without being noticed, get off the steamer at Montevideo, and come on by the river boats, which enter at another Dock, south of the town. Again, other boats come into La Plata, and passengers come to Buenos Aires by train, about two hours distant. To do the work thoroughly, therefore, at least five or six workers would be necessary. Then again workers would have to speak many languages, for a more cosmopolitan lot of immigrants I have never seen.[83]

The diminution of immigration to Argentina after 1914 seemed to make little difference to those who were concerned about conditions in Buenos Aires. Europeans continued to accuse the Argentines of immoral behavior. Sensationalist tracts like *In the Grip of the White Slave Trader*, published in London during the war, warned Englishwomen that "one cannot escape . . . from one thought in connection with the traffic as regards English girls. On all sides it is admitted that the hotbed of this abominable trade is the Argentine."[84] This anonymous publication then reported that a guide to the bordellos of the world, published in France, listed addresses of seventy expensive Buenos Aires bordellos where "the English girl commands the highest price, and it is to the Argentine that she is generally exported." Yet according to the British minister at Buenos Aires, Sir Reginald Tower, who had received letters urging all women leaving England for South America to be registered for their own protection:

Upon my arrival in England [in 1914] I was asked on behalf of the Bishop of Kensington to receive one or two people to discuss the question of the White Slave Trade with the Argentine Republic. . . .

I explained to them in considerable detail the various and effective steps which have been taken in Buenos Aires to control the traffic, and showed them that the consensus of opinion was that very few British girls ever come into the country for immoral purposes, the principal reason being that there is little or no demand for them![85]

Rosalie Lighton Robinson kept herself busy during the war obtaining permission to board incoming ships. Then she had to figure out what to do with the women she helped. One of her first accomplishments was to establish a vacation site for immigrant working women, and between 1914 and 1916 fifty-three women had pleasant two-week vacations. In addition to this effort, the British social worker met 176 ships and helped sixty-six girls, mostly by putting them in contact with relatives or finding them suitable employment. While all this was very commendable, it had little to do with the threat of white slavery.[86]

When Lighton Robinson visited London in 1916 and reported on her work in Buenos Aires, Right Reverend Bishop Ryle's introductory comments clearly indicated he thought Buenos Aires was still a problem: "We are all of one mind in our desire and zeal to promote the cause of social purity both in our country and in those dependencies which are in intimate relation to our Empire, and we are going to have the privilege of hearing . . . from one who has been actively at work in one of the most difficult regions so far as the work of purity is concerned."[87]

Bishop Ryle's alarmist description was a sharp contrast to Lighton Robinson's account of her Buenos Aires experiences. She told her British audience that in 1914, one year after Socialist deputy Alfredo Palacios had successfully sponsored the national antipimping law, he approached her to find out what other appropriate measures might be undertaken to end white slavery in Argentina. Her suggestions, later written down at Palacios's request, were published in a local paper.[88]

Soon after meeting with Deputy Palacios, Lighton Robinson, with the help of the United States consul and the secretary of the Sociedad de Beneficencia (Beneficence Society), the officially subsidized women's charity organization of Buenos Aires, obtained permission to board incoming ships. She then helped the Catholic International Association obtain a similar permit. When they found girls in danger or without jobs, the two groups worked together to find them housing in either Catholic- or Protestant-sponsored shelters, including one operated by the Salvation Army. The needs of Jewish girls were also considered, and Lighton Robinson cooperated with the local Jewish Association.[89]

In all, Lighton Robinson's report demonstrated the eagerness of Argentine philanthropic and official agencies, Catholic and non-Catholic, to cooperate with the international campaign against white slavery. Women's groups had been especially willing to work with her. A case in point was Lighton Robinson's meeting with the local branch of the National Union of Women Workers, "composed of the leading Argentine ladies in Buenos Aires." They promised to use their influence in securing the appointment of a female physician to the criminal law courts.[90]

The report was received with great enthusiasm by the British audience, but many dismissed the possibility that Argentines wished to improve moral conditions. Instead, they agreed with Mrs. Harold Sandwith, a former resident of Buenos Aires, that Lighton Robinson's unique talents caused the changes. In her opinion, Argentines were very exclusive people who "very much resent anybody approaching them with a view to improving the condition of affairs."[91]

It would eventually take more than two national Argentine laws as well as two world conflicts to persuade British and European reformers that white slavery could be prevented in Buenos Aires. In the meantime, as long as Buenos Aires allowed bordellos to operate, Argentina would be accused of offering a hospitable climate for international traffickers in women and children.

The link between Buenos Aires and sexual slavery is a complex one that needs to be examined more closely. Just how unusual was the situation in this South American city? Was prostitution truly an immigrant problem, or was it a chapter in cultural or religious hysteria? Were women merely passive victims, or were they direct participants in this process? What happened to Argentine women in such circumstances? And how did legalized prostitution affect Argentine culture and politics?

Buenos Aires was certainly not the only Latin American city where prostitution was rampant. Mexico City was reputed to have a larger proportion of prostitutes than any European or South American city in 1905 — 21 percent of the adult female population. Nevertheless, Mexico was less worrisome to Europeans because few foreign-born women were involved.[92]

Rio de Janeiro was occasionally mentioned by moral reformers, but European immigrants did not constitute a majority of either the urban population or the prostitutes there. Brazilians tolerated prostitution, but officials there had deported a Jewish white slavery ring of eastern European origin in 1879 and thereafter did not sanction the operation of large houses of prostitution. They were also quick to ratify international agreements pertaining to white slavery, thus paying lip service to international law. In response to this situation reformers often mentioned Rio, but they made less assiduous efforts to complain about white slavery there, even though foreign prostitutes, particularly Frenchwomen, were highly prized in that city.[93]

The situation in the Argentine capital contrasted sharply with that in Rio and Mexico City. The influx of female immigrants, added to its predominantly male population, made the city an ideal target for European reformers. Equally important, after 1875 Buenos Aires licensed brothels, which initially were large, filled with foreign women, and run by many of the same men expelled from Brazil. And despite claims to the contrary, until the Ley Palacios was passed in 1913, Argentina never formally adhered to any international white slavery agreement.[94]

Argentines as well as Europeans agreed that white slavery existed in Buenos Aires. They disagreed about its extent and about whether municipally licensed prostitution was the major cause. World trends in female migration patterns, as well as the particular situation of prostitutes in both industrialized and developing countries, indicated that Buenos Aires was just one of many port cities suffering from an influx of prostitutes. Argentines therefore could easily blame exogenous forces for the influx of pimps and prostitutes.

Although they disagreed about the role of legalized prostitution, both groups were sure that immigrant European women, rather than native-born Argentines, were the principal victims. There was both fact and fantasy to such perceptions. After 1880 immigrant women did constitute the majority of legally registered prostitutes in Buenos Aires, but they were not alone. Thousands of native-born Argentine women faced the same fate as their foreign-born counterparts in Buenos Aires, but proportionately fewer registered. Instead they plied their trade in the streets, cafés, and tango dance halls.

As for Jewish prostitution, white slavery definitely existed, but it was not unique to Buenos Aires. That refugee Jewish women were inmates of bordellos in port cities all over the world, regardless of whether or not bordellos were state licensed, indicated that push rather than pull factors were primary explanations. These women suffered from the consequences of European religious bigotry, rigid Jewish laws, and their combined impact on family structures and poor Jewish women. Under such pressures the network of Jewish prostitution expanded all over the world to Latin America, the Middle East, Asia, the United States, and South Africa. And as it was seen in the cases of New York City and Johannesburg, South Africa, bordellos run by such groups could flourish as easily in cities where prostitution was not municipally regulated as in those where elaborate laws had been enacted.[95] A large contingent of Jewish prostitutes in Buenos Aires was subjected to forces that were unrelated to local conditions, yet their plight and presence was used by moral reformers to condemn Buenos Aires officials for creating the conditions leading to the sexual enslavement of Jewish women.

Why then did Buenos Aires become so central to the white slavery debate? Prostitution and white slavery debates identifying Buenos Aires as the "Sin City" of South America had a particular symbolic content that sent important messages to Europeans and Latin Americans in modernizing societies. For Europeans, Argentina—despite its pretensions and attractiveness—could never replace the immigrants' homeland. To make it undesirable, Argentina was accused of being an accomplice to the loss of family control over innocent foreign women. Once girls slipped away from parental authority, evil men and governments took advantage.

For Argentines, the white slavery issue was manipulated for other purposes. Physicians used it to teach urban inhabitants about the dangers of venereal disease and the need for new forms of social control. Socialists exploited it to gain voters' support. Nevertheless, at the same time that they railed against the existence of legal bordellos and immoral work, Socialists refused to enact tariffs to promote more acceptable forms of female employment.

The central issue that united anti–white slavery campaigns in Europe and Argentina was the way unacceptable female sexual conduct defined the behavior of the family, the good citizen, and ultimately national or religious honor. They all perceived women who sought employment as typical targets of sexual slavery, yet none explored ways to create more acceptable work for them. Women could not be independent under the way they defined family and nation, just as men could not victimize women. Therefore coercive measures to control pimps and prostitutes were justified by national and foreign governments as a necessary restriction of individual civil liberties for the sake of the entire community. Rather than reflecting a completely verifiable reality, white slavery was the construction of a set of discourses about family reform, the role of women's work in modernizing societies, and the gendered construction of politics.

2

Dangerous Women:
Legalized Prostitution

The lurid white slavery stories about Buenos Aires were only partially true. But traditional histories of the capital city, which barely mentioned the prostitution problem, were also inaccurate. Could Buenos Aires be both the city some described as the "Paris of South America" and the place others scorned as "Sin City"? Moral reformers and urban historians looked at the Argentine capital through a stereoscope that held two completely different pictures. To reconstruct an image that incorporates both perceptions, we must return to Buenos Aires between 1869 and 1914 to trace the impact of urbanization, immigration, and white slavery and examine their relation to legalized prostitution.

In 1869 Buenos Aires was a bustling port city with great potential for economic growth. Ruled by dictator Juan Manuel de Rosas until his overthrow in 1852, in 1862 the city was named the temporary national capital. Though it was still marked by colonial architecture, narrow, muddy streets, and an often insalubrious climate, after 1870 the appearance of streetcars and new urban construction allowed its physical dimensions to expand.

From this modest but promising start, Buenos Aires soon blossomed. After 1880 it became the permanent national capital, and bold *intendentes* (mayors) redesigned old colonial streets to permit construction of wide avenues, government offices, theaters, and subways. Fashionable stores, cafés, restaurants, and banks soon dotted the elegant downtown, adding to the glamour and glitter of this apparently opulent capital.

Argentine residents fabulously wealthy from commerce and land speculation went to Europe to acquire culture and buy merchandise unavailable at home, inspiring the phrase "rich as an Argentine," and in response to rags-to-riches stories, millions of Europeans emigrated to the Río de la

37

Plata in search of wealth. By 1914 Buenos Aires was a showcase of the Western Hemisphere. Yet the greater the influx of Europeans, the stronger the rumors of sinister events. The city gained a dubious reputation as a major entrepôt for white slavery and legalized prostitution.

As the population grew, so did the number of prostitutes. They were just one of many groups of social and economic marginals scrutinized by municipal authorities, and the 1875 decision to legalize prostitution in Buenos Aires stemmed from local conditions. Traditional methods of handling social problems buttressed the resolve of city elders to restrict the activities of reputedly dangerous women. A political legacy of arbitrary social control, added to economic forces that fostered rapid urban growth without creating a significant demand for women's labor, had a direct bearing on the handling of gender and class issues in the capital city.

To European reformers, the presence of foreign-born prostitutes in Buenos Aires bordellos constituted an international scandal. To city police and government officials, suspicious women, native and foreign, were just one part of the urban demimonde. In the daytime officials dreaded political subversives; at night they had to deal with all those who defied cultural, moral, and legal order. Marginal men and women helped define social, economic, and political acceptability.

Most poor inhabitants of Buenos Aires, male and female, posed a constant challenge to the governing elite. Native-born residents competed with Europeans for scarce jobs, inadequate housing, and expensive consumer goods. Between 1869 and 1914 the number of city dwellers mushroomed from a modest 180,000 to more than 1.4 million, mostly immigrants and migrants seeking work and a new life. They all brought their own cultural values, and the task of urban government was to find ways to transmit acceptable political, social, and cultural norms to this amorphous lower class. The surveillance and enclosure of prostitutes served many purposes: defining the parameters of power among urban officials, protecting public health, ensuring public order, separating sexual commerce from leisure activities, reinforcing appropriate patriarchal and class values, and determining the gender structure of urban labor.

Municipal officials in Buenos Aires had a long tradition of dealing with social disorder in an arbitrary fashion. Before 1852 urban problems in Buenos Aires were frequently resolved by unauthorized police action, often instigated by neighbors. During the twenty years when Rosas was provincial governor and nominal head of the nation, "public and official attitudes in Buenos Aires about disorder and criminality took on an urgency in the absence of codified legal norms and continued arbitrary practices."[1]

Police officials, in these circumstances, competed with judicial and municipal authorities for the right to control social unrest. By the 1870s each had power that emanated from a different source: the police from alliances with neighbors and their ability to use violence; judicial authorities from their ability to interpret or apply laws; and municipal authorities, particularly health officials, from their right to create new ordinances based on knowledge of medicine and disease.

The history of legalized prostitution in Buenos Aires reflected the diffuse nature of urban political power. City officials after 1852 devised new and often conflicting ways to deal with prostitutes and disorderly women. Public officials "controlled" prostitution as part of contesting each other's authority. What changed over time was the nature and theory of control, as well as the balance of contending powers.

Throughout the nineteenth century, women accused of selling sexual favors came under the surveillance of the police. Initially, poor urban women, regardless of evidence, either were ignored or were rounded up and sent to military outposts for alleged sex trafficking, even though prostitution was not a criminal offense. In 1832, for example, city police simply seized three hundred women "of doubtful character" and deported them to the southern frontier of Buenos Aires province "without any notice or investigation of their offenses."[2]

Fears of uncontrollable, unemployed women continued to haunt urban officials. After 1852 prostitution was believed to be practiced in dance halls (*academias de baile*) or nightclubs (*peringundines*), where fighting and scandalous behavior were frequent forms of diversion. These "sites of lower-class damnation" led police to close down such establishments at the request of neighbors.[3]

Before 1875 urban women accused of licentious or suspicious behavior were treated like *gauchos* (cowboys), who were arrested for being unemployed. Both were monitored by legal officials and persecuted for the crime of poverty. Rural codes turned gauchos into vagrants, a criminal state that could lead to military service or forced labor for a large rancher. Alleged prostitutes faced similar penalties. They could be arrested and sent to provide sexual services to troops on the frontier.

After 1875 an unacceptably employed woman could be accused of solicitation and fined or arrested, but she could not be forced to register as a prostitute. Once she officially declared her occupation, however, she was as

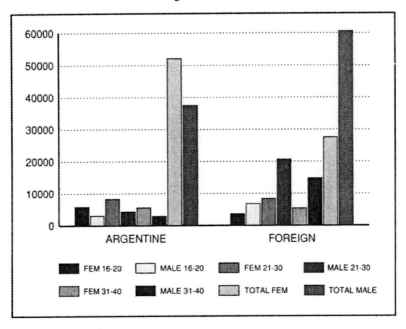

Population of Buenos Aires City, 1869, ages 20–40 years
Source: Argentine Republic, *Primer censo de la república Argentina verificado en los días 15, 16, y 17 de septiembre de 1869* (hereafter *Primer censo*) (Buenos Aires: Imprenta del Porvenir, 1872), pp. 26–27.

closely monitored by police and health authorities as gauchos were by justices of the peace. Like the gaucho, the prostitute was both admired and feared for her freedom and independence, the only response either could muster in a world that exploited them. A contemporary explained the situation of the gauchos in the following way: "Pampean crime resulted from the exclusion of a vast proportion of the rural population from access to permanent employment. 'Our gaucho is not a thief by profession or nature,' . . . but rather out of necessity. . . . Administrations responded not with schools, jobs and land, but with conscription and vagrancy laws, the stocks and the lash, and the autocratic justice of the peace."[4]

The world of the urban prostitute was not much different. Excluded from participating in the export economy based upon ranching and cereal production, rural women migrated to the capital city. Initially they were also marginal to the urban industrial sector. According to the first national census in 1869, more native-born women than men resided in the capital city. The influx of female immigrants had not kept pace with that of males,

Dangerous Women

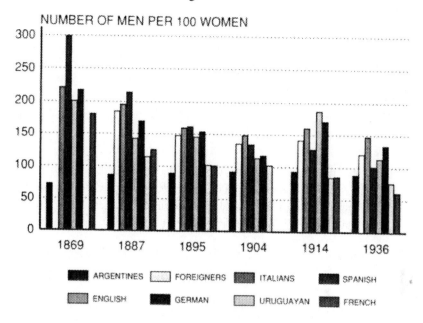

Masculinity index in Buenos Aires City

Source: Ruth Freundlich de Seefeld, "La integración social de extranjeros en Buenos Aires: Según sus pautas matrimoniales, ¿Pluralismo cultural o crisol de razas? (1860–1923)," *Estudios Migratorios Latinoamericanos* 1, 2 (April 1986), p.209.

mostly between the ages of twenty and forty. The result was an overabundance of young males.

Between 1869 and 1936 the proportion of immigrant males to females in the city of Buenos Aires generally declined. At the same time the proportion of native-born males to females increased until 1914 and then began to decrease. The masculinity index of each national group, however, had its own dynamics, and while some had high masculinity indexes, others had low ones.

Throughout this period Argentines as well as Europeans were concerned about the consequences of large numbers of immigrants living and working in Buenos Aires. Although Argentine leaders originally believed foreign workers were a distinct improvement over the rebellious mestizo masses, they soon identified immigrants as the source of urban disorder, and promiscuous and employed immigrant women as part of both the problem and the solution.

Work prospects were scarce in Buenos Aires in 1869, when approxi-

41

mately 16 percent of all female inhabitants worked in textiles, sewing, or cigarette manufacturing, the most common form of female artisan labor in Argentina. In contrast, approximately half of all women were employed in similar pursuits in the northwestern city of San Miguel de Tucumán, where traditional cottage industries still provided subsistence employment. For poor women in the capital city, domestic service and sewing at miserable wages were the major alternatives to prostitution.[5]

At the time the census was taken, Buenos Aires was on the brink of modernization. The colonial dimensions of the city had been expanded by the advent of beef-salting factories and slaughterhouses in the Corrales district and the influx of sailors and Italian immigrants in La Boca and other waterfront areas near the city. There were a significant number of troops lodged in the Parque de Artillería to the west.

The excess of males in Buenos Aires made it an exceptional city in Argentina and explained its attractiveness to immigrant and creole females. Poor women might find work entertaining immigrant bachelors and native-born males who sought illicit sexual congress. In the year the census was taken, 185 self-proclaimed prostitutes and 47 pimps worked in Buenos Aires. In contrast, nationally only 361 people, mostly women, declared employment related to commercial sex. Only Rosario, Santa Fe, claimed a significant share of this dubious honor, with 86 prostitutes and no pimps. San Miguel de Tucumán, one of the most densely populated inland capital cities, listed only 10 female prostitutes. These three cities alone harbored almost 91 percent of self-identified prostitutes and pimps, and Buenos Aires appeared to be the favorite workplace.[6]

Census takers had no illusions about having counted all women who might have been labeled as prostitutes by others, if not by themselves. In fact, they estimated that these 361 individuals represented only one-tenth of the total, and they were particularly noticeable in the growing cities. Officials also realized that any efforts to repress prostitution without trying to improve family and economic conditions would be futile.[7]

The rapid growth of a resident foreign-born population in Buenos Aires heightened anxiety about white slavery. By 1895 three out of every four adult males in Buenos Aires were foreign-born; nineteen years later 60 percent of the city's adult females and 70 percent of adult males were foreigners.[8] The overrepresentation of Europeans among the prostitute population was explained as a deleterious consequence of immigration.

The sexual mores of immigrant and migrant women reinforced fears that they would be susceptible to procurers' wiles. In Europe, rural sexual customs among some peasants included premarital sex and childbearing as a sign of fertility. In the Argentine countryside abduction of women was a prelude to consensual marriage, and there were strong traditions of wives' sexual abuse by the husbands' employers.[9] Women might have had cultural or religious inhibitions, but political and economic circumstances made them consider commercial sex a viable survival strategy. The progression from early sexual encounters, both forced and voluntary, to commercial sex was probably less traumatic than imagined by middle- and upper-class reformers on both continents.

The situation of female inhabitants, both native-born and foreign, could not be attributed solely to immigration and migration. Argentine social patterns and laws also had their impact. According to traditional Hispanic custom, family heads, particularly husbands or fathers, were responsible for the needs of women, but there might be few marriages among the poor, and children were often abandoned by one or both parents. By 1887 there were 6,564 children under fourteen in Buenos Aires who had only one parent or were orphaned, and 8,635 widows were responsible for 20,792 children. The number of widows was equal to 15.6 percent of the married women in the city at that time. In 1910 Roberto Levillier characterized the streets of Buenos Aires as filled with unsupervised hooligan children who were poorly instructed and "morally abandoned" by parents. Throughout this period the proportion of illegitimate births had increased from 13.89 percent in 1890–99 to 14.15 percent in 1900–1909, and this too was seen as a factor that encouraged unstable families.[10]

The problems of illegitimacy and child abandonment were compounded in that until the twentieth century, native-born lower-class males were often conscripted into the army as part of antivagrancy laws. Left behind and often widowed, many native-born women faced lives of persistent poverty unrelieved by the growth of the capital city. Among the foreign-born women, many had migrated alone, and others struggled with their husbands to make a living in the New World. To survive, some desperate women from both groups turned to prostitution.

Even if the census takers were correct and some 3,600 prostitutes inhabited the urban landscape of Argentina in 1869, and even if all the uncounted were in the city of Buenos Aires, they still would have represented less than 5 percent of the city's adult female population. It was not, then, the sheer volume of identified female prostitutes that concerned city elders and census takers alike, nor the nationality of the women involved, but rather the relation between commercial sex, women's work, and other elements of changing urban and family life.

Prostitution became a metaphor for upper- and middle-class fears about the lower class and the future of the Argentine nation. If it were possible to alter and control the sexual mores of poor women, then these reformed women could clarify gender relations between classes, reshape the lower-class family to fit more bourgeois models, and define women's work as reproduction and nurturing rather than production. Yet the real basis for all these fears—the relation between women's work and the Argentine economy and the unwillingness of public authorities to curb male sexual desires—was rarely confronted. Instead, female prostitution was seen as the origin of urban disorder instead of its economic and social consequence.

Because of its geographic situation and its attractiveness to European immigrants, Buenos Aires was in some senses unique. Nevertheless, in the 1860s all of Argentina was in a state of political, economic, demographic, and ideological flux, and these currents combined to affect the situation of women in urban areas. Civil wars and the War of the Triple Alliance (1864–70) had drained the nation of its male resources, directly affecting the men's families.

The enactment of new national laws after 1852 did little to protect women's legal right to work. The constitution of 1853 abolished the remnants of black slavery and guaranteed all inhabitants the right to work, but the civil code enforced after 1871 severely restricted women's civil rights, especially if they were married or had not attained majority. Considered minors, they were completely under the control of husbands or fathers and technically could not manage their own money or property; nor could they work without patriarchal permission. Furthermore, until the 1913 Ley Palacios, family heads who forced women into prostitution committed no crime that affected their rights of patria potestad as defined by the civil code.[11]

The more liberal 1862 commercial code gave young unmarried women more economic rights than its civil counterpart, but it was used in an ironic fashion in enforcing prostitution ordinances. Whereas the civil code determined that a young woman could not marry without permission until age twenty-two, the commercial code set the age of majority for women at eighteen. Since licensed bordellos were legal businesses after 1875, women between the ages of eighteen and twenty-two could sell their bodies but could not marry without parental consent.

When these codes were applied in a country affected by years of war, followed by decades of unfettered urban growth that often ignored the economic needs of women, porteño women had few family, economic, or legal resources to protect them. Prostitution became a real alternative for many poor urban women, one that helped keep some families together while tearing others apart.[12]

By the time the second national census was conducted in 1895, no attempt was made to list the number of self-identified prostitutes in the national capital. Nevertheless, from other sources we know that there were 344 women registered for the first time in a city of more than 200,000 adult females. Perhaps women had been deterred by the greater availability of honest work. In fact, there were more jobs for women in the capital city in 1895 than in 1869, though most still involved domestic service and the needle trades. Nevertheless, 65 percent of all women over age fourteen had no job whatever. These unemployed cared little that women fared better in Buenos Aires than elsewhere since nationally females constituted 78 percent of all adults unemployed.[13]

In response to limited employment prospects, female prostitution became an integral part of the quasi-legal economy and culture of different neighborhoods in Buenos Aires. In the southern district of La Boca, sailors and Italian immigrants were attracted to seedy businesses along Brandsen, Suárez, Olavarría, and Necochea Streets. The *cuartos de chinas* near the army encampment on the western outskirts typically had mulatta (*parda*) creole women. In the central city new types of massive family-dwelling tenements (*casas de inquilinato*) began to be constructed in 1867, and prostitutes were found there too. Initially built in the parish of San Nicolás, the immediate downtown area, such buildings were later erected on Libertad Street in the midst of the Jewish neighborhood, and all were considered foci of clandestine prostitution. The Paseo de Julio (now Leandro Alem Avenue) in *El Bajo* was yet another urban area where prostitution was rife.[14]

✳ In these neighborhoods men found employment, and wages were reputed at times to be high, but women who sought work in the same public places were always suspected of supplementing their income with the proceeds of sin. In this way neighbors stigmatized women who operated tobacco stores, forerunners of contemporary kiosks, or who owned cafés and music halls or worked there as waitresses. Those who took in laundry or sewing were also suspect. Many of them *did* supplement their incomes, as did their European counterparts, as clandestine prostitutes.[15] Others did little to arouse such suspicions, but their visibility as working women led to accusations. In a society where working women were the exception, female wage labor in public places was equated with sexual commerce.

Police may have rounded up suspicious women in the streets before 1875, but they left those in dance halls and houses of prostitution alone. One reason police were reluctant to respond to complaints about bordellos was that sexual entertainment was as popular among elite males as among lower-class men. Adolfo Alsina, a popular Buenos Aires political leader after Rosas, was well known for his penchant for frequenting establishments like the Alcázar Theater, notorious for auctioning off foreign prostitutes like cattle. Members of the upper-class Club del Progreso used to adjourn to these cabarets and bordellos. Men of all classes before 1936 often received their sexual initiation in a bordello. A hierarchy developed among the nightspots and bordellos; it became clear that some were frequented by the upper class and some by the poor, and in others males of both groups were likely to rub shoulders as they danced, conversed about politics, or slipped away to other rooms.[16]

For upper-class men there were famous houses such as the one run by Concepción Anaya at Lavalle 2177 and Laura Monserrat's establishment at the corner of Paraguay and Puerreydón Streets. Everyone, including the police, knew about the bordellos, and rarely were measures taken to prevent their operation. Concepción Anaya was given the nickname "Mamita" in recognition of her strong motherly influence. Who could arrest a mother?

Occasionally violence would erupt, but the women who ran the houses were known for both their courage and their temper. It was the exceptional policeman who dared arrest them. Laura Monserrat reputedly threw a fit when one of her clients committed suicide. Apparently she was enraged because as her client fell he accidentally broke a bottle of beer. María "La Vasca" charged clients high prices for the privilege of dancing with her women. To protect her establishment she kept close guard at the door, selecting who could enter and who could dance. While she remained in charge, there was little need to call the police.[17] Lower-class madams were also infamous for their daring. "Parda" Loreto, a mestiza midwife, was known for her willingness to get into a fight. Enriqueta "the whore" (*la conchuda*) also boisterously defended herself if a fight broke out in her bordello.[18]

In both upper- and lower-class bordellos during the early years most prostitutes were native-born. Gradually, however, much to the consternation of the pardas and the creole native-born, white foreigners, usually French or feigning French accents, began to command higher prices. By the 1880s the women who ran the upper-class-oriented houses of prostitution were mostly foreigners and became replacements for elite women who had previously been able to gather men in their houses to discuss politics and art in traditional *tertulias* (salons).[19]

The 1869 census manuscript offers a composite portrait of self-identified prostitutes before municipally licensed bordellos. They lived with other women or with groups of men and women in *conventillos* (tenements). Some lived with family members—siblings, parents, or husbands. There was no red-light district or, for that matter, any statutes regulating either prostitution or pimping. Consequently there was no physical separation of these women from the general population.[20]

Rural migrants, immigrant women, and native-born daughters of city dwellers were all represented. They most frequently lived with foreign pimps, though some like Ana Dupont, a French national residing at Florida 339, chose to live alone. The bordello near the waterfront at 25 de Mayo Avenue 163 was typical of larger houses. Eleven women, mostly from the Argentine interior, lived with a German pimp. Nearby at Parque 51, María and Federico Cruser, married German citizens, lived with Federico's brother and operated a bordello that housed three Argentine women and one Italian woman. In a house at Moreno 397 there were eight native-born prostitutes.[21]

Police, with the aid of neighbors, were clearly in charge of keeping order in these disorderly establishments. The absence of relevant laws did not deter them. They simply arrested customers who got into fights and created disturbances. In 1867 the chief of police authorized "incessant prosecution" on charges of vagrancy of all disreputable men who frequented pool halls, boardinghouses, and "houses of immorality." Police created a list of hotels, boardinghouses, dancing establishments, and bordellos in each district to identify unsavory businesses. According to the 1873 police report, they continued to claim jurisdiction over bordellos.[22] After the city introduced the system of licensed bordellos, however, police found themselves competing with physicians and city council members for the right to monitor suspect businesses. From that time onward, officers turned their attention to the women rather than their clients.

Like many other nineteenth-century cities in the throes of modernization and industrialization, Buenos Aires legalized female prostitution to isolate and, it hoped, control the social and medical consequences of commercial sex. Modern government-controlled prostitution began in 1802 as part of an anti–venereal disease campaign in Napoleonic France. Designed to lower the incidence of syphilis among troops, a frequent preoccupation of military commanders, by the 1870s licensed brothels monitored by police had been declared a success in many European cities. Even Great Britain, soon to oppose all state-regulated prostitution, experimented with the system under the Contagious Diseases Acts of the 1860s in the aftermath of the Crimean War.[23]

Police and public health doctors continued to operate prostitute clinics and registration offices in many parts of Europe despite the lack of definitive cures for either syphilis or gonorrhea until the twentieth century. It was not known until 1837 that syphilis and gonorrhea were two separate diseases. Even after that, because doctors knew little of gonorrhea's dangers and because they could make the primary symptoms of syphilis disappear with a long and painful course of mercury injections (and just as often without such treatment), physicians believed that syphilis was the most dangerous venereal disease but that it was curable.

Nevertheless, not until 1905 did scientists identify the cause of syphilis, an advancement that shortly led to the invention of Salvarsan, the "magic bullet." As for gonorrhea, only in 1879 did Albert Neisser discover the responsible organism, and until twentieth-century penicillin there was no completely effective treatment for either disease. Despite the absence of definitive cures and some highly questionable assumptions, physicians knew that prostitutes transmitted venereal disease, and thus they decided that public health would be more secure if these women were examined regularly.[24]

With such a strong European movement for medically supervised legal prostitution to protect soldiers, it was not surprising that Buenos Aires followed suit. Argentine municipal authorities were more concerned, however, with the spread of venereal disease within the city than with the infection of troops. By the 1870s the need to extend the city into the *arrabales* (suburbs), where prostitution flourished, meant that those neighborhoods had to be sanitized. Tenement buildings in the central city posed a similar challenge. Municipal officials also believed that the alarming rate of infant mortality resulted from venereal disease brought on by prostitution. If the city's population was to develop in a safe and healthy fashion, prostitutes had to be identified and separated from the general female population.

The Buenos Aires municipal council licensed bordellos in 1875. It had been debating the issue since March 1864, when it was declared that prostitution control laws were imperative because "as it exists today prostitution enervates, sterilizes and even destroys . . . all classes of society," although it was impossible to extirpate entirely.[25] Councilmen also claimed

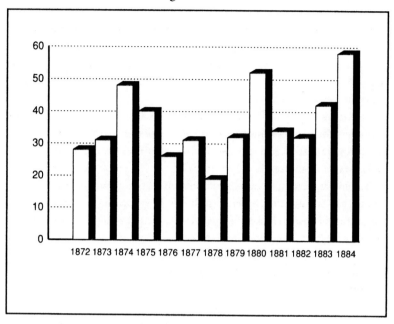

Deaths from syphilis
Source: Emilio R. Conti, "Algunos datos relativos a la mortalidad de la ciudad de
Buenos Aires durante el año 1876," *Revista Médico-quirúrgica* 14, 12 (September
1877): 271–72; idem, *Causes de la morbidité et de la mortalité de la première enfance à
Buénos Ayres* (Buenos Aires: Paul-Emile Coni, 1886), p. 154.

there were no philanthropic organizations that could provide work and
food for desperate women. If the government could not stop prostitution,
at least it could control its more deleterious manifestations. A thorny political problem emerged, however, one that thwarted rapid action. Because
Buenos Aires was both a national and a provincial capital, no one was sure
who should dictate a prostitution control law. Consequently council members refused to license prostitution.[26]

By 1869 two important articles about prostitution in Rosario and
Buenos Aires had been published in the first Argentine medical journal, the
Revista Médico-quirúrgica. Both contained proposals for medically supervised licensed bordellos. Dr. Carlos Gallarani proclaimed that the purpose
of a law in Rosario was "not to help the miserable women who sell their
bodies, but only to keep better watch over them, and above all, have them
submit to periodic medical examinations." He attributed prostitution in
Rosario to the overwhelming female desire to buy clothing and jewels. Gal-

larani clearly saw social control as a more pressing need than prophylactic medical treatment.[27]

Dr. Luis Tamini, author of the Buenos Aires proposal, viewed the problem from another perspective. He quoted Augustine and Ezek. 23:3 as proof of the inevitability of prostitution and concluded that it exists in "all great centers of population, . . . because it is an industry like begging, for example, which allows one to live without working." For Tamini licensed bordellos were needed to "save, whenever possible, future generations from certain types of illness."[28]

Tamini suggested modifying the French system to ameliorate urban finances while protecting public health. He proposed high yearly bordello license fees of 10,000 pesos and 100 pesos annual registration fee from each prostitute. Clandestine prostitutes faced a 10,000 peso fine and thirty days in jail. While incarcerated they could take comfort in the knowledge that their fines would underwrite the cost of a venereal disease clinic. As for the bordellos, they would have to be far from churches and frequently traveled streets. They would be austere establishments where sex would be separated from public entertainment, and thus gambling and the sale of alcoholic beverages would be banned.[29] Tamini was very influential within the Buenos Aires council, and he forced councilmen to confront the prostitution issue. He successfully proposed on October 25, 1870, to prohibit new bawdy houses without written permission of the president of the municipality until a prostitution ordinance was enacted.[30]

In January 1875 the municipal council enacted the first comprehensive prostitution ordinance. Drawn up by politicians and physicians more interested in where prostitution was to be practiced than in protecting public hygiene, the law emphasized medieval practices of keeping pimps out of bordellos and whores away from public buildings, churches, and thoroughfares, and it provided no public facilities to treat ill prostitutes.[31]

The 1875 ordinance identified prostitutes as women who sold sexual favors to more than one man. They could live alone or move into bordellos, but all had to have medical examinations every Wednesday and Saturday. Those who lived in bordellos were treated like part-time jail inmates. Madams (*regentas*) could not leave for more than twenty-four hours, and prostitutes had to return within two hours of sunset. Houses could display no signs, and the women could not appear at windows or doors. When outside, like the rural gauchos, all prostitutes had to carry identity cards. Prostitutes' medical expenses, including those for pregnancy, would be paid by the madam.

Women who reformed and left the bordello were forced to prove their good intentions by "volunteering" services at a charitable institution for one month. Any woman who to failed to register and was suspected by neighbors or police of soliciting would be fined, but not as seriously as Tamini envisioned. And unlike contemporary European legislation, clandestines were neither forced to have medical exams nor placed in bordellos. Nor were there special police squads to search for them. In other words suspected prostitutes were fined if caught, while those who wished to pursue their work legally were taxed and examined.[32]

The new ordinances offered poor women only the legal fiction that they could be free of male pimps and perhaps of venereal disease. What it tried to guarantee to so-called respectable urban inhabitants was something else. It promised men of all classes the ability to distinguish public women from the general female population and the illusion of medical safety in the pursuit of commercial sex. It also attempted to segregate dangerous women from the diverse establishments dedicated to leisure activities. If harlots were to be at work well before dusk, then the casinos, taverns, music halls, and even more important, the streets would be cleared of their presence before the evening commenced.

The real benefits of this law were quite different. Men continued to control women through pimping, usually by having a lover or wife act as madam. Prostitutes also resisted reform as they refused to be excluded from the nightlife of the city, just as they preferred to be ill rather than to remain unemployed during months of often useless medical treatment. Both pimps and independent prostitutes continued to operate illegally.

From the outset police resented having the city council and physicians meddle in prostitution control, because it meant that earlier alliances between neighborhoods and police were challenged. They reacted to the new prostitution laws by violating the ordinances and punishing the businesses, rather than the customers, for creating conditions for scandalous behavior. Within two weeks of the law's enactment, the police chief informed his subordinates that henceforth unlicensed bordellos would be shut down rather than fined. Any woman suspected of prostitution was accused of operating an illegal bordello. Even though this directly violated the ordinance, the mayor and city council failed to censure arbitrary police actions. Unfettered, the police closed down not just known brothels, but also any business run by men or women suspected of harboring clandestine prostitutes. Within a month the chief circulated a list of women who had applied for a bordello permit so that there would be no doubt who had appropriate authorization.[33]

Police were aided by irate urban dwellers who wanted their neighborhoods free of all wanton women, licensed or not. Neighbors cared little whether taxes had been paid; they were more concerned by the indignities their families presumedly suffered in a neighborhood inhabited by prostitutes. When police bothered to crack down on clandestine prostitutes, they often relied on people who lived nearby, whose accusations were sufficient to close down a business or force a woman out of her lodgings. In this way the search for unacceptable women became a witch-hunt as questionable behavior in young women led to the demise of their or their family's business or they were forced out of their lodgings.[34] In 1876 the mayor reported:

> The municipality has attempted to attend to the many complaints expressed by neighbors and the press against these casinos (where clandestine prostitution is practiced); but in many cases it is impossible to resolve the problem for lack of adequate regulations. Frequently the requests of respectable neighbors to close such establishments are passed on to the police; and the chief of police assures me that his department proceeds according to the wishes of the petitioner.[35]

In a short time the municipality developed an approach to clandestine prostitution that relied on both official and arbitrary tactics. To their dismay such efforts only led to more unlicensed establishments. Most of the difficulty stemmed from an extremely high license fee for bordellos. In October 1874 it was proposed that "restaurants, cafés, and casinos frequented or operated by licentious women [*mujeres de vida licenciosa*]" pay a license fee of 10,000 pesos.[36] The 10,000 peso fee became a reality in 1875 when the council ordered registration of all tenement houses. For purposes of taxation, houses of prostitution were classified as first-class operations regardless of size or location. In contrast, hotels, rented houses, inns, and taverns included in this classification had to be in areas serviced by gaslights and had to contain at least ten rooms for rent.[37]

By 1878 the tax on first-class lodgings was raised to 15,000 pesos. Shortly thereafter even city council members had second thoughts about the increase. Voices of reason opposed the measure because "the more taxes are raised, the greater the effort to evade them," and the uniform bordello tax was particularly onerous "as it is unjust: some houses can satisfy it and others not. The ones that cannot, close down . . . only to reopen as casinos and clandestine bordellos." The tax was rescinded, but only for a short time. Subsequent financial readjustment brought on by national economic collapse in 1890 led to new ways of licensing and inspecting businesses that made bordellos pay higher fees than hotels. As late as 1902, 143 bordellos brought in 21 percent of commercial and industrial license fees, although they represented less than 2 percent of porteño businesses. Taxation constituted a special power that the municipal council used to control bordellos, and it did not abandon it until 1919.[38]

The municipality's reliance on the bordello as a source of revenue explains how the police and the municipal council monitored prostitution. Despite many complaints of streetwalking and scandalous behavior by not too clandestine prostitutes, public officials were much more concerned with women purportedly working out of bars, casinos, or unlicensed bordellos. These businesswomen might have the capital to pay the city tax, whereas streetwalkers could not.

By 1876 the municipal council claimed that all clandestine bordellos had been closed down, and registered prostitutes in the seventy-one legal houses complied with the required twice-weekly medical examination. To the council's surprise, however, the number of syphilis cases had increased that year. The change was attributed to clandestines working in "casinos, cafés, eating establishments (confiterías), and tobacco stores."[39] Within four years a similar annual report indicated that illegal bordellos were again operating and that 105 establishments had been closed down.[40] In 1889 the municipal council finally managed to modify the 1875 prostitution ordinance. In the meantime a critical political event, the revolution of 1880, turned Buenos Aires into the permanent national capital. Initially the revolution did little to change the arbitrary behavior of the police and the municipal council. The new intendente, Torcuato de Alvear, is best known for beautifying the city. His accomplishments in the field of prostitution control, however, have been less well studied.[41]

Within one month of Alvear's appointment, the new city council authorized medical clinics for prostitutes and passed measures to expel prostitutes from the entire downtown area.[42] Although the need for medical dispensaries had been recognized for years, their construction, as well as the hopes of ridding the young capital of prostitutes, were wishful thinking at that time. Nevertheless, the plan to beautify the city and stamp out venereal disease went hand in hand with the idea of hiding or pushing away the marginal population.

Undaunted, the mayor and city physicians proceeded with plans to construct venereal disease treatment centers. The *casas de sanidad*, as they were initially designated, were envisioned as places that would serve as "a reformatory that would redeem as many as possible of the women who were sent there" as well as a hospital.[43] Such plans did not include medical sponsorship of workhouses and training programs for destitute women, however. Sympathy did not translate into the kind of aid that would have really deterred poor women from sexual commerce.[44] By 1884 Alvear had publicly announced his intention to establish a *sifilicomio* (venereal disease hospital) for both sexes, but the plan for the hospital as well as a *dispensario de salubridad* (prostitutes' registry) were not implemented until after Alvear had left office.[45]

The police continued to close businesses and evict almost anyone accused of clandestine prostitution during Alvear's administration. Municipal officials authorized similar punishments to improve public health, but they still resented police efforts to evict prostitutes. On June 1, 1881, the four physicians on the municipal council's hygiene committee told the chief of police to limit his force's actions to preventing the opening of new houses and keeping prostitutes away from bordello windows and doors.[46]

Neither police actions nor complaints about illegal sexual commerce abated. Rather, once the 15,000 peso fee was reinstated, the problem became more critical. For that reason the *asesor municipal* (municipal attorney) was called upon from time to time to clarify prostitution laws. In April 1885 the city council ordered a business at Cerrito 177–81 closed as an illegal bordello. The police refused to carry out the order. They chose to interpret the infraction as clandestine prostitution, for which the punishment was either arrest or a fine. The asesor sent the matter to the national Ministry of the Interior because the 1875 ordinance was too vague and could be interpreted to support either the police or the city council. Obviously not all cases of clandestine prostitution could be treated this way, and arbitrary law enforcement was sure to continue.[47]

A September 1885 raid in San Nicolás parish resulted in the arrest of twenty-five madams and eighty-four prostitutes. Most lived in the 300 block of Tucumán Street, and the rest on Suipacha and Esmeralda Streets. This mass arrest, instigated by neighbors, led to a legal rebellion by regentas. On December 4, fifteen operators of unlicensed bordellos complained that they had been evicted although the law mandated only fines. All signed the petition, indicating literacy, and most had eastern European surnames. In response, council members admitted that, indeed, the women had not been treated correctly and ordered that they all pay fines. Thereafter any bordello still unlicensed would be closed. It was a Pyrrhic victory for the outspoken regentas, who, along with their employees, ended up vindicated but poorer.[48]

Summary arrests and closure of businesses continued as usual. In July 1886 Candida Buschini, an Italian who ran a cigarette store on 25 de Mayo Street, complained of being closed down by the police for clandestine prostitution. Even though she accompanied her petition with signatures of neighbors and merchants who attested to her good character, the police inspector stated unequivocally that clandestine prostitution was practiced there. The business had to be shut down.[49]

Buschini's right to petition the municipality had been guaranteed by the asesor. A judgment handed down in September 1880 maintained that these businesses only used the pretext of selling drinks and cigarettes, and that such activities were public knowledge (*de pública notoriedad*). Even though the asesor defended police actions by stating that "it is impossible to believe . . . that public officials' application of the ordinance in so many cases of businesses [was] without due cause," he acknowledged the right of each individual to complain.[50]

Arbitrary procedures were not followed when the police were at odds with the city. In October 1886 the municipality ordered the eviction of residents at Talcahuano 201, 203, 211, 225, and 227 for clandestine prostitution. The police inspector cynically informed Intendente Alvear that such action could be taken only after it was determined that the residences were too unsanitary to be converted into licensed bordellos. Therefore the police refused to carry out the orders.[51]

Clearly prostitutes were caught in a continuing power struggle between the police, the physicians, and the municipal government. Sometimes these battles occurred because of real issues: fear of urban crime, desire to promote public health, and the need to create new municipal revenues. At other times, however, prostitutes were victimized by men who used the prostitution control issue to assert their authority over other men. By the time Alvear left office, the battle lines had been drawn in the war against urban vice. Unlicensed prostitutes continued to seek customers despite police threats. Women who evaded the law by entertaining clients in business or residential establishments that did not pay a bordello tax could expect arrest, eviction, or both. As indispensable as prostitutes might have been to the sexual entertainment of males, their refusal to be licensed and taxed turned them into criminals who were often castigated far beyond the letter and spirit of the law.

The next intendente, Antonio V. Crespo, a public health physician, tried other tactics. Instead of closing down clandestine bordellos, his officers fined unlicensed prostitutes.[52] Furthermore, under his administration the municipal council finally sanctioned the legislation necessary to open the Dispensario de Salubridad and the Sifilicomio. In 1887 Crespo sent a draft of legislation, as well as an accompanying message, to proceed with these projects. Finally in September 1888 the municipal council authorized the expenditure of up to 100,000 pesos to construct a venereal disease hospital to treat men and women. There a special office would inspect all licensed prostitutes once a week. If declared ill, they had to remain in the Sifilicomio until cured. Each prostitute would pay thirty centavos if the exam took place at the clinic and fifty centavos for a bordello visit. Until the Sifilicomio was constructed, the city would rent buildings for the prostitutes' examinations.[53]

The Dispensario de Salubridad opened in late January 1889 to register new prostitutes. It was operated by physicians, not police. On April 22, 1889, the Sifilicomio opened. More specialized than had been envisioned in the 1888 legislation, the hospital was dedicated solely to the treatment of prostitutes, and infected customers or anyone else who manifested symptoms of venereal disease had to seek treatment with private physicians or at other hospitals.[54] Once these two municipal institutions assumed control of licensed prostitutes, the system of legalized prostitution in Buenos Aires finally took on a structural resemblance to its European counterparts. It also reaffirmed the increased power and authority of municipal public health doctors.

The initial success of this new system can be measured by the fact that in 1889, the first year for which detailed statistics about prostitutes were published, 2,007 women registered for the first time, far more than those mentioned in earlier municipal reports.[55] The system's success was short-lived, however, because the municipal council insisted in the early 1890s that bordellos honor the two-block distance from churches and schools, comply with new hygiene regulations, and move from certain downtown streets. In 1891 alone 250 bordellos were closed to appease neighbors' complaints.[56] As a direct result of municipal harassment of bordellos, the number of women registering for the first time declined drastically until 1904.

The opening of the prostitutes' registry and the Sifilicomio satisfied doctors' concerns only temporarily, because they failed to solve basic problems

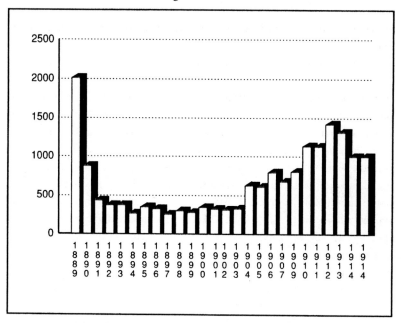

Number of prostitutes registered for the first time
Source: Buenos Aires Municipality, *Anuario estadístico de la ciudad de Buenos Aires,*
1900, p. 225; 1905, p. 216; 1907, p. 210; 1909, p. 95; 1911, p. 185; 1913, p. 94;
1914, p. 100.

of women's compliance. Not only did prostitutes distrust physicians, they continued to defy the municipality. In the midst of all these deliberations pimps and traffickers became more powerful, using coercion and political corruption to protect what became an increasingly illegal operation. From 1891 to 1914 the city of Buenos Aires attempted to reform, rather than discard, legalized prostitution. The results were disastrous as far as city officials were concerned.

No matter how well intended the ordinance, each new measure was as counterproductive as the one it replaced. Councilmen envisioned a system that would be noncoercive but still restrict prostitutes. Women were not to be harassed or humiliated, merely registered and treated. To keep pimps and white slavers away all sorts of schemes were devised, from hiring interpreters at the registry to closing bordellos with more than one woman. Plans that might have pleased prostitutes offended pimps. When bawdy houses opened in new neighborhoods, residents complained. If the downtown was to be cleared of bordellos, outlying neighborhoods complained.

In a city with so many unmarried men and poor women, bordello regulation could never eradicate prostitution but could only hide its more obvious manifestations.

The reform process began in March 1891, when Intendente Francisco Bollini complained to the municipal council that his campaign against clandestine bordellos had experienced severe setbacks. Eighty houses had been shut down in sections 3 and 5, and some eighty-six cases were pending. These accomplishments, however, did not prove that the city had been victorious. Swift eviction notices were difficult to obtain because madams resisted and hired legal counsel. Many houses had been established before the construction of new schools and churches, and madams claimed the right to remain within the two-block limit. The intendente was furious that his orders were challenged by some of the city's most distinguished lawyers, judges, and policemen.[57]

Bollini asked the council to consider what he called "radical" measures to enable him to "free the municipality of such shameful matters." In response, councilmen questioned whether Bollini really contemplated major reforms. After all, as one councilman put it, there were few alternatives: "To suppress [prostitution] would be impossible because it satisfies one of the necessary brutalities of life . . .; to designate a special neighborhood is a good idea that should be studied further. However, it is unclear what rights the municipality has in such matters. Of course, what is really needed is the strict enforcement of the 1875 ordinance while we study other measures."[58] Few councilmen cared to reform prostitution ordinances. By the 1890s they could not agree on who was a prostitute, let alone how to regulate her activities. For them, the best approach to the matter was to avoid it altogether.

Occasionally the council did take action, but its decisions were often ignored either by the intendente or by the prostitutes. On June 2, 1891, the Hygiene and Treasury Commission lowered fees for weekly medical inspections after several madams argued that reductions would encourage women to be examined more often. After all, the council argued, the Dispensario de Salubridad was not supposed to be a money-making venture, particularly when revenues encouraged clandestine prostitution. The intendente curtly reacted by challenging the council's right to adjust fees and insisted on the measure's withdrawal.[59]

It was not until the following year that the council began to discuss serious revisions of the 1875 ordinance, and the revisions took two years to complete. The final document, sanctioned on November 7, 1894, carefully defined the age of majority as eighteen for prostitutes with permission from their parents. Minors attempting to register would be remanded to the *defensoría de menores* (defender of minors). Most restrictions of prostitutes' behavior in public places were removed, as was the requirement that the reformed volunteer for charitable work. Bordellos were still prohibited within two blocks of churches, theaters, and schools, except those with fewer than three prostitutes. Women accused of clandestine prostitution would no longer be arrested and instead faced fines and the temporary or permanent demise of their business.[60]

Superficially the 1894 ordinance was a victory for those who had argued that prostitution ordinances violated women's civil rights. The relaxed regulations and lighter penalties, according to their theories, would encourage registration. When added to Bollini's 1892 decree authorizing Dispensario officials to ascertain if any woman had been forced to lie about her age or to register against her will, the threat of white slavery should have been reduced. Instead, reports of clandestine prostitution, as well as incidents of white slavery, increased as the number of newly registered women decreased. After registrations rose to 344 in 1895, the numbers declined until 1898, when they leveled off at 205. At the same time increased deaths attributed to syphilis in 1880–1910, compared with the 1870s, also alarmed public officials.

In September 1902 Intendente Adolfo Bullrich appointed a committee consisting principally of public health doctors to devise new ordinances that were completed in November 1903. Just before the law was passed, the Asociación Nacional Argentina contra la Trata de Blancas urged legislators to raise the minimum age from eighteen to twenty-two. The resulting 1904 law conformed to the association's request, and shortly thereafter reformers were also given permission to interview women at the Dispensario de Salubridad.[61] The new laws reflected the concerns of anti–white slavery groups and public health physicians. They clearly defined registration procedures, medical inspection, and venereal disease. This time, however, medical control won out over individual liberty. Registered prostitutes once again had to carry identity documents and refrain from working while ill, though they no longer faced mandatory incarceration. To prevent future illness, all prostitutes treated for venereal disease would henceforth be told of the prophylactic measures available to prevent future illness and informed of the consequences of syphilis and gonorrhea.[62]

Public health doctors continued to be preoccupied with bordello sanitation and isolation. Houses were required to have appropriate doors, con-

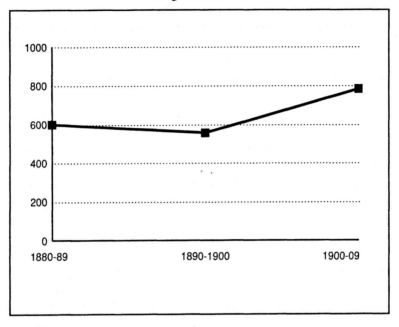

Infant (0-2 yrs.) mortality from syphilis
Source: Buenos Aires Municipality, *Anuario estadístico de la ciudad de Buenos Aires*,
1900, p. 225; Statistics on syphilis mortality rates, particularly among children, can be
found in Buenos Aires Municipality, *Censo general*, 1910, 2:115. See Irizar, "Servicio
sanitario de la prostitucíon," p. 111; Pareja, *Prostitución en Buenos Aires*, p. 176.

struction, and interior design. Described in hygienic and moral terms, bordellos, from the outside, were supposed to be unobtrusive and inoffensive.
Inside, houses had to be clean and to have adequate ventilation, a bath and
toilet, and signs describing symptoms of venereal disease and tuberculosis.
In many ways these rules demanded that prostitutes conform to sanitation
and housing standards that were advocated for all poor urban inhabitants.[63]

In 1904 the municipality first went on record against large houses of
prostitution. Between 1904 and 1908, the next time the law was changed,
bordellos could house only two prostitutes, a female servant, and a male
concierge. If women chose to live alone, they could not reside in buildings
with others engaged in sexual commerce. Clandestines, under the new regime, were treated more harshly. They were fined at a higher rate than before and always evicted from their lodgings. Furthermore, bordellos, even
legal ones, could be forcibly closed temporarily or permanently if they became the sites of disorderly conduct.[64]

In contrast to the 1894 ordinance, the 1904 law gave pimps, traffickers, and financial backers of city bordellos little to be pleased about. Business would diminish as fewer women were allowed in legal bordellos as well as in independent dwellings. Eighteen- and nineteen-year-olds could not be put to work without falsifying their ages. In response, according to the Asociación Nacional Argentina contra la Trata de Blancas, traffickers met and contributed 50,000 pesos to ensure that the ordinance would not be implemented. The Asociación duly informed the city council of the pimps' plans. Not only did the traffickers fail to have the law changed, but in July 1904 the intendente decreed that lodgings for prostitutes who lived alone would be restricted to one per city block instead of two and that they could not be contiguous with bordellos.[65]

The new laws proved unsatisfactory to many, including those who had devised them. More bordellos did not produce more order. The 621 newly registered women in 1904 were supposed to live in a maximum of 311 bordellos, compared with the 119 houses that in 1903 housed 640 women. The proliferation of houses, added to the costs pimps incurred in renting more than twice as many lodgings as before, led to a crisis where no one was pleased by the laws.[66]

Political pressure and more frequent incidents of scandalous behavior by streetwalkers prompted city officials to revise the law once again in June 1908. This time the municipal council created an exclusionary zone. Rather than declare a specific red-light district, it banned bordellos in the immediate downtown area defined by San Juan, Entre Ríos, Callao, 25 de Mayo, and Balcarce Streets, except those on side streets shorter than 301 meters. Houses on side streets could contain as many women as bedrooms. Elsewhere in the city, bordellos were limited to five women. Prostitutes once again had to be incarcerated in hospitals until they were cured, and to leave the business, women had to produce the testimony of two honest persons and a police certificate so they could have their names erased from the Dispensario de Salubridad. Even then the physicians would still have the right to examine the women.[67]

This time pimps and the influential backers of Buenos Aires bordellos benefited most from the new laws. For a short time, women between eighteen and twenty-two could register, and pimps and madams were allowed to recruit as many women as they wanted for downtown houses and have at least five legal women ensconced in their suburban businesses. No mention was made of the need to keep the houses away from churches or schools in suburban neighborhoods. Evidently hiding the bordellos on side streets in the downtown area satisfied the municipality's desire to obscure their presence while still keeping them under surveillance.

Prostitutes and neighbors suffered most under the 1908 laws. Women lost much of the freedom some physicians argued was necessary, and neighborhood complaints were ignored. Legal prostitutes could not remain in the bordello if ill, and they were no longer trusted to live decently after they reformed. These changes were sharply criticized by the local press. Journalists noted that Intendente Piñero Sorondo absolutely refused to close any bordello that fulfilled the requisites of the new law, regardless of neighborhood opposition. And unlike tobacco stores and commercial establishments, bordellos did not have to comply with Sunday rest laws. Newspapers demanded to know what kind of morality ordinance allowed such inconsistencies.[68]

Resentment toward pimps increased. Anti–white slavery groups began street demonstrations in Buenos Aires. Traffickers were occasionally sighted and threatened with physical violence, but they protected themselves by organizing people to disrupt anti–white slavery meetings. City officials even protected flagrant clandestine activities in illegal bordellos. Although the Paseo de Julio was added to the exclusionary area in September 1913, most houses there were still allowed to operate. On the same day the city council denied the petition of the National Education Council to close down two bordellos near schools. Similar decisions were made about two more houses in December of that year.[69] The numerous exemptions granted by public officials gave the impression that any powerful pimp could bend the law.

It was in this context that William Coote and Samuel Cohen traveled from England to Argentina to investigate the Buenos Aires connection to international white slavery. Unaware of specific changes that had ensured favorable working conditions for bordello owners, both men presumed that the situation of legalized prostitution after 1908 was typical, though it only reflected municipal ordinances between 1908 and 1919.

The system of legalized prostitution implemented in nineteenth- and early twentieth-century Buenos Aires was blamed for most of the problems European women experienced in the Argentine capital. As soon as the municipality began to keep track of self-identified prostitutes, it became evident that there were many foreigners in porteño bordellos. According to the 1878 report, for example, forty licensed bordellos housed 202 women. Most madams in the twenty houses mentioned were foreign-born. This might have meant they were more willing to register, but more likely it reflected the reality that they had male backers who could pay the 15,000 peso license fee.[70]

Those who wanted "proof" of white slavery had only to look at the nationality of the madams. Yet at the same time, the number of Argentine women working for European madams was almost twice that of foreign-born women. This more realistically evaluated both the proportion of native- to foreign-born prostitutes and the economic resources of creole women, who could not go into business for themselves even if they had a foreign-born pimp. Nevertheless, no explanations of white slavery made these distinctions. Instead, they claimed that the presence of foreign-born women in New World bordellos verified claims of an extensive international traffic in women.

Among the twenty bordellos listed in the 1878 Buenos Aires report, the number of inmates varied from one to sixteen. This meant that women like Dolores López and Consuelo González, both Spanish immigrants who lived alone, had to pay the 15,000 pesos from their own wages. Ana Dupont, who in 1869 had lived alone, now in 1878 operated a bordello where the wages of five women—one Argentine, three French, and one Spanish—could pay the tax man. Fanny Bader, a German madam who had sixteen women working for her (ten Argentine, five French, one Austrian), could pay her municipal obligations much more easily.[71]

Even though the impact of license fees on the nationality of bordello operators and organized pimping rings could be easily discerned in reports like this, prostitution statistics were constantly misinterpreted. European observers did not see the native-born women who worked for foreign madams, walked the streets, or stayed in bordellos outside the capital city. As Judith Walkowitz has pointed out, the British anti–white slavery frenzy was almost unjustified.[72] Nevertheless, British moral reformers were mortified that their women might end up in Argentine whorehouses. Instead of hiding a necessary evil, the licensing of prostitution accomplished the opposite: it offered "proof" of the fate of all immigrant women.

Accusations of white slavery were also supported by exposés of accommodations made between the police and foreign procurers. An 1880 newspaper article claimed that the municipal council allowed an illegal bawdy house, operated by an Italian woman, to conduct business on Venezuela Street. "This house continues to operate clandestinely due to the protection, or one might say, the *condescension* of some public official . . . because adolescent boys, of good family, are freely allowed to enter." Besides alluding to juvenile male customers, it also made guarded reference to the seduction of young males for prostitution: "We know that on more than one occasion poor young boys have been allowed to enter, attracted by the thousands of false promises made by the *madam*." The newspaper thus accused officials of allowing upper-class boys to have sexual initiations in the bordellos whereas lower-class boys were lured in to satisfy pederasts or the special predilections of some prostitutes. The municipal government's response to the matter was that no evidence existed to warrant such allegations.[73]

Not only did Buenos Aires condone bordellos as a legal business, it refused to acknowledge culpability for the existence of white slavery. In a legal judgment released in 1892, the asesor municipal defended the intendente's view that

> it is impossible to confirm that a group of individuals control this traffic, even though it is public knowledge that such is the case. . . .
>
> It is within the countries where these women are seized by means of deception and forced into prostitution that better means of dealing with this problem could and should be adopted. . . .
>
> Since those countries are not taking more precautions so that their citizens are not deceived by traffickers, we should applaud the efforts of the municipality, especially the measures adopted by the head of the Dispensario de Salubridad and the director of the Sifilicomio to attenuate and eliminate these evils.
>
> The municipality cannot prevent the importation of deceived women from Europe who end up in houses of prostitution because its authority does not extend beyond the national capital.[74]

The most the municipality could offer was the services of a translator who could ask immigrant women if they were being forced to register and offer asylum to innocent victims.

In 1895 Buenos Aires' reputation was further tarnished by special rulings for politically powerful groups. As had happened on other occasions, the municipal council from time to time exempted entire neighborhoods (*barrios*) from complying with prostitution regulations. A case in point was the parish of San Juan Evangelista (La Boca), which in December was allowed to have bordellos one block away from schools instead of following the customary two-block rule.[75]

Relations between the municipality and legal bordello operators, however, were far from idyllic. Yearly changes in license fees or periodic reforms of bordello ordinances created financial and political insecurity for all but the largest and wealthiest brothels. Houses opened and closed, women entered and left with incredible rapidity. Many houses that had once been legal closed up and reopened elsewhere. Madams and their financial backers simply refused to pay the license fee. They preferred to take their chances or buy police protection.

Regardless of what tactics police and municipal authorities used to monitor prostitutes, most failed. In 1894 the municipality's annual report observed that between 1889 and 1893, out of 3,984 women who had registered, only 744 still came for weekly exams. This poor attendance rate was explained by the "great mobility of the population, its majority immigrant, by the city's commercial nature . . . as well as because of things such as clandestine prostitution." At that time there were seventy-seven bordellos with 581 women, and another 163 prostitutes lived alone. Of the 368 women registered for the first time in 1893, one-third were Argentine, and 41 percent claimed they were literate. When asked about their previous employment, the most common answer (32.3 percent) was that they had never worked before. Among those who had worked elsewhere, the most frequent professions had been maids (21.9 percent), followed by seamstresses (14.7 percent) and dressmakers (8.69 percent). Jobs as cigarette saleswomen and café attendants did not lead women into bawdy houses, nor did work in the public sector. Instead, the unemployed and those who worked in private homes or behind the scenes in businesses were most at risk. Unemployment and poorly paid domestic service, rather than employment outside the home, drove women into prostitution.[76]

The implications of these facts were far reaching. To control prostitution, according to the evidence presented by self-identified prostitutes, urban authorities had to eliminate female unemployment and supervise domestic service more rigorously. They were unwilling to do either. City officials also had no intention of arresting every woman suspected of streetwalking or operating a clandestine bordello. One key function of legalized prostitution in Buenos Aires was the persecution of working women in order to drive them out of occupations that were later redefined for men.

The dynamics of women's employment in Argentina, at least until the turn of the twentieth century, diminished opportunities for female inhabitants. Traditionally women contributed to family income more frequently in rural than in urban areas. As part of sheep raising, textile making, and home food production, rural women had been able to protect their families from destitution when men were sent to war or migrated elsewhere in search of work. The modernization of Argentine agriculture and livestock production after 1870, accentuated by reliance on machinery operated by immigrant male laborers, brought a drastic decline in rural women's employment.[77]

Working-class men may have been hired in Buenos Aires with greater frequency than women, but both had to deal with the consequences of economic uncertainty. Real wages fell in Buenos Aires between 1874–78 and 1890–93. The years that followed were not much better. As James Scobie writes: "During the long periods of recovery that followed each of these depressions, immigrants and laboring people in the city made do by reducing the quantity and quality of their food, by mending and remending worn-out clothing and by seeking out miserable low-cost hovels of tenements. Even in boom years, living costs bit deeply into apparently handsome wages."[78]

Women in late nineteenth-century Buenos Aires had few prospects of supporting families, or even contributing to family income. A study of porteño commercial establishments in 1887 showed that 58 percent of 12,291 male sales clerks earned less than forty pesos per month, but 86 percent of 242 females were paid those low wages. Commercially employed *peones* (day laborers) received even less. Of 6,985 males, only 17 percent earned twenty pesos or less, while 75 percent of the 134 females eked out an existence with such paltry wages. [79]

Female industrial labor suffered the vagaries of business conditions. In some cases they benefited temporarily from economic depressions because they were willing to work for low wages. Thus men who had received a daily wage of 4.5 pesos for making cigarettes in 1887 were replaced ten years later by women who would work for half that amount. For the same reason, women and children gladly packed cigarettes, hoping that their piecework would net them the maximum amount of three pesos. Possibly hiring these women while men remained idle reinforced the traditional resentment against women who made or sold cigarettes, even though machines would soon replace cheap labor, both male and female.[80]

For a while the police and the city council responded to poor women's need to work by tolerating clandestine bordellos. The 1894 municipal report noted a reduction of licensed bordellos and medically supervised prostitutes at the same time it delineated the extent of clandestine operations in certain Buenos Aires neighborhoods:

In some *barrios* there are stores [*boliches*] where liquor is sold. . . . in La Boca, for example, there are three hundred to four hundred women within eighty to one hundred houses that, under the name *café* or *despacho de bebidas*, are in reality detestable bordellos.

In the Corrales district (section 12), we also have another group . . . consisting of fifty to sixty women in fifteen huts [*ranchos*]. . . . They used to be on Caseros Street, but have now abandoned their dwellings and moved out to Flores.

Even beyond these sites . . . unlicensed madams gather their hordes of prostitutes in furnished houses [*casas amuebladas*], hotels, inns, cafés, private residences, as well as their wandering through the streets, theaters and public ways.[81]

At the turn of the century men's as well as women's unemployment rose to new levels, and many immigrant bachelors returned to Europe. In late 1901 *La Prensa* claimed that families could not survive on one salary alone. "Survival, of course, lay in putting wife and children to work and cutting living standards."[82] What kind of work was available for women, particularly when city officials tended to deny that there was an employment crisis?

Within a few years, as in the past, the municipality returned to its policy of driving women out of the commercial sector. This time special attention was given to waitresses. A campaign in 1903 attempted to rid the city of these centers of clandestine prostitution where "men are wrested from useful occupations . . . [and] are poisoned whether with alcohol or with venereal disease." The municipal council enacted high license fees for such establishments and made waitresses have venereal disease exams as if they were bordello inmates. The ordinance was sanctioned in October 1903. It was further amended in April 1910 by banning any more cafés with waitresses except by permission of the intendente. In the meantime no one under age eighteen, male or female, could enter a café served by waitresses. Soon there were few waitresses left in the city, and since then the occupation has remained one reserved for males.[83]

The declining participation of women in the porteño commercial sector before 1895 is difficult to document because the 1869 census did not distinguish employment by sex. Fortunately the two subsequent censuses identified the gender structure of the city's labor force. An analysis of commercial employment reveals that between 1895 and 1914 the proportion of female employees declined from 21 to 11 percent. The shift is particularly noticeable within the category of food and lodging. In 1895 there were 6,994 women who represented 25 percent of that labor force. By 1914 only 6,621 women worked at similar jobs, and they constituted 14 percent of all employees. As for cafés, 370 women labored there in 1895, whereas only 197 had similar employment nineteen years later. Similarly, in 1914 only 202 women continued to work in bars compared with 521 reported in the earlier census. Despite the immense population increase Buenos Aires experienced between 1895 and 1914, fewer women worked in food and lodging. The antiprostitution ordinances had been quite successful in taking jobs away from women in commerce.[84]

Given the absence of diaries and censuses that focused specifically on women's work, it is difficult to measure exactly how women responded to these conditions. Several indirect methods, however, can reconstruct a female response. One way is to measure increased clandestine prostitution during these years. The only estimates available come from the physicians who created and enforced prostitution ordinances. In 1880, for example, Dr. Emilio R. Coni, a city council member, claimed there were 3,000 clandestines in Buenos Aires. By 1903 Dr. Enrique Revilla of Asistencia Pública (Municipal Public Assistance) estimated that the number had risen to somewhere between 8,000 and 10,000. Such calculations increased to 18,500 by 1915, a year when 510 women registered in legal bordellos for the first time while 1,045 either changed residences or left the business completely. The estimates of clandestines can be partly accounted for by the increase in the city's female population, partly by the arbitrary enforcement of legalized prostitution, partly by the conventional methods physicians used to estimate clandestine prostitution, but mostly by the reality that women had to do something to put bread on the table for themselves and their families.[85]

Another way to measure the ways women would defend their families or themselves was their participation in the rent strike of 1907. Even though unemployment had taken its toll among the working class, no relief from high rents had been forthcoming from owners of conventillos and casas de inquilinato. A rent strike started in one building and soon spread throughout Buenos Aires and into working-class cities in the province. Women were pivotal organizers. They defended buildings when men were working, often by threatening to pour boiling water on landlords who attempted to solve the problem by the forcible eviction of striking tenants. They threw all kinds of objects at meddling police. Ultimately the courts defended landlords' rights to evict. They also used the law of residence to deport dangerous immigrant anarchists and others who had led the strike.[86]

Women's continuing search for employment constitutes another response. By 1914 women were entering the porteño labor force in greater numbers than before. Among them were 13,429 schoolteachers (44 percent of all who claimed this profession), 79,781 domestic servants (82 percent female), and 68,574 industrial workers (25 percent female). Thus, while the proportion of employed female adults declined nationally from 58.8 percent to 27.4 percent, women in the national capital found employment at a faster rate than men in that city and women in the rest of the country. The antiwaitress campaign may have caused the proportion of women in food and lodging trades to decrease, but some women found work in other sectors of the economy.[87]

Women as well as men organized to increase wages and improve factory conditions. The Socialist *La Vanguardia* reported formation of labor unions for female domestic servants, canvas shoe makers, and garment workers. Women went out on strike to support demands made by male co-workers, as well as for their own advancement. In these early years the weakness of Argentine industry compared with European competitors made it difficult for porteño workers to defend their rights successfully. Furthermore, the dire necessity of women's wages to sustain relatives sometimes led families to refuse to support strikes that resulted in the loss of women's income. Such an incident occurred in 1904 when twenty-one female textile workers were forced by their fathers to return to work.[88]

The situation of textile employees is significant because that industry became a major employer of women in Buenos Aires. By 1914 more than 4,700 women had found jobs in large garment, fiber, sack, and canvas shoe factories, constituting 51.7 percent of employees. And even though textile manufacturing had been a female-focused cottage industry in the Argentine interior, in Buenos Aires strong disapproval developed of women's working in these and other factories. Part of this disapproval stemmed from loss of family income if females went on strike, as well as the belief that women were taking jobs away from men. Men's fear of losing jobs could be seen in the 1906 decision of the Unión General de Trabajadores to support the exclusion of all women and children from factories. They based this decision on the ease with which employers, parents, and husbands could prevent women and children from organizing. The fear of cheap competition was most likely another factor.[89]

Male heads of families and factory workers were not the only people who worried about women's increased factory employment. Insalubrious and hazardous factory conditions stirred moral reformers to sponsor protective labor legislation for women and children. Another factor shaping the view that women should not work in factories was the belief that such places exposed women to immoral influences, among them nonrelated males.

In 1902 the Socialist Gabriela Laperrière de Coni presented the municipality of Buenos Aires with a proposal to monitor women and minors in city factories. Among the safety provisions were guarantees that women of childbearing age, as well as nursing mothers, would have special privileges. Other clauses ensured that women would not be forced to work in immoral businesses and that they would not have to be supervised by males, "thereby preventing promiscuity with men."[90]

Laperrière de Coni defended these provisions by explaining that most countries enacted morality clauses to prevent women from working in establishments that produced obscene books, pictures, or objects. As for the insistence upon female supervision, she explained that while she was inspecting factories women had confided their fears to her, as had their parents.

Her conclusions were similar to those of Juan Bialet-Massé, who examined labor conditions in the Argentine interior two years later. He deplored the plight of home work for females but also believed that no women of childbearing age, except widows, should work in factories. In both cases reformers preferred that women reproduce rather than help support the family, as if the two tasks were interchangeable.[91]

Although these proposals were well intended, they show that reformers perceived the place of work, as well as the productive methods, as unhealthful and unsafe. Subsequent studies of women who worked at home or in sweatshops apart from the factory, conducted by the National Labor Department, showed a more complex situation. Although factory working conditions were less than ideal, women were more endangered by home labor.

In 1913 two major studies were published. The first dealt with sweated home labor. The investigator surveyed 1,088 home workers, of whom 899 were women. The most typical jobs for women were seamstress (201) and pants makers (219). Seamstresses worked from three to seventeen hours every day except Sunday for salaries that ranged from 50 centavos to 5 pesos a day, or 15 to 150 pesos per month. Most lived in one-room dwellings with other family members, for which they paid a monthly rent of 10 to 138 pesos. Only eight families earned between 200 and 300 pesos a month. In other words, women who sewed piecework could barely afford to pay for one-room flats, let alone feed themselves and their families.[92] Pants makers fared even worse. They earned less than seamstresses, and the great majority received no more than 2.5 pesos a day. Most could afford to spend no more than 30 pesos a month on lodging. They lived in 265 houses inhabited by 1,238 people.[93]

Carolina Muzilli's study of women's work, presented to an international exposition in Belgium in 1913, confirmed the dismal conditions of female laborers who worked outside the home. Besides factory and home laborers, Muzilli also investigated telephone operators, saleswomen, and working mothers. No matter what type of work, women received miserable wages and labored under deplorable conditions.[94] If factory work was unacceptable, then prostitution, legal or clandestine, rather than staying at home, was the only alternative for the woman who had to work.

Another way to measure the impact of economic conditions on women is to analyze the work history and family connections of women registering at the Dispensario de Salubridad. Obviously the number of women correlated not with economic conditions, but with the politics of municipal councils, intendentes, and the police. Nevertheless, except in 1889, more women sought legal registration in bordellos from 1910 to 1914 than in the 1890s.

After 1889 physicians began to collect and publish data about the prostitutes not only in annual municipal reports, but also in statistical yearbooks and medical journals. Their diligent efforts have left us a legacy of fascinating data about the women who registered in Buenos Aires from 1889 until 1934. It must be kept in mind, however, that prostitutes were forced to answer questionnaires administered by public authorities, whose control they constantly resisted. Therefore we must assume that they often gave evasive answers to extremely personal questions. Over the years there is a consistency to the answers that suggests the women gave the responses authorities wanted to hear. They may refect not a completely accurate group portrait, but rather the ideal biography that would allow them to work without undue harassment. Despite these uncertainties, this body of information is also the most extensive collection of data on women engaging in a specific occupation in Buenos Aires, and for all these reasons it offers insight into their lives and further clarifies the debate about women's work and prostitution.

In the early years consistent responses may have been accounted for by brief questionnaires. This trend became more pronounced after surveys became more sophisticated, however, and the number of women registering increased after 1909 when, instead of 600 to 700 women presenting themselves at the registry, 800 appeared. By 1910 there were 1,128 new recruits.

Newly registered women came from the same national groups as before. Among the 1910 group 22.3 percent were Russian (253), 20 percent were French (226), and 20.4 percent (230) were Uruguayan. Argentines constituted only 14.2 percent (160), followed distantly by 91 Spaniards (8 percent) and 76 Italians (6.7 percent). The high numbers of Uruguayans came as a shock to public health officials, and most likely they were not native-born South Americans, but rather Europeans who entered Argentina indirectly from Uruguay in order to attract less attention.[95]

Most women were between eighteen and twenty-five (72 percent), although 10 percent were over thirty. Their rate of literacy was almost the same as in 1893, about 40 percent. Since workers at the Dispensario now asked more questions, we have a better understanding of their situation. For example, although 87 percent were single, 34 percent had children; 31 percent had a living parent, and 39 percent were orphans. Over 50 percent of these women had never had a regular job before registering, and among those who had, the most frequent professions had been seamstress (10.1 percent) and dressmaker (10.3 percent). Domestic service had been either unattractive or unavailable to these women compared with those who registered in 1893.[96]

This group portrait shows that more than one-third of these women had children to support, and some might have been financially responsible for siblings or parents. Thus even though prostitution was often viewed as an occupation scorned by a woman's family, it was clear that some prostitutes used their income to support family members. Although 75 percent admitted to having been prostitutes before registering, all refused to list it as a previous occupation. Their adamant position on this point could be interpreted in several ways: they may have perceived previous activity as a survival strategy rather than an occupation. They might have been afraid of police harassment because of clandestine prostitution. Or they might have claimed they had engaged in prostitution before to ensure that there would be no bureaucratic obstacles to registration. Each of these possibilities points to the ways prostitutes used the registration system for their own purposes.

When asked what led them to prostitution, the great majority, 63.7 percent, answered money: 15 percent said they enjoyed the work, and only three women (0.2 percent) blamed it on abandonment or seduction. Once again, it is difficult to discern the veracity of these responses. For example, the three women who claimed they had been seduced would have been approached by authorities and offered rehabilitation rather than registration. How many women lied about spousal coercion in order to work? And of the majority of women who needed money, just how many had sought other employment? Only six cited lack of work as a reason to register, but this may be explained by the fact that most jobs available in Buenos Aires simply did not pay enough money so a family or an individual could survive on one woman's income.[97]

By 1912, out of more than 1,400 recruits, 50 percent of whom were either Russian or French, 804 (56.84 percent) claimed unemployment as their previous profession, followed by seamstress (17 percent) and various needlework and domestic service occupations. Though 70 percent had practiced prostitution before registration, once again none considered it a profession. For all these women, the act of registration turned prostitution into a job, and it might have been motivated by pressure from pimps or by their saving enough to move off the streets. From this perspective registration might have separated the poorest from the poor.[98]

These questionnaires were conducted on the eve of the arrival of European reformers like William Coote, Samuel Cohen, and Rosalie Lighton Robinson. Like Percy Bunting before them, Coote, Cohen, and Lighton Robinson relied on statistics of nationality as proof that legalized prostitution in Buenos Aires led to the degradation of European women. They blamed municipally supervised bordellos for the situation, rather than dwelling on the economics of female employment and brothel keeping, the fact that most European women claimed to have been prostitutes before registering in Buenos Aires, and the absence of data on clandestine prostitutes.

There is little evidence to support the notion that most women "fell into" prostitution because of immoral influences. If a woman said she had been coerced into prostitution, by the late 1890s translators and eventually social workers were able to help her escape the grip of the white slaver. Such aid did not, however, ensure employment elsewhere at a fair wage, nor would it guarantee her family a subsistence income. It also might have resulted in repatriation and hence the return to impossible living conditions in her homeland. For these reasons a woman might not have made such an admission to the survey taker, and thus the debate about the extent of white slavery could continue.

What the surveys did demonstrate was that women who could manage to get factory jobs in their native land or in Buenos Aires rarely ended up in a city-operated bordello. Registered prostitutes were not direct castoffs of industrial capitalism, but rather those who had been unable to enter the modern labor force. Equally important, factories did not necessarily create environments that would produce immoral women. Similarly, fears of women's mixing commerce with sex were exaggerated, based more on unwarranted fears of women's taking jobs away from men.

These anxieties manifested themselves in other Argentine cities that were grappling with urban growth and economic conditions even less dynamic than those in Buenos Aires. Out in Buenos Aires province, for example, the towns of Tandil, La Plata, and Ensenada legalized prostitution. For women who did not migrate to the capital city, work in provincial bordellos like those of Tandil became yet another alternative to unemployment. By the turn of the century houses in Tandil were filled by creole women between twenty-five and thirty-five years old. In 1910 four bordellos operated in the provincial capital of La Plata, where there were forty-one native-born and forty-three immigrant prostitutes out of an adult population of more than 18,000 females.[99]

Outside Buenos Aires, provincial cities with prospects of attracting male workers used legalized prostitution to monitor the female population, whose employment was less certain. The capital of Córdoba province enacted legislation in 1883 to create a red-light district. Bordellos unlicensed or outside the zone were subject to closure. Women accused of clandestine prostitution were arrested or fined. At the outset most Cordobese prostitutes were "*chinas*" (poor Indian or mestiza women), and their pimps were usually their creole lovers. By the turn of the century immigrant women and their pimps made their way inland. And, as in the case of Buenos Aires, police frequently ignored the infractions of upper-class clandestine bordellos and nightclubs.[100]

Municipal authorities in Rosario instituted a system of licensed bordellos in 1874. They initially rejected the idea of a red-light district, although Rosarinos later changed their minds. In 1893 they identified the geographic boundaries for bordellos, and in 1906 they expanded the zone. In 1890 the city constructed the Dispensario de Salubridad to centralize prostitutes' exams. The women exacted revenge on the system by behaving as outrageously as possible outside the Dispensario. At that time there were eighteen authorized houses with 125 women, 56 percent Argentine, 18 percent Italian, 10 percent Spanish, and 10 percent German. Most of these houses were on Suipacha and Pichincha Streets, and the price per visit ranged from one to three pesos. One particularly notorious establishment,

Madame Safo's, had a merry-go-round where women clad in nothing but shawls entertained prospective customers.[101]

Another major provincial city that legalized prostitution was San Miguel de Tucumán. Site of a prosperous sugar industry that attracted large numbers of male workers but offered little employment for women, the city passed a prostitution ordinance in 1890. Bordellos could be anywhere within the city except near a church or within four blocks of the main square, the Plaza de Independencia. Prostitutes were supposed to be examined once a week by a private doctor.[102]

Not all Argentine provincial capitals and cities legalized prostitution. Those that did not tended to be urban areas that experienced large-scale male migration to more economically active areas. The capital of Corrientes is an example. In 1898 Dr. Antonio B. Pont made a study of the prevalence of syphilis and suggested that the number of cases in Corrientes could be lowered by legalizing prostitution. At the same time Dr. Antonio B. Pont, a resident, believed the city would never bother to implement such a law because, as he put it, "there's simply too much competition." Of all children born in the city, 71 percent were illegitimate, and the proportion of married people in Corrientes was far lower than in Buenos Aires. Pont also claimed that not only was there a tremendous amount of commercial sex among adult females in Corrientes, but minors walked the streets and parents were known to sell the sexual services of children as young as two years old.[103]

Throughout Argentina prostitution control was symbolically associated with fear of disease and the more general issue of what to do about the potentially revolutionary working classes—the *problema social.* In reality prostitution patterns responded more to immigration and urban-based activities that partially integrated women into the paid labor force but rarely provided working-class families a decent wage. In modernizing Argentine cities, the plight of the woman who flaunted herself and sold her body—along with those who might—haunted the politically powerful and attracted extensive discussion. The municipal council began the debate, and police and physicians soon joined in. The issue exploded in the late 1800s with the advent of the international campaign against white slavery, but its nationalistic emphasis obscured the specific economic, political, and cultural issues affecting the Argentine case.

Between 1875 and 1936 various participants joined in the local debate and made their opinions public. Each had a different perspective, and they proposed diverse solutions, most of which rarely challenged the economic and patriarchal order. Nevertheless, together they constituted one of the most volatile debates about political authority, gender, and class relations in Argentine history, one that continued long after 1936. In fact, all subsequent Argentine political issues related to women's work, family reform, and women's rights have been indelibly touched by the history of legalized prostitution.

3

Venereal Disease, Public Health, and Criminality

Prostitution threatened Buenos Aires and other Argentine cities through the spread of venereal disease to sexual partners and subsequent offspring. What was less clear to nineteenth-century urban reformers was what to do about this problem and who would take charge. The struggle began with the municipal council and the police force, and they were soon joined by public health physicians (*higienistas*). It was a battle not taken lightly by any of the interested parties, and consequently aggrieved politicians, physicians, and policemen began to justify their views in articles, books, and reports. The nature of their dispute revealed the political and social tensions that were manifest in Buenos Aires during this period, as well as showing how illness and crime were identified and constructed in terms of class, gender, and morality.

Few groups had more to say about prostitution, disease, and social control than the higienistas. Unlike physicians in private practice, higienistas devoted most of their lives to public service. They often worked in municipal hospitals and on the city council, and their knowledge about the causes of communicable diseases probably gave them more influence on urban planning and social control than any other group of trained professionals. Their expertise was both recognized and sought by the Buenos Aires municipal council after its reorganization in 1856. From then on physicians were present on the council and staffed a hygiene board that provided technical information and made public health recommendations.

Much of what physicians recommended for urban health, however, transcended their task as healers and reflected their role as social reformers. Doctors identified lower-class residents as both the cause and the victims of disease. Although higienistas campaigned for treatment for smallpox, yellow fever, and cholera and insisted that municipal government treat leprosy, tuberculosis, and venereal disease, their proposals emphasized lower-class moral reform.[1]

Their methods included efforts to instill better sanitation and health practices among the poor. They initiated programs for child care and maternal education in hopes of improving the reproductive strength of the immigrant and native populations, and they trained parents to assume more responsibility for the appropriate socialization of their children. To achieve these various goals, new behavioral norms had to be inculcated in the working class for the sake of future generations. Higienistas targeted women more frequently than men as objects of reform because they were most responsible for child rearing.

Several generations of Argentine physicians helped shape public health policies in Buenos Aires and other Argentine cities. After national unification in 1852, Drs. Guillermo Rawson, Eliseo Cantón, and Edwardo Wilde served dual roles as both political leaders and doctors, and in this way politics became inseparable from issues of public health. In 1873 the medical faculty of the University of Buenos Aires created a chair in hygiene, and Rawson was appointed to teach the courses. By 1880 the Departamento Nacional de Higiene (National Hygiene Department) was established to replace an earlier national Consejo de Higiene Pública (Public Hygiene Council). Intended to monitor the ports and the country generally for signs of epidemics and infectious diseases, the Departamento Nacional de Higiene gathered and analyzed statistics and information from higienistas all over Argentina. Public health had become so important to the future of the nation that in 1898 Eliseo Cantón announced rather egotistically that physicians "who attempt to diminish mortality statistics serve the nation better than increased immigration statistics."[2]

Medical students at the University of Buenos Aires were exposed to contemporary European social and medical theories, especially French ideas. Among those who designed and implemented prostitution ordinances for the national capital in the 1870s, Emilio Coni, Telémaco Susini, and José María Ramos Mejía received their medical training at this time. Since 1880 all three had been proponents of a municipally sponsored public assistance program like the one Adolphe Thiers had presented to the French Assembly. The purpose of the Buenos Aires Asistencia Pública was to centralize responsibility and control over the city's hospitals and public health facilities.[3]

The subjects offered at the university's medical school encouraged student interest in public health. Emilio Coni specialized in leprosy, which, like venereal diseases, was often first diagnosed as a skin condition. Dermatology and its diverse aspects thus constituted a common career for many higienistas. Several had training as pharmacists before they began their medical education. These specialties prepared them to tackle the problem of venereal disease control in Argentine cities, particularly Buenos Aires.

For the new generation of higienistas, the prostitutes' registry directed by municipally appointed physicians and a city hospital to care for ill prostitutes were essential. As Emilio Coni noted in his memoirs: "In 1879 I published a plan to organize a prostitutes' clinic . . . but it was not acted upon. My plan was designed to correct the unfortunate consequences of an 1875 ordinance (which must have been designed by profane and incompetent people because it taxed bordellos so exorbitantly that [the tax] became prohibitive and it gave the madams the right to select physicians who made the required examinations)." [4]

Coni fought long and hard to revise the 1875 ordinance because he believed that inadequate medical treatment for prostitutes had led to alarming increases in venereal disease. In 1877, while still a medical student, he published an article discussing the relation of syphilis to mortality in the city of Buenos Aires. He noted that between 1872 and 1876, 173 deaths were attributed to congenital syphilis, and most of these had occurred among infants at the city orphanage. He directly blamed the illness and its tragic consequences on "this social evil so ignored among us, one called prostitution." [5] In 1887 he presented a demographic study of Buenos Aires that once again blamed increased incidence of syphilis and venereal disease on lack of interest in reform of prostitution ordinances. [6]

In 1880 Drs. Coni, Ramos Mejía, and Ignacio Pirovano suggested the creation of a prostitutes' registry based upon the 1877 Belgian model, one operated by physicians rather than the police. There women would identify themselves to city authorities and have weekly medical inspections. Clandestine prostitutes would not be arrested and taken to the office until there was definite evidence of public scandalous behavior. Furthermore, police were not to harass women known to have consensual relationships with one man ("acciones de libertinaje privado [relaciones habituales con un hombre])." [7]

Most of the plan was designed to take the surveillance and treatment of prostitutes away from police, city officials, and private doctors and to empower municipally appointed physicians. No longer would police be able to label a woman a prostitute without presenting evidence. To study the causes of prostitution, henceforth registered women would be asked about their backgrounds and their reasons for becoming prostitutes. Furthermore, there would be no more onerous bordello taxes. From this perspective Argentine physicians harked back to their early nineteenth-century French counterparts, who believed that the "first task of the doctor is . . . political: the struggle against disease must begin with a war against bad government."[8]

Despite their desire to rectify past injustices, higienistas initially were adamant that prostitutes be segregated from the general public. To that end they included provisions that prostitutes be banned from frequenting "confiterías, cafés etc., in other words, pretending to be involved in a lawful business." These women were also denied the privilege of walking in public in an offensive manner, standing about in doorways or hanging out windows, gathering in public places, and luring men. If they wanted to leave the bordello, the only way a prostitute would automatically receive permission would be through death or marriage.[9]

Much of their philosophical rationale came from a study that appeared shortly before the triumvirate went to the municipal council. Written by Dr. Benjamin Dupont, a French-trained physician who had moved to Buenos Aires, and titled *Pornografía de Buenos Aires*, it justified curtailing prostitutes' civil liberties because "prostitutes violate various fundamental social laws, therefore they cannot expect the freedom that society assures all its members." To prove his point Dupont cited the classic French prostitution study of Parent Duchatelet, the Bible, and Montesquieu's commentary on prostitution, thereby showing that medical, religious, and liberal sources agreed that prostitutes could be treated differently from the rest of the population. The only disagreement related to how many of their civil rights could be violated. Dupont's arguments were implicitly incorporated into Coni's 1880 plan as well as into another proposal introduced to the municipal council in 1884 by Dr. Juan de Parras Castañeda. In this way higienistas reaffirmed the view of European moral reformers that female prostitutes defined the parameters of social acceptability and citizenship.[10]

In 1880 higienistas won a partial victory with the temporary reduction of the 15,000 peso fee, and they persuaded Intendente Alvear to propose venereal disease clinics in Buenos Aires. Basic reforms of the 1875 ordinance, however, were not passed, and Emilio Coni, who had been appointed to the hygiene section of the municipal council in February 1880, resigned in protest the following year.[11]

While Coni awaited passage of new prostitution legislation, other higienistas devised strategies to expand municipal treatment of venereal disease.
Dr. Telémaco Susini suggested that the new municipal Hospital San Roque
designate a room to examine prostitutes. As he put it, not only would this
plan help resolve a long-standing issue related to legalized prostitution, it
would also advance medical knowledge of syphilis and its various manifestations. Susini's response from the city council was that the hospital did not
have adequate facilities.[12] Dr. Juan de Parras Castañeda's 1884 plan met a
similar fate.

Although the city did not authorize construction of treatment facilities
for ill prostitutes in 1884, that October a new set of municipal ordinances
was enacted. The law represented a compromise between the liberal concerns of higienistas and their agreement with traditionalists that prostitutes'
physical mobility should be curtailed. Women were still restricted in their
activities outside the bordello, but henceforth clandestine prostitutes were
supposed to be protected from unfair police accusations. The new ordinance, in fact, did little to protect them against arbitrary treatment.[13]

The creation of the long-awaited Asistencia Pública in 1883 helped but-
tress medical campaigns by placing all municipal public health agencies under a central authority. Initially run by Ramos Mejía and later by Coni, Susini, and other graduates of the University of Buenos Aires medical school,
Asistencia Pública was responsible for the management, budget, and admis-
sions policies of all the city's medical facilities and hospitals under its control.

The Dispensario de Salubridad was the first medical facility dedicated to
venereal disease control. Opened in October 1888, it was headed by Dr.
Eugenio Ramírez and staffed by physicians and aides, all male. In a period
of twelve years the Dispensario changed directors three times and was
moved on five occasions to different parts of the city. Originally it was in
the heart of the downtown area at Esmeralda 76. In 1891 city officials re-
located the clinic twice, first to Entre Ríos 1492 to the southwest, and then
to San José 15, a more central location not far from the Plaza Lorea. Eight
years later the Dispensario was moved back to the southwest to Sarandí
1440, only to change location again in 1900 to Larrea 1500, in the more
fashionable northern area not far from Recoleta Cemetery.

Most likely these relocations were the city's response to neighborhood
anger and inadequate facilities. Nevertheless, they raise the question whether
prostitutes could even find the Dispensario from year to year, and whether
this might have been a factor in the declining number who came to register.

When the various post-1891 Dispensario sites are considered from a geographic perspective, they form the edges of the urban zone where bordellos were banned after 1908.[14]

Despite the opening of the Dispensario de Salubridad and expanded powers, one area of medical care continued to elude the heads of Asistencia Pública: public hospitals where women could receive long-term care for venereal disease.[15] Until this problem was circumvented or resolved, the city had limited authority to treat venereal disease in prostitutes. This obvious gap in municipal control stemmed from the historic right of the Sociedad de Beneficencia (Beneficence Society) to operate orphanages, hospitals, schools, and prisons for women. Organized by the liberal government of Bernadino Rivadavia in the 1820s, the society replaced religiously sponsored charitable institutions with ones operated by elite women and subsidized by the government. Although suppressed during the Rosas dictatorship and heartily criticized by liberal reformer and future president Domingo Sarmiento when it began to operate again in the 1850s, the society took over the management of the Hospital General de Mujeres (Women's Hospital), when no one else wanted the responsibility.

Thereafter the hospital that served the city's poor women was maintained under multiple handicaps of perpetually insufficient funding, shortages of facilities and supplies, and open political hostility by higienistas. The women in charge often complained of their financial handicap, but they were thoroughly unwilling to be relieved of the responsibility. Instead they relied upon other socially minded physicians and the unpaid help of female religious orders and female prison inmates to staff many of their institutions.[16]

The issue at stake was who operated the hospitals and determined which patients would be admitted rather than whether there was appropriate medical care. It was not that the society refused to treat syphilitic women; on the contrary, they were among the principal patients at the Hospital General de Mujeres. Neither was it a question of adequate medical training. The Sociedad de Beneficencia hired as many physicians as its budget would allow, and the doctors tended to support the women's organization when it came under criticism. It was the question of just how many ill prostitutes would be cared for at the Hospital General de Mujeres, and whether hospital beds should be dedicated to patients with chronic rather than treatable illnesses that brought the brunt of higienista criticism of the society.

Caught in the midst of proposing mandatory municipally supervised medical treatment for prostitutes, public health physicians realized they

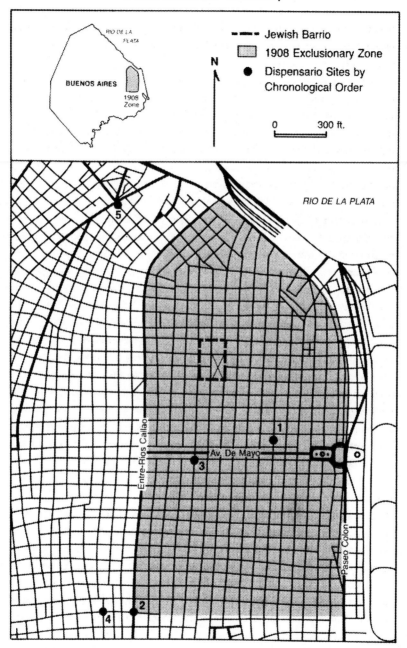

Map of prostitution by geographic restriction and Dispensario sites in Buenos Aires.

needed a location where they could commence treatment immediately. The only public hospital specifically designated for women was the one run by the society. For higienistas it was the ideal location for their temporary prostitutes' clinic. Requests for such facilities had been made by the municipal council since 1877, and in 1880 Emilio Coni once again inquired about the feasibility of designating ten beds for the care of prostitutes. Coni was informed that the only way such a commitment could be made, given the shortage of beds, was to reduce the care of chronically ill women, something the Sociedad de Beneficencia was unwilling to allow. Ultimately a compromise was effected after the beggars' asylum agreed to take ten terminally ill patients from the Hospital General de Mujeres.[17]

The refusal of the Sociedad de Beneficencia to admit ill prostitutes for short-term care was seen as the consequence of inappropriate hospital management by untrained women. It is not at all clear, however, that the Hospital General de Mujeres would have been better off under the control of the municipal council. Cooperation might have accomplished far more than the hostile attitude of the higienistas. From the outset, however, the public health physicians adopted Sarmiento's position that women were unsuited to wield public authority. Undaunted, the women of the Sociedad de Beneficencia continued to operate the city's women's hospital after the old one was torn down and replaced in 1887 by the Hospital Rivadavia.[18]

Even if the higienistas were better trained than the society's doctors, it is still doubtful whether they could have offered prostitutes better medical care in their new Sifilicomio because venereal disease treatment was still so rudimentary. Until the 1930s a possible cure for syphilis depended upon a long and costly course of medical therapy. If the Buenos Aires city government wanted to keep all infected prostitutes in the Sifilicomio, or any other hospital, patients had to remain there for months. According to Dr. Brito Foresti, in 1919 no one with gonorrhea could ever be considered cured. If women were hospitalized they needed perpetual care, although it is clear that higienistas did not openly admit this to the society. As for syphilis, cures could be guaranteed only after a patient had been free of sores for four years. In those circumstances it was too expensive and coercive for prostitutes, and it is highly unlikely that Argentine public hospitals were any different from British lock hospitals, which often discharged patients early to make room for new ones.[19]

The Sifilicomio opened in 1889 with two hundred beds. The type of room a prostitute received depended on her ability to pay, and none were turned away. Whether the women came for weekly examinations at the Dispensario or for medical treatment at the Sifilicomio, their physicians designed the rules and regulations that governed relations between themselves and prostitutes.[20]

Emphasis on submissive and deferential behavior by prostitutes was notable in the procedures for the Dispensario and the Sifilicomio. Prostitutes were not to speak except in response to questions from the attending physician. Legally no prostitute was ill until a doctor made such a determination, and any woman resisting the physician's authority during an examination could be declared unwell as punishment and forcibly incarcerated in the Sifilicomio. Within the walls of the medical clinic prostitutes were to exhibit moral and socially appropriate behavior or else they were as guilty of illness as the infected. In this way the physician gave disease a social, moral, and medical construction.[21]

The stringent regulations also invested higienistas with questionable police powers, and the municipality again relied on the municipal attorney to resolve jurisdictional boundaries. On July 6, 1889, Asesor Basavilbaso ruled that doctors could transport recalcitrant and badly behaved women to the Sifilicomio, and they could call for police help if necessary. Four years later the police were complaining that Dispensario officials demanded too much from them, and the asesor agreed that it was not intended that the police act as a private force for the Dispensario, for several reasons. First of all, the municipality was no longer authorized to jail women at the request of the Dispensario. Second, it was futile to send the police out to chase recalcitrant women, so long as they were not guilty of scandalous behavior or interfering with traffic. Unless the municipality passed a new prostitution ordinance, police powers were not be abused by physicians. Higienistas may have complained about the coercive powers of others, but they also relied upon police help to enforce their own authority.[22]

The most dubious aspect of the higienista campaign, and one that directly affected the way they planned to deal with prostitutes, was their reluctance to dismiss a commonly held nineteenth-century belief that prostitutes transmitted venereal diseases to men but men had little to do with contaminating the prostitutes. Since these women were perceived to be the transmitters of venereal disease, it is understandable why doctors like Coni were so frustrated with a system of prostitution regulation dependent on the whims of mayors and the honesty of physicians hired by madams. The right to monitor prostitution guaranteed neither compliance nor cures; but confident and undaunted, many doctors continued to insist upon limiting public medical treatment to prostitutes despite germ theory and the evidence that customers infected women.

Despite the evidence of extensive male prostitution and the role of males as sources of contamination for healthy prostitutes, no men were ever subjected to municipal licensing or mandatory medical examination until the advent of mandatory prenuptial blood tests after 1936. Higienistas knew that Buenos Aires had a significant homosexual population and that male prostitutes were found not only among streetwalkers soliciting sex but also within the supposedly all-female bordellos. Although these men were studied as medical curiosities and efforts were made to identify the environmental causes of their homosexuality, they were ignored as a source of illness.

A case in point was the Paraguayan transvestite male prostitute named "Aurora" whose life history was analyzed by Dr. Francisco de Veyga in 1903. Aurora arrived in Buenos Aires as a young adult and became a homosexual prostitute after being propositioned and seduced at the Paseo de Julio, a part of town renowned for its female streetwalkers. According to de Veyga, hunger helped the man overcome his scruples, and soon Aurora was cruising downtown Buenos Aires. Aurora was arrested for scandalous behavior only if he dressed as a woman or was found brawling in cafés or on the streets. In other words, Aurora's activities were considered criminal by police only when he demonstrated male sociopathic behavior.

Once Aurora entered the homosexual world, his compatriots urged him to become a women's hair stylist, a job that led him to work for prostitutes. Evidently this was a common event, and males often provided sexual as well as nonsexual services in bordellos as prostitutes, servants, and business associates. De Veyga had the opportunity to study Aurora after he was placed under "preventive arrest" for having angered clients at a costume ball in a public bordello. Evidently his costume was too realistic for the offended customer.[23]

Throughout the study of Aurora, the higienista refrained from placing the prostitute's behavior in a moral context. Nor did he refer to Aurora as a prostitute. Rather, he preferred to call him a "professional" and explained men like Aurora and "Rosita de la Plata" (the other transvestite analyzed in the article) as examples of acquired mental disorientation caused by misunderstanding of female sexuality.[24]

Several months later de Veyga published his findings about another transvestite prostitute whom he labeled as a merchant (*tipo profesional: un invertido comerciante*)! According to the physician, the man "fell into" homosexual practices. Luis D., a Spanish immigrant who renamed himself

"La Bella Otero" after a famous Parisian courtesan, had been seduced by a neighbor in Madrid. After his initial revulsion, Luis decided such sexual contact was pleasurable and eventually went to work for a homosexual bordello owner (*meretricio homosexual*).

"La Bella Otero" prepared an autobiography for the doctor that clearly refuted the contention that Luis's sexual preferences had been accidental. In Luis's own words he had always considered himself a woman and worn women's clothing. He claimed to have married another man and given birth to two children before becoming a widow. He was obsessed with suicidal thoughts and fascinated with the cult of Santa Teresa ("like all aristocratic women") but gave up both because of his intense desire for physical pleasure. The autobiography suggested a tremendous amount of fantasy or delusion rather than the impact of accidental factors. De Veyga reproduced it without comment.[25]

When de Veyga studied female prostitutes, he had a totally different view of their activities. They were as immoral as the politicians who sanctioned legalized prostitution and the pimps and white slavers who also benefited from sexual commerce. Even more important, he characterized female prostitutes as *auxiliares del vicio* (abetors of vice), people who lived on the edge of the criminal world and crossed over when they helped rob or defraud their customers. Yet he barely mentioned male prostitutes in his study of urban evil.[26]

De Veyga was not the only higienista aware of the distinctions made between male and female prostitution in Buenos Aires. Dr. Eusebio Gómez, a criminologist and popularizer of contemporary criminal anthropology, in 1908 published an article and then a monograph entitled *La mala vida en Buenos Aires* (The Profligate Life in Buenos Aires). Gómez depicted the male prostitute as motivated more by money than by sex, and for this reason nearly all of them also engaged in thievery. Like de Veyga, Gómez identified female prostitutes as vectors of disease, ignoring the transmission of disease by male prostitutes and heterosexual clients. Neither labeled male sexual professionals as prostitutes, but Gómez's view of female prostitutes differed in that he viewed them as inherently immoral and linked to the criminal world.[27]

Not only were physicians unclear about the exact relation between prostitution and gender, they also mixed science with gender-based moral issues to define female prostitution. In 1894 the Buenos Aires municipal council was debating prostitution ordinances and discovered that councilmen, many of whom were physicians, could not agree on a definition of who was a prostitute. After a lengthy discussion of possible definitions, one member of the council, a physician, commented: "When the council created an ordinance to regulate dairies [*tambos*, also a term for bawdy houses], there was no need to begin by defining what they were. Nor was it necessary to identify who traveling salesmen were in order to regulate their trade. Now that we are deliberating a prostitution ordinance, it should be unnecessary to define who is a prostitute."[28] Most of Dr. Montes de Oca's colleagues disagreed, and the discussion continued by defining the difference between a profligate (*libertina*) and a prostitute in terms of ability to transmit reputedly "female" diseases:

> The woman who, owing to her instinctive nature, sometimes chooses this class of life and gives herself to many men without pecuniary need is a profligate; the woman who sells her body and does it constantly and transmits venereal and other female illnesses [*enfermedades sóricas*] is a prostitute. Therefore there is a need to establish two separate categories.
>
> When it comes to defining prostitution, the final question is how to differentiate between one and the other. One can monitor the profligate or lost woman . . . but one cannot isolate her [*secuestrársele*].[29]

Dr. Berutti, on the other hand, was more concerned about the class and marital identity of the woman involved than about whether she accepted money for her deeds or infected men. To that end he recounted the story of Messaline (the third wife of the emperor Claudius, who worked in a common bordello). He asked whether married and upper-class women should be forced into houses of prostitution. His query was based upon the presumption, totally unfounded and contrary to anti–white slavery claims, that only unmarried women showed up at the Dispensario de Salubridad.

In response to Berutti's comments another physician, Dr. Spuch, gave the group a higienista's solution to the problem by recounting the tale of the *curandero* (healer) Talmos, who knew how to cure fevers but could not define them. When subjected to the scrutiny of the French court, he proclaimed: "You define it and I'll cure it." The object lesson of the story was obvious—the council could solve the problem of prostitution with appropriate ordinances or waste its time deliberating who was a prostitute.[30]

Up to this point in the debate, council members had been most interested in identifying the relation of prostitutes to morality, class, marital status, disease, and the economy. The last stage of the discussion dealt with sensuality and sexual gratification. The topic was brought up with the presentation of a new definition: a prostitute is a woman who sells her body and enjoys the experience. Some women prostituted themselves not only for money, but also for pleasure. This definition was so fraught with controversy that it probably convinced legislators that it was better to drop the subject.[31]

When it became clear that no definition of prostitution would satisfy all council members, they began to discuss the real dilemma that faced them. What separated the good woman from the fallen woman? What about the half-fallen woman? Where could one draw the line? What was sinful behavior to one was an act of contagion to another, but only the beginning of immoral activities to a third. Out of frustration and in recognition of the dangers inherent in categorically labeling women, they finally had to agree with Dr. Montes de Oca and Justinian that "all definitions are dangerous," and the ordinance passed later that year, unlike the original one of 1875, contained no definition of prostitution.[32]

Clearly what was taking place was more than the implementation of a public health program. Higienistas had their own conceptions of illness and deviant behavior, both of which were developed to instill class- and gender-directed norms through legalized female prostitution. They saw no medical or moral threat in male prostitutes and thus never contemplated the medical examination or legal registration of men.

At the same time many higienistas continued to search for ways to make legalized prostitution palatable to female prostitutes. Emilio Coni was among the staunchest proponents of "enlightened" medical supervision. In 1893, after wealthier prostitutes refused to be incarcerated in the Sifilicomio with the poor ones, Coni drafted an ordinance accepted by the city council to allow richer prostitutes to be treated at other hospitals or clinics in the city. He did this with the expectation that these reforms would encourage more prostitutes to seek medical care. Later he was in the vanguard of the medical education movement, and in 1907 he founded the Sociedad Argentina de Profilaxis Sanitaria y Moral. The society had intended to provide free venereal disease medication to all who sought it and to publish a series of pamphlets designed to inform everyone of the dangers of venereal disease. Unfortunately the organization collapsed within three months from lack of public support.[33]

No matter how much Coni believed in public education and free medical treatment, he still affirmed his faith in the efficacy of municipally regulated prostitution. This was clearly seen in 1909 when he presented a report to the Fourth Latin-American Scientific Congress in Santiago, Chile. He supported advocates of legalized prostitution while simultaneously admitting that "despite all the objections to the contrary . . . I believe that a prostitute is an indispensable element of modern society and should not be oppressed by absurd regulations." The question remained how to create ordinances that would ensure public health through prostitution control without forcing prostitutes to submit to unfair regulations.[34]

Coni's concerns about class differences among prostitutes were reexamined in reforms later proposed by other higienistas who wanted to exempt wealthier prostitutes from onerous regulation. In 1912 Dr. Silvestre Oliva, a director of Asistencia Pública, asserted that it was counterproductive to regulate prostitution among women who worked out of their own homes or who met men in *casas de citas*, small hotels renting rooms by the hour. According to Oliva, these women still had a certain degree of modesty (*recato*) and therefore would have little difficulty returning "to an honest life and the tranquillity of work and family." Since they were the group of prostitutes least likely to "become disorderly and offend morality," they did not warrant municipal supervision. On the other hand, women living in bordellos not only should be overseen, but should have no more than three colleagues working with them at any time.[35]

As late as the 1920s higienistas were still struggling to find the ideal way to control prostitutes. Dr. Enrique Rosés Lacoigne published a study of prostitution in Buenos Aires following the Socialist reforms of 1919. According to Rosés Lacoigne the situation had deteriorated because of the proliferation of bordellos. Therefore he recommended allowing larger houses to reopen rather than abolishing municipal licenses. At the same time he expressed a strong desire to protect the rights of prostitutes from coercive police and medical control.[36]

Not all higienistas, however, approved of the system of licensed prostitution in Buenos Aires, even after the reforms of the late 1880s. Those who ultimately supported the campaign to abolish legalized prostitution did so for two basic reasons. First they recognized that prostitutes refused to be treated in a coercive fashion, and second they began to accept empirical data that venereal disease could be halted only by providing medical education and treatment to the entire community, not just prostitutes.

Higienistas opposed to legalized prostitution were less sanguine about the prospects of creating just ordinances, let alone ones that incorporated class concepts identifying high-class prostitutes as medically less dangerous than streetwalkers. Dr. José Manuel Irizar, who had firsthand experience with this issue as the director of the Dispensario de Salubridad in the 1890s, lambasted the system in 1902 when he categorically stated that "any ordinance that stresses a coercive spirit will be counterproductive as a method of prophylaxis." Rather than relying on the health of the prostitute, he recommended public education and treatment of all the infected.[37]

The following year Dr. Enrique Prins, secretary of Asistencia Pública, published a short but concise indictment of legalized prostitution. He categorically refuted the notion that written laws influence a woman's decision to engage in commercial sex: "They do it when the tendency and opportunity are suited to their necessity," and not at the age the municipality defines appropriate. He questioned whether the organization and location of legal bordellos had any effect on public morality. More than anything else, however, he criticized the mandatory hospitalization and incarceration of diseased prostitutes. Instead he argued that prostitutes would be less dangerous when allowed to make their own decisions. He concluded his short but emphatic essay with the opinion that nonlicensed prostitution among consenting parties would elevate the moral condition of prostitutes in Buenos Aires.[38]

Many physicians approached the prostitution problem by applying positivist principles, ones that could be made sensitive to gender and class relation. Positivism and public health in Buenos Aires were further linked by local philosophical developments and practical applications. Two of Argentina's most famous positivists, José María Ramos Mejía and José Ingenieros, were also physicians who specialized in urban reform: one by organizing the city's medical services, the other by analyzing urban crime. In addition, both examined the consequences of mass behavior in Argentina from biological, historical, and psychological perspectives.[39]

Ingenieros, an early adherent of socialism, directed the Mental Health Observation Service (Servicio de Observación de Alienados) of the Buenos Aires police force from 1904 to 1913. There he and his associates investigated conditions considered to be "morbid and antisocial" in the capital city. The results of their research became the basis of modern Argentine criminological theory as well as a justification for subsequent urban reforms such as the abolition of legalized prostitution.[40]

By the first decade of the twentieth century, Ingenieros and his colleagues had gathered enough empirical data on the nature of crime in Buenos Aires to justify new forms of urban social control. Although Ingenieros adhered to a Darwinist faith in biology and the struggle for life, he believed that criminality and deviant behavior were not immutably based on biology or morality. Instead, many concepts of crime were in fact based on class or group interests. The application of positive science to criminology would identify these factors and result in reform of the legal system. As Ingenieros noted:

> Each group or class has its own morality, and there is no way to claim that the one espoused by the dominant class at any time or in any place is superior to any other; rather, it is more useful to the governing class. . . . These types of moral definitions are particularly perceptible in the realm of crimes against the social order as compared with crimes against property. . . .
>
> Undoubtedly the advent of a new morality must be accompanied by a transformation of the notions of honesty and delinquency, of virtue and vice, of good and evil. From this perspective the diffusion of scientific philosophy will eventually subvert the legal concept of crime and ultimately force the law to approximate biological reality.[41]

Ingenieros's assertion that social crimes were not rooted in biology gave criminologists and fellow Socialists a clearer understanding of how to approach class and gender issues. If no provable biological explanation for a crime existed, then the decision to define the act as a crime was politically and ideologically inspired. He also suggested that females, regardless of their crimes, be housed in their own prison.[42] Nevertheless, he did not delineate in detail his ideas on female criminality.

Ingenieros published research on the criminality of prostitutes carried out by his mentor and colleague Dr. Francisco de Veyga. Dr. Fermín Rodríguez, another Ingenieros associate, examined the relation of prostitution and suicide to the sexual imbalance in the city as well as to the low rates of marriage. Presumably if women were less frequently exposed to immorality and more people married and established responsible families, suicide and prostitution would decrease. In the analysis Rodríguez replaced biology and class with moral danger.[43]

Although Ingenieros went further than most of his colleagues on this issue, the hesitancy of some Argentine criminologists to blame many crimes on heredity and race put them in disagreement with European theorists. Studies by Tarnowsky, Ferrero, and Lombroso posited that female prostitutes were physically distinct from so-called normal women and that anatomical measurements verified the differences. Female desire to engage in prostitution thus presumedly stemmed from biological defects, and prostitution was viewed as the female counterpart to male biology that drove men to engage in violent crime. In fact there were no biological abnormalities, but the theory that prostitution was the female form of criminality continued to influence legislators and criminal anthropologists. It remained the task of Ingenieros to defend his group's acceptance of criminological relativism to European positivists, and he accomplished it successfully at a European scientific congress in April 1905.[44]

Three years later Ingenieros made similar assertions in his introduction to Eusebio Gómez's *La mala vida en Buenos Aires*. Gómez's work adhered to European positivism and repeated Lombroso's theories that prostitution was a consequence of biological flaws that led to moral insanity. At the same time, however, Gómez utilized data published by Ingenieros's colleagues and suggested that environmental influences such as "poverty and a lack of moral education" could also drive women into sexual commerce. Male prostitutes, on the other hand, engaged in similar activities "not only to satisfy their inherent desires, but equally important, to make money." Like Rodríguez, Gómez viewed male prostitution from a class perspective while linking female prostitution more to morality than to economic need.[45]

Ingenieros responded to Gómez's views by emphasizing class and gender concerns. He reiterated that social crimes are defined by the norms of the moment and that crime is defined by the "limits the collectivity places on the individual in the struggle for life." Thus, from his perspective the decision to monitor female prostitutes for moral purposes while perceiving male homosexual prostitutes to be mentally ill or in need of cash was gender based.[46]

In a later study of marriage and the family Ingenieros clarified his position on prostitution and betrayed his biological determinism. Deeply opposed to monogamous marriage as contrary to natural selection and love, he saw prostitution as a form of biological and economic liberation for females. According to him: "In primitive societies wives were slaves and prostitutes were free women considered socially more acceptable than wives. . . . Later female slaves destined for sexual exploitation [prostitution] were set apart from concubines and the legal wife. . . . In very recent times women have reconquered their right to exercise this profession, enjoy the profits of their work, and share these profits with any man they choose."[47] Ingenieros accepted the right of women to earn money through sexual commerce and to be equal with men in having multiple sexual partners, though he ignored the economic circumstances that drove women to prostitution. Prostitution for Ingenieros was not a criminal activity as long as women were not forced into it by men, nor was it the result of economic desperation. He made no references to homosexuality or male prostitution.

What compelled Argentine positivists to devise studies of criminality, male and female, that would challenge European criminal anthropology? The answer lay in the belief that social science could cure the problems that beset Buenos Aires, problems caused by immigration and urbanization. Among the earliest Argentine positivists, Esteban Echeverría, Juan Bautista Alberdi, and Domingo Sarmiento all had elicited confidence that European immigration, mass education, and liberal economic policies would civilize Argentina and prevent a return to the dark days of a Rosas type of dictatorship. If reforms had produced only political and social turmoil, and if immigrants who committed crimes or engaged in prostitution were biologically defective, there was little hope that the great *problema social* would be resolved so that a strong and healthy Argentine nation could evolve.[48]

Much of the debate about the future of legalized prostitution, regardless of ideological position, was carried on by male reformers. In contrast to their European and North American counterparts, Argentine feminists entered the debate about prostitution, venereal disease, and family morality long after politicians, physicians, and police began to formulate their attitudes. This did not imply, however, that their views went unnoticed or that they did not participate in the discourse. Furthermore, feminists were not united in their analysis or theoretical stands. This fragmentation served to diffuse their impact, but they still buttressed the general campaign to abolish legalized prostitution.

The main way women became concerned with this issue was through the study of medicine. Once again positivism, concern for public health, and the application of medical and social theories had their impact on the analysis of gender issues. The first Argentine woman to receive a medical degree was Cecilia Grierson. After receiving her degree in 1889, she worked in municipal hospitals in Buenos Aires, initiated the first school for nurses, and also developed programs in obstetrics and child development (*puericultura*). In 1900 she founded the Argentine chapter of the International Council of Women. It was this group that responded to Rosalie Lighton Robinson and her efforts to prevent white slavery, and the council devised many programs to promote social and educational programs for working women.[49]

Although Grierson's Council of Women was often scorned by more politically radical women's groups, her own interests in improved prenatal and child care, along with the council's advocacy of training programs for working women, inevitably linked the physician and the organization to other feminist groups. Some, like Dr. Julieta Lantieri de Renshaw, a naturalized citizen who had studied pharmacy and medicine in Buenos Aires, were staunch political feminists whose role models were British and United States suffragists. Lantieri became the first woman to run for the Chamber of Deputies in 1920. Nevertheless, her interest in child development led her to also organize the Children's Congress in 1913.[50]

It was Lantieri rather than Grierson who directly integrated the prostitution issue into feminist discourse, and she did it in a rather brash fashion. In 1910 Argentine women organized their first international congress, where the question of what to do about legalized prostitution was discussed. Lantieri introduced the topic by expressing the hope that prostitution would disappear as men evolved "toward an ideal of sincerity, purity, and love, and learn how to dominate their instincts, which today place them on the same level as beasts."[51] To reach this goal she was firmly opposed to government-regulated prostitution because it prevented women from responding to their natural instincts of "maternity and child care" and encouraged their "sensuality and ignorance."

The description of male sexuality as animalistic, the implicit assumption that it was the fault of men rather than because of economic circumstances that women were forced into prostitution, and the fear of government intervention were all typical of anti–white slavery views expressed by Josephine Butler. They were not, however, commonly found in anti-prostitution speeches in Argentina at this time. For that reason Lantieri's radical stance was questioned by others, and when the vote was taken on her motion to oppose legalized prostitution, more than 30 percent of the women opposed her view despite entreaties from the Asociación Nacional Argentina contra la Trata de Blancas as well as from Lantieri.[52]

Other women physicians joined the ranks of anti–white slavery groups. Dr. Petrona Eyle, who had to study in Switzerland to receive her degree in 1891, validated her title at the University of Buenos Aires two years later and began practicing medicine and feminist politics. After Dr. Arturo Condomí died in 1917, Eyle became president of the Asociación Nacional Argentina contra la Trata de Blancas and continued to direct its activities until 1928, when it was disbanded. As one of the few women to direct a moral reform association with a large male contingent, Eyle's acceptance by her male colleagues showed that many Argentine inhibitions about women's leadership in the resolution of female-focused problems were beginning to weaken.[53]

Among all the various women's groups that discussed female-focused social issues, the one that became most committed to taking up the question of legalized prostitution was the Argentine Socialist party. Although women could not hold office in the Socialist party so long as they did not have political suffrage, the party was deeply committed to women's issues and offered women a supportive environment within which they could organize for political action.

In the first years of the twentieth century Socialist women formed their own centers in Buenos Aires. Dedicated activists like the Chertkoff sisters—Fenia, Mariana, and Adela—Raquel Messina, Gabriela Laperrière de Coni, and Carolina Muzilli investigated the living and working conditions of poor women in Buenos Aires and then led the fight to improve them. They had three principal goals: raising women's salaries to equal men's; improving the safety and healthfulness of the workplace; and providing working women with adequate education and child care for their children.[54]

By the early 1920s Socialist women finally approached the prostitution problem in the same way male feminists had in earlier years: they listened to the arguments presented by their colleagues who were physicians and higienistas. The most famous female opponent to legalized prostitution in Argentina was Dr. Alicia Moreau de Justo. Born in England in 1885, as a young child she came to Buenos Aires, where in 1914 she received her medical degree. Daughter of staunch socialist parents, Moreau married Juan B. Justo, founder of the Argentine Socialist party, and dedicated her life to medicine and socialism.

Prostitution and white slavery were the topics of one of her first publications. In 1919 she reported on the white slave trade in Argentina to the International Conference of Women Physicians. Buenos Aires had become a prostitution center because "we are a country of immigration, and the mistress of the house of prostitution must offer to her clients of different nationalities varied ethnical types in harmony with their tendencies or speech. On the other hand, the Argentine is a country where money is made. That is the mirage for which so many poor people expatriate themselves and that is what attracts the girl or the young woman who has the promise of a fine position."[55]

Dr. Paulina Luisi, higienista, feminist, and socialist reformer from Uruguay, was a contemporary of Moreau de Justo and often helped Argentine reformers in their battle to abolish legalized prostitution in Argentina. To that end she traveled to Buenos Aires in 1919 to address the Argentine chapter of the International Abolitionist Federation, which had recently been founded by Petrona Eyle. Her speech emphasized the Argentine situation and reflected her close contacts with Argentine physicians and politicians.[56]

From the outset, Moreau and Luisi recognized that white slavery could never be eradicated without identifying local, as well as international, causes of prostitution. To them, most of these factors stemmed from unsatisfactory working and family conditions, which would remain as long as women did not have political, economic, and social equality. Furthermore, family conditions, particularly problems associated with adolescence, could be ameliorated through sex education and special counseling for abnormal children.[57]

Fifteen years later Moreau de Justo was still advocating sex education and family reforms to remove the need for women to engage in commercial sex. In a speech given in honor of Anti–Venereal Disease Day in Buenos Aires, she told the audience at the Teatro Colón that only the "transformation of society in some of its most fundamental aspects" would eliminate the causes of prostitution. These included family reform, individual development, and social, economic, and political reforms.[58]

It was no coincidence that Moreau de Justo's views were similar to those Luisi expressed. Despite their respective nationalities, both were physicians and committed Socialists. They were also ardent feminists in the Latin American tradition, one that encouraged women to seek political and social reforms to enable them not only to develop their own potential as individuals, but also to discharge their social and family responsibilities as mothers.

While Moreau de Justo devoted most of her energy to the suffrage campaign, Luisi worked with men of the Argentine Socialist party, who were eager to reform Buenos Aires municipal prostitution ordinances. In 1919 she joined with Dr. Angel Giménez and several others to form a joint Argentine-Uruguayan Committee of the International Federation of Abolitionists. Their platform advocated the abolition of legalized prostitution, the formation of a system of free medical treatment for all venereal disease patients, absolute divorce, reform of paternity laws, improved working conditions for mothers and children, sex education in primary and secondary schools, and the closing of obscene forms of entertainment. This program effectively integrated family reform issues with the abolition of municipally regulated bordellos.[59]

In the 1920s Paulina Luisi became active in presenting women's issues in the League of Nations. Although a delegate from Uruguay, her Argentine contacts put her in an ideal position to defend Latin America from undue European criticism as part of the League of Nations Special Committee on the Traffic in Women and Children, while Angel Giménez continued to lobby for the abolition of legalized prostitution in Buenos Aires.

Just as Alfredo Palacios had been the principal activist in the passage of anti-pimping laws in 1913, Giménez was the most important Socialist and the leading proponent of venereal disease legislation after World War I. Sensitive to the gender issue, he was always willing to work with feminist groups, both socialist and nonsocialist. He often began his legislative debates by praising the efforts of Josephine Butler and the women's anti–white slavery movement, and he undoubtedly would have considered it a compliment had a contemporary called him a feminist. Like his female counterparts, Giménez's expertise as a higienista helped him avoid the pitfalls of moral and criminological debates that often did little but provoke controversy. And without ardent male feminists as dedicated as Giménez, the few successful socialist and feminist demands for public health reform and legal equality of Argentine men and women would not have been implemented so soon.

After World War I immigration to Argentina resumed, and questions of white slavery and prostitution in Buenos Aires once again became the topic of inquiry for many international moral reform societies. Within Argentina the pioneering higienistas were ending their careers just as a new generation took up the cause of public health, venereal disease control, and the prostitution debate.

One indication of the changing generations had been the establishment of the Argentine-Uruguayan Committee of the International Federation of Abolitionists. Much like Asociación Nacional Argentina contra la Trata de Blancas, this committee was a response to international pressures and nationalist concerns. Significantly, by this time the notion of abolitionism had shifted from keeping out the traffickers to changing laws and customs associated with prostitution and venereal disease.

The group that ultimately proved very effective in promoting the programs of the Argentine-Uruguayan Committee was the Liga Argentina de Profilaxis Social (Argentine Social Prophylaxis League). Organized in May 1921, the Liga was committed to waging war against venereal disease by advocating a campaign of public education, improved medical treatment, and prenuptial blood tests. In addition to an executive commission that consisted of notable higienistas, all male, it also created a consulting board that included Emilio R. Coni, Alfredo Palacios, José Ingenieros, and conservative politicians Estanislao S. Zeballos and Joaquín González.

The Liga's activities paralleled efforts of higienistas in the Socialist party. They approached members of Congress and suggested appropriate legislation. They sent information to the Ministry of Public Instruction concerning the availability of suitable materials for sex education and requested a subvention to underwrite the costs of disbursing the information. In both cases their efforts were initially rebuffed. When they approached their third target, the Ministry of War, they found a fertile environment in which to advance the cause of sex education. The ministry was quite willing to experiment with distributing pamphlets explaining the dangers of venereal disease and the precautions to be taken by soldiers, but initially it lacked the resources to defray publication costs. Fortunately a patriotic publisher printed the pamphlets without charge, and for the first time Argentine soldiers began to learn about sex hygiene as part of their military experience.[60]

The Liga did not limit its battle to the armed forces or its resources to those of the national government. With help from other organizations with similar goals, it obtained educational movies with subtitles and had pamphlets translated from French and English into Spanish. It brought this information to workers' associations and to the Unión Feminista Nacional (National Feminists' Union), headed by Alicia Moreau de Justo, taking care to adapt lectures on sex hygiene to female audiences. They also went beyond Buenos Aires to provincial cities, and soon groups in other provinces had access to their programs.[61]

Once the Liga's educational and informational programs commenced, politicians no longer had to defend the idea of sex education. Thereafter it became a question of who would operate these programs and how many people would be exposed to the information. The final test of sex education would come from people's willingness to seek medical treatment for venereal disease once it was demystified and no longer a "secret shame."

While higienistas and criminologists debated the relation between prostitution, venereal disease, and the legal inequality of women, urban authorities temporized by accusing prostitutes and disorderly women of encouraging crime in Buenos Aires. Police statistics for Buenos Aires confirmed that disorderly women, including those who drank too much as well as those who committed acts of violence, were a minor concern compared with their male counterparts.[62]

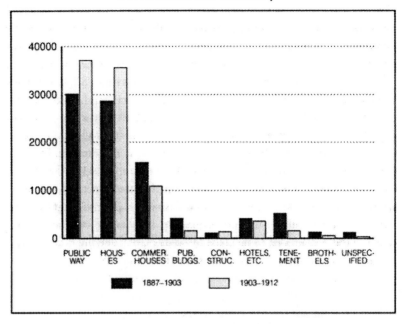

Offenses classified according to where they took place
Source: Buenos Aires Municipality, *Anuario estadístico de la ciudad de Buenos Aires*,
1903, p. 243; idem, *Statistical Yearbook for the City of Buenos Aires*, 1913, p. 246.

As in other modern cities, men rather than women were the main per-
petrators of major crimes. Misdemeanors including disorderly or scandalous behavior were also principally male crimes. In the early 1880s, for
example, women constituted from 9 to 11 percent of those arrested for disorderly conduct. In 1893, at a time when legal bordellos were being closed
down, only 3 percent of those arrested were women, and only thirty-two
(26 percent) of them were identified as prostitutes. In terms of all misdemeanors including drunkenness, in 1881, 1882, and 1883, women constituted 11, 17, and 18 percent of the total. In 1893 they constituted only 4
percent.[63]

Not only were women far more law-abiding than men, but the places
where women supposedly were inciting men to violence were not the
scenes of most crimes. Between 1887 and 1912 most crimes took place in
the streets, private homes, or commercial businesses, not in cafés, bordellos,
tenement houses, or bars.

When one reads the police *Memorias*, it is difficult to correlate arrests
with the amount of attention paid to prostitution. In 1881, for example,

surveys of different city police districts were published in an effort to justify staff increases. The report for section 5, which included the Parque de Artillería, noted that the population of 14,700 resided mostly in tenement houses and that the area was dotted with sixty-three cafés, twenty-nine houses of prostitution, and a variety of inns and lodging houses. Such conditions produced all kinds of scandalous behavior, and according to the police, liquor and women incited the troubles. Women lured men into cafés, illegal gambling establishments, and dance halls, most of which had access to bedrooms. These businesses were such an attraction that on the weekends the district's population swelled to more than 19,000, all overseen by twenty police officers. Reports on other areas in the city also cited the presence of commercial sex as a fundamental cause of sociopathic behavior.[64]

The police continued to worry, but they did not arrest many women, as is seen in the percentage of females brought in for misdemeanors throughout the 1880s. Nevertheless, police officials went out of their way to warn the public about female criminality. The 1884–85 *Memoria* included a letter from the policeman in charge of section 3 who had arrested a mother for selling her daughter's sexual services to a bordello. It is unclear what crime she was charged with, but the arrest was made as the mother patiently waited outside with another, younger daughter. To the policeman's dismay, the judge dismissed the charges. The case of the immoral mother was just the tip of the iceberg as far as he was concerned, since in his district he claimed there were more than one hundred clandestine bordellos with over five hundred women. He accused women of luring young girls in the streets and then raffling them off to the highest bidder. The police may have complained and accused, but they only occasionally arrested, because in the entire city that year only 7 percent of those arrested for disorderly conduct (364) and 5 percent (1,448) of arrests for drunkenness were of women.[65]

The letter was unusual because individual cases were rarely printed in annual police reports and because it accused a woman of pimping for her own child, unlike the typical complaint of husbands' or fathers' procuring. It also portrayed the women accused of clandestine prostitution as independent of males, as devoid of principles, and as threats to the community. These, in essence, were the same descriptions of working-class women who dared to work in a public place where their lack of virtue could not be restrained. It was these women, rather than passive white slaves, who corrupted their children and lured men into trouble, infecting them with diseases and encouraging them to commit crimes.

Not all policemen agreed, however, that women were the cause of urban crime. The year after the immoral mother sold her child to a bordello, two members of the city police force published an exposé, *La prostitución en Buenos Aires*. It began with an open letter to their chief, Marcos Paz, complaining about the impossibility of maintaining social order as long as housing shortages led to conventillos wherein "disorder prevails . . . in habitations shared by various families and individuals of both sexes and all ages, most of whom do not know how to restrain their baser instincts. . . . It is logical that from these places are recruited victims, many of whom have been influenced by the immoral conditions there."[66]

Public authorities were also to blame for the disgraceful situation in Buenos Aires. Few legal bordellos operated, because of municipal harassment and overly stringent regulations. Young women could work in bordellos before reaching the age of majority. City officials did nothing to prevent pimps from financing houses that technically were operated by women, and a pimps' club with two hundred members operated openly from a restaurant and café. In such circumstances these two policemen believed the municipality had no right to insist that police hector prostitutes and deprive them of their civil rights.[67]

A contemporary and fellow policeman, Adolfo Batiz, also attempted to explain the factors that led to prostitution, both official and clandestine, in Buenos Aires in the 1880s. Like the others he saw two supposedly distinct patterns, one associated with an organized international traffic (white slavery) and another, also based upon family coercion but rooted in Argentine socioeconomic conditions. Police had little hope of rescuing many women because "their own parents and relatives have forced them to sell their bodies, and they agree to do it because of their extreme poverty. Under these conditions young girls who dedicate themselves to commercial sex believe they are doing a good deed, since the product of their dishonest work feeds the members of their families."[68]

If police were pessimistic about their ability to rescue women, they could not put all the blame on ineffective government. Part of the problem stemmed from their of lack of authority, but mostly the police were unwilling to arrest men for sexual and family-based crimes other than child abandonment. Between 1904 and 1913, not a single man in the city of Buenos Aires was arrested for bigamy, rape, corruption of minors, or ravishment. In contrast, 857 people were arrested for child abandonment and 24 for child abduction (presumably not their own children).[69]

After 1900 policemen continued to voice their opinions in a variety of ways. In 1913 Laurentino C. Mejías, a retired officer, published *La policía por dentro: Mis cuentos* (An Insider's View of the Police), in which he described the police response to white slavery. He accused the municipality of having exacerbated the prostitution problem by refusing to create a red-light district and by hindering effective police control while Polish and Hungarian traffickers took control of the houses.[70]

In 1930 policeman Julio L. Alsogaray turned his attention to the Jewish element among white slavers in Buenos Aires. After years of accumulating evidence, he published the *Trilogía de la trata de blancas: Rufianes — policía — municipalidad* (The White Slave Trilogy: Pimps—Police—Politicians). The book documented the many ways porteño politicians and fellow police had been corrupted by Jewish pimps.[71]

The abolition of municipally regulated prostitution in Buenos Aires in 1934 did not deter police from writing about it. In 1937 Ernesto M. Pareja followed in Alsogaray's footsteps and published a study of legalized prostitution in Buenos Aires until December 1934, particularly from the perspective of religion. Once again the Jewish role in legalized prostitution was the principal concern of a policeman turned author. But in contrast to Alsogaray, Pareja chose not to dwell on police complicity.[72]

When the battle over the legality of municipally regulated prostitution was finally joined in postwar Buenos Aires and on the national level, higienistas, positivists, police, and political ideologues all had the opportunity to present their cases. By that time the Argentine public was well acquainted with their country's reputation as a haven for white slavers. They also knew that legalized prostitution was seen as the cause of this problem, yet politicians and many Argentines, male and female, were still reluctant to force municipalities to refrain from enacting prostitution ordinances. The result was a slow and rather tortuous effort at political reform and social education. And caught in the middle of this were not just the pimps and prostitutes, but Argentine gender relations.

The behavior of the Buenos Aires municipal council served as a weathervane for the political campaign against legalized prostitution. It was one of the groups least willing to entertain the notion of abolishing legalized prostitution. For many years its members listened to their higienista colleagues who criticized the system as unworkable and to those who argued that legalized prostitution was the only way to combat venereal disease. Until 1919 the city council as a group refused to contemplate abolishing licensed bordellos. They were equally loath to propose reforms. Part of their reluctance was due to pressure from powerful pimps, but a good deal of resistance sprang from the embarrassment many suffered when forced to discuss the issue. Their discomfort stemmed from the inconsistencies that accompanied the debates, along with the realization that each council member had his own reason, often indefensible, for believing that legalized prostitution was appropriate.

Subsequent municipal councils were no more united or coherent in the way they approached the relation between prostitution, morality, and venereal disease. Gradually both council members and intendentes acknowledged the need to expand inexpensive venereal disease treatment to the community, but until 1919 most council members still believed it was wiser to keep intact an inefficient system of licensed bordellos and prostitutes' clinics than to examine the real reasons they were anxious to monitor prostitutes.

Their exaggerated fears paralleled those of the city police and the public health physicians, all of whom cringed at presumed threats posed by these dangerous lower-class women who might sell their sexual favors out of economic desperation or, even worse, enjoy themselves while they earned their immoral wages. As late as 1910 Buenos Aires municipal reports still discussed prostitution under the category of morality. There was no mention of men or venereal disease, only of unacceptable female behavior patterns. Until the medical campaign became more important than public morality and the city was willing to admit that there was no gender construction to venereal disease, efforts to eliminate municipally regulated prostitution would be unsuccessful.

4

The Final Battle?

Pre–World War I white slavery and female prostitution debates captured the imagination and attention of politicians, physicians, and policemen as long as European women migrated to Buenos Aires. Even though the dynamics of economic and social relations within Argentine families were occasionally identified as critical factors, these would not be addressed as long as foreigners could be blamed. By the 1930s neither deviant foreigners nor native-born social marginals were acceptable to governing elites. Rising nationalism and the intrusion of the military into Argentine politics made it imperative to eliminate the foreign criminal element and the internationally unacceptable houses of prostitution. For these reasons, Jewish pimping associations were taken to court and municipally licensed bordellos were abolished by national law.

Although these measures attempted to end white slavery once and for all, the symbolic relation of prostitution to female work remained and became increasingly important. The outbreak of the World War in 1914 drastically reduced the number of Europeans, male and female, who could migrate to the Americas. After 1914 more women than men migrated from inland provinces to Buenos Aires in search of work. The successful entry of women into the industrial labor force reinforced traditional concerns that women would be exploited in the workplace. Even though women performed the same work at home as in the bordello, factory, or cabaret, remuneration for sexual, economic, or social services was often criticized. As in the case of legalized prostitution, civil rights issues prompted the Argentine government to define the boundaries of acceptable employment for women, native-born or foreign-born, opting for supervised female work in the factory and the cabaret. But the gender tensions resulting from this decision meant that these establishments soon replaced the legal bordello as the symbolic site of immoral female employment.

The outbreak of World War I, along with the subsequent enactment of new Argentine immigration laws in 1921, did more to halt the influx of European pimps and prostitutes than any well-intentioned efforts of boat inspectors or the Ley Palacios. Many traffickers who had left Argentina in the wake of the 1913 law became trapped in Europe. In general, few immigrants arrived in Buenos Aires between 1914 and 1918, and Argentine women registered more frequently than in the prewar years.

Jewish immigration plummeted. High urban unemployment, added to anti-Semitic aspects of the Semana Trágica (Tragic Week), the repression of strikes in Buenos Aires in January 1919, further discouraged Jewish immigration. From 1915 to 1922 fewer than 1,000 Russian and Polish immigrants entered the country compared with 18,000 between 1905 and 1913. Subsequently the number of eastern European immigrants began to rise, though they were still held down by the price of steamer tickets, which rose 300 percent from 1923 to 1926 and increased another 25 percent in 1930.[1]

The decline of Russian immigrants was reflected in the marked decrease in the number of registered Russian-born prostitutes. In 1910, for example, 22 percent of licensed prostitutes claimed to be Russian, and that figure increased to 26 percent in 1913. In contrast, between 1914 and 1923 the proportion of Russian women never exceeded 15 percent, while the representation of Spanish and Argentine prostitutes increased.

Since 1908 politicians had protected the investment of organized and independent bordello owners in the national capital as long as they stayed away from downtown main streets. That situation, however, changed radically in 1919 when the Socialist party became well represented on the municipal council. Led by the dedicated Angel Giménez, abolitionists on the city council were determined to ban licensed prostitution once and for all within the city and to create an improved system of venereal disease treatment centers.

Giménez was elected to the municipal council in 1919 after serving two years as national deputy. In 1917 he had launched a crusade to abolish municipally regulated prostitution wherever it existed in Argentina. To that end he introduced national legislation to punish anyone who "in any way is involved in the traffic of women, promotes or facilitates their corruption and prostitution with the intent to make money, even with the permission of the victim."[2] He also included provisions to punish any national, provincial, or municipal authority that allowed such crimes to occur. In this way Giménez managed to criticize gender relations and associated political alli-

The Final Battle?

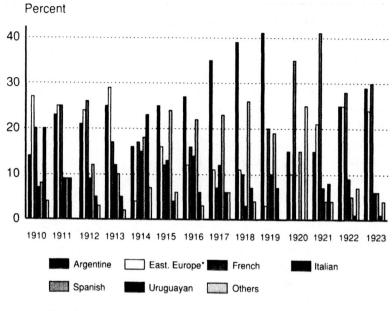

Nationality of newly registered women, 1910–1923

Source: "Nationality of Newly Registered Prostitutes in Buenos Aires for the years 1910 to 1923, Inclusive," in League of Nations, *Report of the Special Body of Experts on Traffic in Women and Children*, 2:19; Mirelman, "Jews in Argentina (1890–1930)," p. 13.

ances in a direct fashion. Giménez's legislation was supported by other Socialist deputies who proclaimed a full-scale war on licensed bordellos and directly blamed them for white slavery in Argentina.[3] But like Palacios's earlier attempts to enact the first anti–white slavery law, Giménez's bill was buried in congressional committees.

Undeterred, Giménez moved his campaign to the local arena. Elected to the Buenos Aires municipal council in 1919, he fought to ban licensed prostitution while creating ten municipal clinics to treat victims of venereal disease and offer sex education classes. This time Giménez offered a clearly developed class and gender argument against licensed prostitution, one that expanded on concepts developed by Ingenieros. He questioned why upper-class courtesans never went to the prostitutes' registry and why better-paid women workers were not compelled to do so either. He showed how low wages led to sexual exploitation of domestic servants, the job most fre-

quently obtained by women, and similar conditions faced female entertainers and "artistes" in the city. The explanation was the link between women's
poverty, job opportunities, and prostitution. Legalized prostitution ignored the causes of female sexual commerce, just as it failed as a prophylactic measure. He concluded that "licensed prostitution is . . . an obstacle to
medical treatment" because it offers the public only the illusion of protection against infection. Furthermore, the system would never work as long
as women evaded medical treatment.[4]

Initially Socialists thought victory was at hand. Unfortunately, on June
6 Intendente Joaquín Llambias went to the council and threatened to veto
any attempts to abolish prostitution or to implement the Giménez program. The ordinance still passed with the minimum number of votes. Again
threatened with a veto, the council reached a compromise with the intendente.

The new law satisfied Socialist demands to close bordellos and open venereal disease clinics without ending legalized prostitution. After December 31, 1919, all licensed houses were banned. Thereafter female prostitution was permitted so long as the woman lived neither in a conventillo nor
on a street where other prostitutes conducted their business. The only other
person authorized to live with the prostitute was a maid or housekeeper,
who had to be female and over forty-five. The municipal law also authorized the creation of venereal disease treatment centers to be open after
working hours and provide free care.[5]

The 1919 ordinance created unexpected public relations problems because it conflated prostitutes and bordellos. Since all prostitutes had to live
alone and most people regarded their residences as bordellos, the number
of bordellos in Buenos Aires increased in direct proportion to the number
of prostitutes. The opening of "bordellos" continued in a precipitous fashion until 1926, when new municipal laws banned new houses, meaning
that no new women could declare themselves legal prostitutes. The publication of statistics gave the impression that the prostitution business in
Buenos Aires was flourishing until that date.

The effect of the 1919 laws on prostitutes was far less benevolent than
Socialists imagined. Closing larger bordellos meant that pimps and madams had to work more clandestinely in Buenos Aires after 1919 or else assume the financial burden of operating one-woman bordellos. They also
had to rely more on police corruption. Under-age women needed falsified
documents. If more than two women lived and worked together, then traffickers had to rely on the silence of the police. From 1919 onward, Buenos
Aires was a paradise for white slavers so long as they could control the po-

The Final Battle?

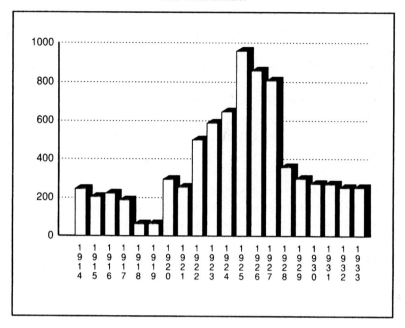

Number of licensed bordellos

Source: Statistics for 1914–19 come from "Statistics from Health Department, Buenos
Aires, on Number of Houses of Prostitution," in League of Nations, *Report of the
Special Body of Experts in Traffic of Women and Children*, 2:19; Statistics for 1920–33
come from "El problema de la prostitución," *Archivos de la Secretaría de Salud Pública* 4,
5 (November 1948): 419.

lice. Provincial cities with more liberal municipal regulations became even
more attractive.

Prostitutes fared even worse than pimps and madams under the new Socialist ordinances. Designed to help free women from the social tyranny of
third-person exploiters, the new laws did nothing to resolve the problem of
high rents and police corruption. In economic terms, living alone meant
that one woman had to pay all the expenses heretofore shared by several.
Exorbitant bordello taxes were eliminated, but even with one economic
problem resolved, expensive housing costs in Buenos Aires meant that tax
relief had solved little, and the financial situation of prostitutes after the Socialist reforms was ironically similar to the situation between 1878 and
1919.

Pimps took advantage of conditions in Buenos Aires, as seen in testimony given to the League of Nations in 1927:

I'll admit that everything in Buenos Aires is supposed to be in favour of the girl, but you can see for yourself that a prostitute must have a man. There are supposed to be no *madames*, no *souteneurs* [pimps], no brothel-keepers, but we really have it all our own way here.

A girl cannot afford to have a house fixed to do business in. Houses that would answer the purpose are not always available. The rent is high, and unless the girl has someone to put up the money she cannot start up. . . .

I have several houses. I went out and bought each property. I re-modelled it to suit my tenant. My tenant is a prostitute and she gives me half of what she makes. . . . I put a housekeeper in each house for the girl. Sometimes she is my wife; always she is someone whom I can trust. . . .

When a girl registers, she shows a paper to the effect that the owner will sell her the house. . . . Naturally when I give her a paper and she is supposed to be the owner, I have to have some protection. . . . The way we protect ourselves is to get 1,000 pesos from the girl as security, and in addition she signs a paper. . . . I have nearly 50 of them. . . . I keep it. . . . If she refuses to obey, then I can write in here whatever I want, give it to my lawyer, and make it so hot for the girl that she has to leave town.[6]

Under the new regime all prostitutes had to work harder to pay their rent. Another pimp interviewed by representatives of the League of Nations Committee on the Traffic in Women and Children told a chilling tale about what it took to be a successful prostitute in Buenos Aires in the 1920s. A woman who refused to engage in "perversion" (fellatio) could not earn sufficient income to sustain herself and her pimp. A successful woman might have an average of three hundred customers a week, each of whom paid five pesos. From these encounters she earned an equivalent of U.S. $500, half of which she turned over to her pimp. The League report concluded that "these profits stimulate the *souteneur* [pimp] and the house-owner to get more such girls from Europe and to educate the new generation of growing boys in these practices."[7]

Pimps were not the only individuals to exploit prostitutes after 1919. City policemen were easily persuaded to ignore the illegal methods traffickers used. They were also quite willing to harass prostitutes who incurred the wrath of their pimps. Policeman Julio Alsogaray wrote about a number of incidents where the police did pimps' dirty work. In one case a municipal inspector informed him that two unauthorized women were working at a house on Lavalle Street and that they should be arrested. At the same time he admitted, "I know that this is the work of pimps and that I am the instrument of their policies, but what else can I do? I received an anonymous complaint, and I cannot deny his accusations. I have no other choice."[8]

Policemen stimulated business for bordellos by rounding up streetwalkers at the request of pimps. They harassed men and women who tried to separate themselves from organized prostitution. According to Alsogaray, police reinforced the coercive actions of pimps: "In most cases they terrorized prostitutes with threats that were not always too effective. But since the police would never help the prostitutes, women often had no other choice than to leave the bordello and hide from their implacable persecutors, who sent other women to the abandoned house to engage in clandestine prostitution."[9]

This situation prevailed throughout the 1920s and into the 1930s despite the passage of additional legislation designed to protect women from sexual exploitation. In 1921 a new national penal code was enacted to replace that of 1886. For the first time the rape of a prostitute would be punished in the same way as the rape of a virgin. An entirely new type of crime was declared in new provisions on obscene literature. The new code incorporated the reforms of the Ley Palacios as well as others to deal with crimes of sexual exploitation.[10]

In addition to the penal code, more stringent prostitution ordinances were enacted in 1923. Reacting to the fact that fewer women in houses meant that the number of bordellos would increase, various proposals were presented to stem the proliferation of bordellos, which soared from 61 in 1919 to 585 in 1923. On March 23 three councilmen suggested that a more extensive exclusionary zone would effectively eliminate legal bordellos from the entire downtown area.[11]

Two months later Giménez introduced his own scheme. He wanted to close down the Dispensario de Salubridad and ban new bordellos within city limits. Infractions would be punished by one month's imprisonment. In response, others were less sanguine about the prospects of closing the Dispensario. Since it was common knowledge that many so-called servants were also practicing prostitution, on June 1 Intendente Carlos M. Noel ordered all bordello housekeepers to register at the Dispensario, thereby forcing the women to move into their own lodgings and increasing the number of legal city bordellos.[12]

It was not until 1925 that Intendente Noel openly supported a ban on new bordellos, and he still refused to close down existing ones. To that end he decreed that after January 1926 no new women would be registered at the Dispensario until new ordinances were enacted. This created the appearance of having solved the bordello problem, since each year thereafter, with the exception of 1932, the number of houses declined. But it also encouraged illegal establishments. From 1926 until 1934, intendentes and the municipal council could not agree on what the new ordinances were to be. Legalized prostitution remained in limbo.[13]

From the perspective of immigration statistics and the socialist-inspired 1919 ordinance, there should have been little concern about Jewish white slavery in Argentina in the 1920s. Yet it was precisely during this time that these fears once again obsessed Argentine politicians and journalists. The direct sources of these anxieties were new reports of Jewish traffickers. Rumors made their way back to Poland and caused potential immigrants to stay away from Argentina.[14]

British moral reform groups continued to be concerned about the Argentine capital despite scanty evidence confirming that English women were in danger. In 1920 the *Vigilance Record* reported that sixty-one British women had been aided by Rosalie Lighton Robinson, who had met 103 American and British ships. The typical story of such a rescue was that of a sixteen-year-old girl who lost her purse en route to Buenos Aires. Lighton Robinson telegraphed the girl's father for money so she could get home from the port. Obviously such cases still had nothing to do with white slavery.[15]

Three years later the *Vigilance Record* extracted another case from Lighton Robinson's annual report to the National Vigilance Association and claimed that it proved "the necessity for Workers to be on the spot in cases of emergency." An English girl had traveled to Buenos Aires to get married, but she received a letter from her fiancé before she arrived admitting that he was already married. Intent on seeking work when she got to Buenos Aires, the girl obtained a job through the intervention of the British social worker. Once again there was no evidence of white slavery or sex trafficking, only the reality that the best laid plans often work out in unexpected ways.[16]

It was not until 1927 that Lighton Robinson claimed she could verify a genuine case of white slavery. Even then she had little to do with its discovery. Instead, the local branch of the Jewish Association for the Protection of Girls and Women was responsible for identifying the problem. Within four

The Final Battle?

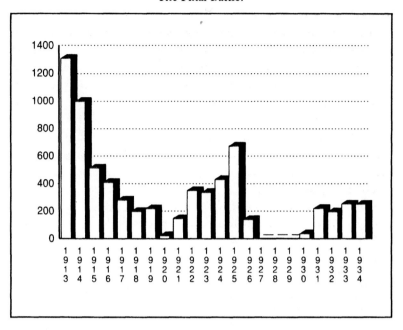

Newly registered women, Buenos Aires
Source: Statistics for 1913–19 come from the Dispensario de Salubridad, in Buenos
Aires Municipality, *Statistical Yearbook for the City of Buenos Aires*, 1913, p. 94; 1914,
p. 100; idem, *Anuario estadístico de la ciudad de Buenos Aires*, 1915–23, p. 133; Statistics
from 1920 onward come from "El problema de la prostitución," *Archivos de la
Secretaría de Salud Pública* 4, 5 (November 1948): 419.

years—and in the midst of the most notorious white slavery scandal in Argentine history—Lighton Robinson retired out of boredom, and the
Buenos Aires Office of the National Vigilance Association was closed
down! On September 11, 1939, she died in Buenos Aires, a well-respected
member of the British-Argentine community.[17] Moral reformers in Buenos
Aires may have had little success in identifying international traffickers in
women and children, but as late as the late 1920s most Europeans still considered Argentina a hotbed of white slavery because foreign women registered at the Dispensario de Salubridad. They ignored the inconsistent pattern of prostitute registration, which was a reaction to factors such as
frequent changes in municipal ordinances and high rents.

International anxieties were directly linked not only to Dispensario statistics, but also to the activities of the League of Nations, which in 1921
organized a special committee to investigate the international traffic in
women and children. The group was not supposed to concern itself with

113

the plight of the native-born, because the League had no right to challenge national sovereignty. The results, however, were quite different. In its quest to "persuade . . . nations to agree on simultaneous concerted action" the League's 1927 report implicitly criticized countries like Argentina for allowing bordellos to operate as legal businesses.[18]

Originally the committee focused on traffic from western Europe to Central and South America. Eventually the research extended to North America, the Mediterranean, the North Sea, and the Baltic countries. Members visited 28 countries and 112 cities and interviewed more than 5,000 prostitutes and pimps.[19]

South America was the first geographic area reported on by the Committee on International Traffic in Women and Children. Argentina provided convincing proof that many foreign-born women registered almost as soon as they arrived:

> In Buenos Ayres 79 foreign-born prostitutes were interrogated; 75 out of the 79 inscribed themselves within a year of their arrival. . . . Even more significant is the fact that 56 per cent inscribed themselves within two months of their arrival, and in one case inscription actually followed within four days of arrival. Assuming, therefore, at a conservative estimate, that 75 per cent of the foreign prostitutes newly inscribed each year have arrived in the country that same year, we may take it, from figures available, that 197 women came or were brought into the country in 1922 and 179 were brought in 1923 for the express purpose of *registering* as prostitutes in Buenos Ayres.[20]

This statement was made without reference to data, presented later, that verified the ever decreasing numbers of legal prostitutes, native-born and foreign.

The League report dwelled on the specific conditions in Buenos Aires at the time of the investigation. If its conclusions were misleading, those who responded to the report were even more alarmist. Albert Londres, author of the 1928 *Le chemin au Buenos Aires* (The Road to Buenos Aires), transformed his favorable observations of French pimps in Buenos Aires into an antifeminist, anti-Semitic, pro-French tract. He truly confused Europeans by contradicting the League of Nations observations that stated:

> The enquiries in the underworld in Paris showed a frequent coming and going of *souteneurs* on the lookout for women and girls who could profitably be taken abroad for the purposes of prostitution.

Most frequently they secure women who are already prostitutes and who are of full age and consenting parties, but they also occasionally obtain minors and inexperienced women. They are in contact with traffickers in many other countries, such as Poland, Egypt and the Argentine, and they act as intermediaries and agents to assist and facilitate this international traffic.[21]

French pimps were active not only in Buenos Aires, but in other Latin American port cities such as Montevideo, Havana, and Rio de Janeiro, as well as in Alexandria, Egypt. Unfortunately more people read Londres' work than the committee report.

According to the League, Italy too was not exempt from an organized traffic in women to Buenos Aires, but Italian authorities made this business difficult to conduct by enacting immigration policies designed to prevent such practices. In response, Italian traffickers often went to France, Tripoli, Tunis, or Algiers and then on to Buenos Aires: "A certain amount of international traffic out of Italy does take place, and official regulations are evaded. . . . A *souteneur* met with in Genoa advised the following method for getting a girl to the Argentine: 'The best way to go is to first go to France and from there go wherever you want to. . . . After she gets to Marseilles, the Italian Consul there will fix her passport so that it is good for the Argentine.'" With the cooperation of consular officials outside Italy, as well as the falsification of documents within the country, Italian women, both experienced and innocent, were being sent to "Tunis, Algiers, Marseilles, Tripoli, Malta and Egypt, and to a somewhat less extent to Mexico, Cuba, the Argentine, Uruguay and Brazil."[22]

Within South America, Uruguay and Brazil were cited as important entrepôts for international traffickers intent on importing women to Buenos Aires. After being sent to other countries to avoid Argentine port officials, an unknown number of victims, for unexplained reasons, were then sent to the Uruguayan city of Salto, where they boarded river vessels that would take them to the nearby Argentine city of Concordia. From there they reputedly made their way to Buenos Aires.[23]

In 1928 H. Wilson Harris published *Human Merchandise: A Study of the International Traffic in Women*, which sought to disseminate the League of Nations report to an even wider audience. His introduction interjected personal opinions about why the traffic existed. He denied that economic factors encouraged prostitution; rather, women's inherent moral weakness and passivity were the principal causes: "Girls slip into prostitution—not

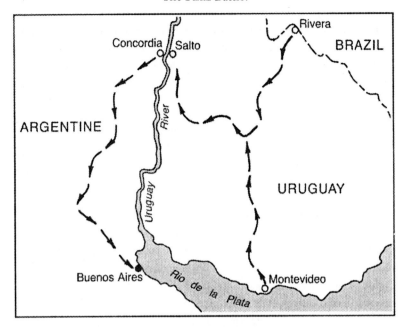

League of Nations map of the Salto-Concordia route

plunge into it—from one cause or another. Rarely, if ever, is it considered a choice. . . . Bad advice, moreover, . . . can have its demoralizing effect." When Harris reported on the South American studies, he once again had his own perspective. He deemphasized the forces pushing women away from their homeland and argued that in Argentina a life of vice was too attractive: "Investigators into commercialized vice in its most systematized and varied forms could find no more fruitful field of enquiry than the Argentine Republic, and its capital city, Buenos Ayres, in particular. . . . The general conclusion emerging is that Argentina is largely a paradise for souteneurs."[24]

As late as 1929 pamphlets such as the *Lettre ouverte addressé par un homme aux jeune filles* circulated, warning women of white slavers who "under the pretext of marriage, promise them a trip . . . to Buenos-Ayres," where they would be forced "to live a life of debauchery and prostitute themselves to men of every color, race and social condition."[25] Written by an overzealous Frenchman interested in preserving the reputation and honor of women abroad, this pamphlet was dismissed by the National Vigilance Association as too alarmist, but the French reading public was most likely unaware of this assessment.

Despite the dubious nature of the League of Nations findings, the combination of renewed local fears of organized Jewish prostitution rings and international revelations of white slavery in Argentina enabled Socialists and other critics of legalized prostitution to push for new local and national laws. Success had been partially achieved in 1919 ordinances for Buenos Aires, though municipally licensed bordellos were not declared illegal in the city until 1934 in the wake of a Jewish white slavery scandal. Two years later a national venereal disease treatment law banned all municipalities from licensing bordellos. By 1936 the final battle against organized Jewish prostitution, unfair public health laws, and legal bordellos supposedly had been won. The inability of such laws to address underlying religious, nationalistic, gender, and economic issues, however, militated against such an easy victory.

There were clear indications from 1913 onward that national laws would not easily solve police problems associated with prostitution and white slavery in Argentina. The Ley Palacios was not an effective threat to potential pimps or traffickers. In fact the law encouraged victimizing of prostitutes by police, as well as by other immoral men and women. Despite its stated goals, the Ley Palacios rarely protected women mistreated by husbands, relatives, and strangers. Instead, Buenos Aires police used it to justify harsher campaigns against unlicensed prostitutes.

As the number of legal prostitutes and bordellos decreased after 1913, the number of women arrested for disorderly conduct increased. In fact, just one year after the Ley Palacios was enacted, scandalous behavior became a female rather than a male crime, since women constituted 80 percent of those detained (1,960). Equally important, 66 percent of the women arrested were self-identified prostitutes, and 47 percent were Argentines. This meant the law was being used principally to control unlicensed sexual commerce, and Argentine women were among those most frequently brought in. Meanwhile traffickers and pimps were almost ignored, because in the same year only twenty-six cases of white slavery were investigated in Buenos Aires. As a result, forty-four people were detained.[26]

Scandalous behavior remained a female crime in Buenos Aires as long as occurrence within authorized bordellos continued to define the difference between legal and clandestine prostitution. This can be seen in the arrest records for 1919 to 1927.

Prostitutes, both native-born and foreign, were the principal targets of these police arrests. Between 1920 and 1930 self-identified prostitutes

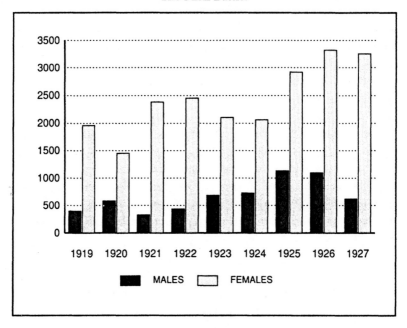

Arrests for scandalous behavior
Source: Buenos Aires Police, *Memoria*, 1919–27, passim.

comprised 50 to 79 percent of all women detained for scandalous behavior. The proportion of Argentine women ranged from 32 percent in 1922 to 73 percent in 1927. During these years more than two thousand women were arrested annually for this misdemeanor, suggesting that women were caught streetwalking as well as working in suspicious jobs.[27]

While all this was happening, Buenos Aires police officials expressed dismay at their inability to arrest pimps and other male undesirables. Police simplistically blamed the problem on the immigrant population and several times advocated passage of stricter anti–immigrant vagrancy and antipimping laws, but national legislators ignored their entreaties. In the meantime, arresting pimps' victims, increasingly native-born, was the only way city police could demonstrate their efficiency. Unfortunately, few people paid attention to adverse consequences of the Ley Palacios.[28]

Although rumors of Jewish white slavery continued to circulate in Buenos Aires, most foreign-born women arrested for scandalous behavior were Spanish, French, or Italian. Few were from eastern European countries. This meant that Jewish women, traditionally seen as victims of white slavery, were infrequently arrested for clandestine prostitution. Given the greater numbers of clandestine than registered prostitutes, the statistics on nationality for scandalous behavior probably more accurately reflect who were prostitutes in Buenos Aires than the Dispensario records.

Despite the decreased numbers of Jewish women engaged in legal or clandestine activity in Buenos Aires, anti-Semites persistently referred to Jewish pimps as a sign of religious depravity. In 1916 Jewish officials felt compelled to respond to an article published in the *Boletín Mensual del Museo Social Argentino*, in which it was "asserted that the most unfitting element for the country was the Russian-Jewish one, because among them were 'many dangerous elements, anarchists, caftens . . . , and prostitutes capable of criminal acts.'" Manuel Bronstein responded in the same journal that there was no contact between respectable Jews and traffickers. Nevertheless, the association between white slavery and Jewish pimps remained very strong.[29]

Annual reports of the Jewish Association for the Protection of Girls and Women did little to promote a more balanced vision of Jewish prostitution in Buenos Aires. In 1924 the association commented on incidents of white

Foreign Women Detained for Scandalous Behavior, 1920–30

	1920	1921	1922	1923	1924	1925	1926	1927	1928	1929	1930
Austrian	2.0	1.0	3.0	2.0	2.0	1.0	1.0	1.0	1.0	1.0	1.0
Brazilian	0.6	—	1.0	1.0	4.0	1.0	1.0	1.0	1.0	1.0	1.0
Chilean	1.0	—	1.0	1.0	3.0	2.0	2.0	3.0	2.0	3.0	3.0
English	1.0	1.0	4.0	2.0	1.0	1.0	—	2.0	1.0	—	1.0
French	12.0	15.0	15.0	13.0	22.0	26.0	26.0	23.0	28.0	23.0	15.0
German	1.0	—	3.0	2.0	2.0	1.0	1.0	1.0	1.0	1.0	—
Italian	13.0	25.0	15.0	29.0	11.0	9.0	21.0	9.0	9.0	10.0	9.0
Paraguayan	1.0	2.0	2.0	2.0	4.0	1.0	1.0	1.0	1.0	2.0	2.0
Romanian	0.4	—	—	—	1.0	1.0	—	—	1.0	1.0	1.0
Russian	11.0	15.0	8.0	7.0	5.0	6.0	8.0	8.0	3.0	4.0	4.0
Spanish	41.0	26.0	24.0	28.0	16.0	30.0	19.0	31.0	30.0	34.0	43.0
Turkish	1.0	5.0	5.0	3.0	1.0	—	3.0	—	—	—	—
Uruguayan	9.0	6.0	5.0	6.0	7.0	6.0	2.0	8.0	8.0	9.0	9.0
Others	6.0	4.0	4.0	4.0	20.0	13.0	14.0	10.0	5.0	4.0	2.0

Source: Korn, *Buenos Aires: Los huéspedes del 20*, p. 142n.

Note: Figures are percentages of the total in each year.

slavery in the Argentine capital during 1923 and 1924. In one case a young girl from Warsaw was lured by a female procurer into traveling to Buenos Aires to get a better job. Interviewed by the local JAPGW inspector when she landed in Buenos Aires, the girl obtained temporary lodgings with the help of Rabbi Halphon. It was soon ascertained that the woman who was supposed to meet her was a procuress. Eventually the local Jewish community found the rescued girl a job as a seamstress. She later married her employer's nephew and sent money to her mother.

Of the five cases examined in detail, this was the only incident involving procuring by nonrelatives. The report concluded that the JAPGW could cite "a great many more sad cases, but the foregoing are surely sufficient to convince even the most skeptical that the Traffic exists." It may have existed, but it was not as extensive as reformers claimed.[30]

The reason Jewish reformers remained apprehensive of the situation in Argentina was the continued operation of the Varsovia Society and the Asquenasum. In 1926, the year before the Varsovia Society renamed itself the Zwi Migdal in honor of the two Migdal brothers, the JAPGW reported that organized Jewish pimps had regrouped since the war and could be found all over South America. Yet within Argentina the committee had helped arrest only three international traffickers. The other cases reported again involved prostitution induced by family coercion.[31]

Throughout the 1920s the Asquenasum, the Varsovia, and subsequently the Zwi Migdal bought protection from public officials to enable their legal and clandestine bordellos to operate freely throughout Argentina. Asquenasum president Simón Rubenstein ran most of the bordellos in San Fernando, Varsovia member Felipe Schon owned a house in Zárate, and Isaac Drayman had establishments in El Tigre and San Fernando. Bordellos in Mataderos, Mar del Plata, and Ensenada were also under Varsovia control. All were in the province of Buenos Aires.[32]

The Varsovia/Zwi Migdal continued its advance into the Argentine interior. Earlier in the century the organization had set up bordellos in Rosario. By the 1920s Córdoba became another center of operation. There Varsovia members cemented firm alliances with local pimps. "El Paisano" ("the Compatriot"), an infamous local trafficker, operated several bordellos in partnership with the Zwi Migdal. Protected by patronage from conservative politicians, El Paisano also had important friends entrenched in the higher echelons of the police force.[33]

The 1920s marked the high point of the Varsovia Society as well as its transformation into the Zwi Migdal. The ending of the war enabled traffickers who had left Argentina in 1913 to return to cities that once again enjoyed the fruits of renewed European immigration. If there were fewer Russian and Polish Jewish women than before, that circumstance did little to dampen enthusiasm. After all, the organization could rely on the demand for new faces by trying to recruit more Jewish women or by rotating prostitutes from one bordello to another, within and among the many Argentine provinces. Yet at no time, even in the 1920s, was the Varsovia or the Zwi Migdal as powerful as their detractors imagined.

The only discordant notes in the otherwise optimistic situation facing the Varsovia was the change in political climate in Buenos Aires after 1919 and the criminal charges leveled against the Varsovia in 1927 by the local branch of the Jewish Association for the Protection of Women and Children. The first event was by far the more serious challenge, but it did little to deter the Asquenasum or the Varsovia, because their bordellos were located throughout Argentina. The second merely caused the Varsovia Society to change its name to the Zwi Migdal.

In sharp contrast to the situation of pimps, the uncertain political situation in Buenos Aires created tremendous anxiety for prostitutes. Each time the municipal council met, a new proposal regarding prostitution might be presented. It was impossible to know what new orders police might receive or whether legal bordello operators would soon have to join the growing ranks of the clandestines. This unease was expressed in a letter written on November 2, 1924, from a Polish prostitute in Buenos Aires to her husband in Europe:

> Dear Husband, you write me to give you a detailed letter. The time is not opportune now, as it is two months before New Year and I do not know yet what is going to happen. . . . I am in partnership in my business, and I say that I must look out well and decide whether I should dissolve or let my partner remain in business, or keep it myself. Because he would want of me a bargain, knowing that I want to depart for home. I toiled hard enough before I could bring it to a business of my own and therefore I must be patient until January. . . .
>
> I wanted, dear Husband, to send you a few hundred dollars, but we do not know what's going to happen here. Each day there are new laws, and I hope to God that they should not close the business [place], because every day it is expected something new; and on account of this I am holding back the sending of money.[34]

While the municipal council grappled with ordinances, a scandal erupted that threatened to embarrass city and national officials at the highest levels. In 1928 several members of the Buenos Aires police were put on trial for having falsified official documents so that underage women could work as prostitutes in the remaining bordellos. According to one German pimp, Herr Koster, "All that was necessary was a photograph, and, after that had been obtained, the certificate was issued with the space for fingerprints and signature blank, to be filled in at a later date."[35]

The charges against the police were eventually dropped, and as soon as Hipólito Yrigoyen was reelected president that year, the men returned to work as if nothing had happened. Only the most naive observer in Buenos Aires was surprised. As Rosalie Lighton Robinson put it: "I was told some months ago by a police official that as soon as Irigoyen came into power that Santiago [chief of the Criminal Investigation Department, accused of complicity] would be re-instated, I did not believe it possible, but you see it has happened! Of course no one believes in his innocency."[36]

The police scandal implicated the highest levels of national and municipal government and incited further public dismay at the extent of corruption in Buenos Aires. The furor over organized prostitution was part of a general anger over the way immigrant criminal elements were believed to dominate political and social life. Whether it was the Italian Mafia or Jewish white slavers, increasingly xenophobic Argentines came to resent foreign presence. Thus by the 1920s it was no longer legalized prostitution that was menacing Buenos Aires society, but rather evil Jews and immigrant mobsters. Consequently pimps and prostitutes alike were forced to conduct their activities more or less surreptitiously, with the connivance of the police, in order to evade new regulations. Rather than recognize the influence of religious discrimination and xenophobia, politicians and the public blamed the crime wave on foreigners and legalized prostitution. The solution to this problem, therefore, was a heightened anti–white slavery campaign accompanied by further attempts to abolish municipally licensed bordellos.[37]

The creation of the Zwi Migdal made Jewish traffickers a perfect target for frustrated reformers. In 1927, just one year before the police scandal came to light, the Varsovia Society was forced to change its name or else be the object of diplomatic opposition. On October 27, Selig Ganopol, caseworker and translator for the local branch of the Jewish Association for the Protection of Girls and Women, officially accused the Varsovia Society of being a haven for white slavers. Based on documented cases collected in

London, the JAPGW clearly identified key members of the Varsovia as pimps and madams engaged in ensnaring unwitting immigrant women.

Although no arrests or convictions were made at the time, enough evidence was available to convince the Polish minister at Buenos Aires to protest the Varsovia Society's legal status. The justification was that the society's name was an insult to the Polish capital. In response, pimps merely formed another organization, naming it the Zwi Migdal after fellow members.[38]

The Zwi Migdal took over the Varsovia's elegant mansion on Córdoba Street, as well as the synagogues and burial grounds in Avellaneda and Santa Fe. The new society and other groups of pimps continued to protect themselves by bribing police and politicians. In the province of Mendoza, for example, politicians were known for celebrating their electoral victories in Federico Glik's bordello in the provincial capital. Asquenasum president Simón Rubenstein reportedly drove a car that used the official license plates of Radical deputy Leopoldo Bard. Bard was a key figure in the Radical party and presided over his party's caucus in the Chamber of Deputies. According to Julio Alsogaray, by the 1930s the Zwi Migdal operated two thousand bordellos with approximately three thousand women, all of which brought an annual profit of 108 million pesos, or 36 million dollars. At the same time the Asquenasum and "operators of clandestine establishments of other nationalities" each reaped 18 million dollars annually.[39]

Albert Londres provided international proof that Jewish pimps were becoming too powerful in Buenos Aires. He believed that "the true White Slave Traffic, as it is conceived of by the popular imagination, is carried on by the Polaks." They took advantage of the poverty in Europe to procure young Jewish women, and Jewish women only, and unlike the French, they relied on ritual marriages and dowries to secure new recruits.[40]

Within Buenos Aires he met Jewish pimps and prostitutes who worked in La Boca, which Londres described as a place "that reminds one of a conscience, which, loaded with all the mortal sins and driven ashore here, survives amid the execrations of the world." There music halls served as antechambers to bordellos, and *casitas* were the pitiful buildings where Jewish women were forced to sell their bodies. He compared these establishments to the "secret haunts of the hashish-smokers, at Cairo." They were places only the poorest or bravest of men dared frequent.[41]

Londres described the role of French prostitution in a very different light. Like the Varsovia Society, the French too operated bordellos in many provincial towns and cities. In contrast to their competitors, however, they considered themselves extraordinary individuals who cared for the women they exploited. Londres was told: "We must be administrators, instructors, comforters, and experts in hygiene. . . . The men of the 'Center,' . . . keep women free from vice. What do they do without us? They smoke, drink, dance, take snow, flirt, and even have affairs with each other."[42] Thus the men of the Center claimed they could save prostitutes from all the horrors of life including drug addiction and lesbianism if the women would only share their profits with them!

After Londres' book became available, derogatory exposés of the Zwi Migdal appeared. Most of the reports about the Varsovia Society, Zwi Migdal, and Asquenasum came from Julio Alsogaray and Victorio Bessero. Their evidence also became the principal source of incriminating documents offered at the trial of Zwi Migdal members. Like the Alsogaray book, Bessero's *Los tratantes de blancas en Buenos Aires* (White slavers in Buenos Aires) focused on the Zwi Migdal's most infamous associates, particularly wealthy madams such as Emma "the millionaire." Both tracts were specifically written to inform the Argentine public of the alleged activities of nefarious Jewish pimps whose political and police protectors had allowed them to continue working.[43]

In 1937 policeman Ernesto M. Pareja published his history of legalized prostitution in Buenos Aires. Building on the other works, his study, frequently quoted, identified so-called racial aspects of prostitution in the capital city. Noting the predominance of foreign-born madams and prostitutes that had characterized licensed prostitution for many years, he further delineated his views on the causes of Jewish prostitution. To understand these women, "it was necessary to understand that they have no moral qualms, and their desire to obtain money . . . was frequently the source of their degradation. European women [on the other hand] were considered to be superior, even those who were Catholic, Orthodox, or Protestant, because it was understood that they entered prostitution after suffering long periods of misery."[44]

These works focused on Jewish prostitution because anti-Semitism was easy to stir up in Catholic, increasingly nativist, Argentina. While they criticized immigrant Jews, they implicitly defended the morality of the native-born even though local pimps, madams, and prostitutes had long been an integral part of both licensed and clandestine prostitution. Regardless of personal motives, these books reinforced a stereotype of the white slaver and the prostitute as typically Jewish.

There were anti-Jewish white slavery campaigns in Europe and the New World, but the Argentine campaign had its own dynamics. Linked to a long-standing desire to blame urban social problems on foreigners residing in Buenos Aires, Jewish traffickers were an ideal target. Nevertheless, Jewish control over prostitution in Buenos Aires and other Argentine cities was never as extensive as imagined. Primary sources indicate that the Zwi Migdal was neither as powerful nor as all-encompassing as heretofore claimed and that women did not spend years in bordellos unless they went on to operate them.

By the late 1920s, just as the Varsovia Society reorganized into the Zwi Migdal, importation of fresh recruits for bordellos had tapered off considerably. According to Lighton Robinson: "Things have changed very much during the last few years, girls no longer come out here to look for positions, and those who do travel are very independent, and do not need help from anyone, least of all an Association, and I am feeling that our work is coming to an end. People tell me that I ought to be very pleased that things are so much better. Of course I am, but it is very dull and tiresome to have nothing to do, that is the hardest work of all."[45]

The prospects for Jewish white slavery were a bit more troublesome, but less than imagined by the press. Between 1930 and 1933 the Buenos Aires committee of the JAPGW interviewed twenty-five Jewish prostitutes, of whom only nine had been lured by traffickers, five by their husbands or lovers, and three by other relatives. The rest registered because they needed to earn money.[46]

As for the native-born pimps (*canfinfleros*), most journalistic accounts tended to ignore their presence or at most to dismiss their importance. Londres accused them of trying to steal women from the French and Polish rings. According to him, once canfinfleros found a woman, they used her wages to indulge in clothing, cigarettes, and all the sartorial splendors attributed to the dandies of the time. Yet Argentine popular culture, whether in the tango, novels, or plays, had a fascination for these men, and by 1900 the foreign pimp was almost ignored in social-realist novels. Which account more accurately reflected Argentine urban conditions?[47]

Another group that should be considered are the native-born prostitutes who worked in legal or clandestine bordellos. Contemporary estimates of clandestine prostitution in Buenos Aires ranged from 25,000 to 30,000. Yet the Argentine government reported to the League of Nations that Argentine women showed "a certain inferiority" that made them less attractive as prostitutes. If the Zwi Migdal controlled 3,000 or even 30,000 women in the entire country, their domination of the business and Argentine allegations that native women were not prostitutes could hardly be considered empirically based claims.[48]

The symbolic aspect of the prostitution issue explains why native-born prostitutes were almost totally ignored by the three authors who published in the 1930s. Pareja went so far as to list the nationality and numbers of all registered women as of December 1934, but he purposely failed to print the Argentine percentage in the chart. Had he done so, it would have revealed explicitly that although 40 percent (seventy) were Polish, 43.9 percent (seventy-six) were locals. Although the percentage of Polish women was still high, registered women were clearly a distinct minority among prostitutes in the city.[49]

Pareja and Alsogaray dwelled on the Jewish presence while they ignored incidents such as the 1929 detention of ten white slavers, of whom eight were French and only two were of eastern European extraction. They never examined scandalous behavior statistics that identified many more Argentine and non–eastern European prostitutes than Jewish women registered at the Dispensario. Instead they, like Londres, tended to emphasize what was important to them.[50]

The decline of white slavery, including Jewish white slavery, as a significant factor in Buenos Aires prostitution can be seen in the later history of the Asociación Nacional Argentina contra la Trata de Blancas. After World War I the Asociación found few cases of white slavery among immigrants. Instead it increasingly realized that its work had less to do with monitoring the ports and more to do with local conditions. In 1917 a young woman wrote the group a letter and signed it "A Victim." She said nothing about the usual complaints about white slavers but rather exhorted reformers to consider the plight of domestic servants who were sexually coerced by their employers. The following year the Asociación reported the case of an Argentine woman with two children who went to register at the Dispensario de Salubridad after a strike at a meat-packing plant had left her without work.[51] For several years local cases continued to occupy moral reformers. Since they could not find typical cases of white slavery, it was useless for the Asociación to pursue traffickers at the port, and in 1928 the committee disbanded.[52]

Police reports for Buenos Aires for the first half of 1924 confirmed that local, rather than international, factors were most often the principal causes of prostitution and related sociopathic behavior. When the police chief was asked by the League of Nations to report on "all cases during the year in which persons have been discovered procuring, enticing, or leading away women or children of either sex for immoral purposes," he presented only six incidents. One involved the seduction of an Argentine boy by several men, and four were cases where Argentine women were threatened with sexual slavery by lovers or relatives. The last case involved a seventeen-year-old Spanish girl whose Argentine boyfriend tried to force her to support him by working in the cabaret Maipú Pigall. The police report challenged the belief that white slavery was a major threat to women in Buenos Aires.[53]

One must also question the degree of control men in the Zwi Migdal and the Center had over "innocent" women they recruited in Europe. Most accounts of the League of Nations and the JAPGW admitted that immigrant prostitutes had often already practiced the trade in Europe. Once in Buenos Aires, the demand for young girls militated against a long career unless they moved to a more remote interior city.

Some of the women were able to amass enough money to go into business as madams. Among the women arrested in the 1930 Zwi Migdal roundup, several told how they had become members of the organization. Unlike many of the men, they did not deny their association with the Zwi Migdal, nor did they deny having engaged in prostitution or having operated bordellos. As in other cases of prostitutes' biographies, they were clearly lying, but they seemed to do so in a fixed pattern.

Rosa Chigalski Wurzerdorf told the court she had arrived penniless in 1899. After working for a time as a dressmaker, she supported herself as a prostitute for two years until she married. Subsequently she operated a café with furnished rooms owned by her husband. When he died in 1928 she went to the Zwi Migdal and paid to become a member so her husband could have a religious burial.[54]

Tauba Pasternak de Rosemberg, like Rosa Chigalski, had been in Argentina for many years. Before she arrived in 1912, she had practiced prostitution in France for five years. In Buenos Aires she again worked as a prostitute, this time in a bordello operated by another woman. She used her earnings to open her own house, and within two years she had earned 40,000 pesos.[55]

Emma "the millionaire," also known as Masha Fischer and María Fizzer, told the court she had arrived in Buenos Aires thirty-two years earlier intending to operate houses of prostitution and had returned to Poland to recruit. After her lover's death in 1914 she became a member of the Varsovia, to which he had belonged, though she claimed ignorance regarding the specific operations of the society. What she did not tell them was that her mother, two brothers, and sister were all involved in organized trafficking.[56]

Other accounts mirrored the ones these women presented. All were remarkably free of accusations of involuntary prostitution, most likely a reflection of their desire to stay out of jail and also to help compatriots. Their stories contrasted sharply with that of Cosía Zeilón, an unwilling recruit who published her autobiography in 1930. She did not become involved in prostitution until her husband, an associate of the Zwi Migdal, died in Montevideo. She was taken back to Buenos Aires by Emma "the millionaire," introduced to pimp Luis Migdal, and kept a sexual prisoner in a downtown bordello for two weeks. For the next few years she was taken to work in Bahía Blanca, Tres Arroyos, Rosario, and then back to Buenos Aires. After all these involuntary experiences, she decided she would be better off working as a madam, and in the 1920s she operated a bordello in Ensenada, in the province of Buenos Aires.[57]

Stories like the one told by Cosía Zeilón, as well as individual cases presented in 1927 accusations against the Varsovia, brought to light the important role women played in procuring other women. Many who had been registered as housekeepers in bordellos were wives, sisters, and mistresses of male pimps, but these women did not rely solely upon their male relatives to gather new recruits. Scheindla Blum, Sara R. Matenburg, Elena Domb de Druzky, Juana Yagodzinska, and Paulina Weitz were all independent procurers. They were known to go on scouting trips to eastern Europe and were members in good standing of the Varsovia Society.[58]

Julio Alsogaray published lists of members of the Zwi Migdal and the Asquenasum, and both included women's names. These women demonstrated that a few could end up as rich as the men who first became their pimps. Emma "the millionaire" was estimated to have a personal fortune of three million pesos and incomparable jewels. It was perhaps the success of a few women as much as the threats of men that kept women in Zwi Migdal bordellos of Buenos Aires and provincial cities.[59]

In any event, neither the occasional protests of unwilling women nor the scandals that rocked the police force and the Varsovia Society affected the operations or the coffers of this small group of organized traffickers. Well entrenched in provincial cities as well as Buenos Aires, groups like the Zwi Migdal and the Asquenasum continued to operate even after the military coup of 1930 overthrew Hipólito Yrigoyen's government and replaced it with a military dictatorship.

In 1930 Raquel Liberman accused the Zwi Migdal and her husband of forcing her back into prostitution years after she had taken her savings and opened an antique store. Her account led to the arrest of Zwi Migdal members not warned by their political friends, but it failed to end the society's activities. The individual acts of Zwi Migdal members charged with operating an organization that conspired to commit illegal acts were insufficient to indict the organization. Those arrested managed to persuade victims not to testify, and all were eventually released. At the time of the great police roundup, the only other pimps arrested were those known to have associations with the Jewish group. They were caught in an obvious attempt to entrap the Zwi Migdal.[60]

For Alsogaray and other contemporaries, the Zwi Migdal represented all that was wrong in Buenos Aires. As part of the xenophobia of the times, it was easier to blame Jews for the entire problem than face the complex relation of prostitution to Argentine society, politics, and economy. After Zwi Migdal members managed to bribe, cajole, and threaten their way to freedom, embarrassed Argentine politicians were more willing to reconsider the abolition of licensed houses. Anti-Semitism did not disappear, but the Zwi Migdal indictments finally brought the Jewish criminals to trial, albeit unsuccessfully.

In December 1930 José Guerrico, the Buenos Aires intendente, issued a decree abolishing municipally licensed prostitution in the national capital. In his prefatory remarks the intendente admitted that Buenos Aires was considered a center of international white slavery. More important, he recognized that legalized prostitution was ineffective and a farce. To rectify the situation, he decreed that the city would no longer monitor bordellos, and he ordered the closing of the Dispensario de Salubridad. Then he created a committee to organize an anti–veneral disease campaign, one that included Angel Gímenez.[61]

It was one thing to issue a decree and quite another to have the order carried out. Between 1930 and 1934 intendentes bickered with members of the municipal council until all came to recognize the inevitability of abolishing legalized prostitution. Finally they agreed to ban bordellos after December 31, 1934, and replace prostitution ordinances with laws that offered medical care, repatriation, or help in finding "honest jobs" for those who left bordellos. More comprehensive municipal anti–venereal disease campaigns were also authorized.[62]

To implement the new law, Intendente Mariano de Vedia y Mitre ordered the burning of all books and papers at the Dispensario de Salubridad that contained personal data about prostitutes. This included all the identity booklets prostitutes and maids were supposed to carry. Then three days later the municipality ordered police to arrest anyone who encouraged licentious behavior (toda incitación al libertinaje o lo que signifique un atentado a la moralidad y buenas costumbres"). This placed the police at a disadvantage because they could not officially identify women who, until recently, had been prostitutes. The ordinance also demonstrated that it remained unclear whether prostitution itself was illegal.[63]

In response to the new laws, during the first year of the ban police created a new category of scandalous behavior, one to which was appended the word *incitar* (to incite). For that crime 2,910 women were arrested, compared with 23 men, whereas 237 women were arrested for scandalous behavior that did not incite, compared with 1,017 men. The new category was clearly designed to keep women from luring men with sexual propositions. Of the 2,910 women arrested, 907 (31 percent) were self-identified prostitutes, and 1,197 (41 percent) were unemployed. In 1936 almost 5,000 women were brought in on similar charges, of whom 51 percent were prostitutes and only 12 percent were unemployed. Police had defined the ordinances in such a way as to make prostitution, rather than bordello operations, an illegal activity.[64]

They justified their actions in 1935 by stating that the police had been systematically excluded from controlling prostitution by the municipality's efforts to rehabilitate women, yet it was their duty to protect the youth of the city. For that reason they believed it was necessary to watch the women who were no longer required to have medical examinations.[65]

Arbitrary police action was only one facet of the problems evoked by local ordinances. The municipal council of Rosario enacted similar legislation in 1932, to the dismay of many. As a United States diplomat noted, "Many of the houses are used as gathering places . . . a commonplace farewell remark among men is 'See you at Saphós.'" In addition to the disappearance of male conviviality derived from socializing in bordellos, he believed the city would lose 100,000 pesos in revenue with the new law.[66]

Many in Buenos Aires also wondered what effect such a law had when suburbs still allowed houses to operate both legally and clandestinely. There were bordellos all over the province, and the provincial government had not abolished licensed houses as Santa Fe had done in 1934. At this point it became evident that municipalities had little control over the prostitution business so long as neighboring cities were reluctant to adopt similar policies.

In these circumstances local governments were unable to stop the activities of many pimps or the flight of prostitutes to the suburbs. Consequently in March 1931 military president General José Uriburu began to contemplate national measures to resolve the problem, and he authorized a committee to study Buenos Aires prostitution. Members were urged to suggest new regulations, but they did not mention abolishing legal bordellos.[67]

In 1933 Socialists led by Angel Giménez introduced the first national venereal disease treatment proposal in Congress. The legislative intent was to have the national government take over all venereal disease treatment centers, make sex education mandatory in primary schools and in the armed forces, prohibit licensed houses, and require prenuptial medical exams. It also established contraction of venereal disease by a spouse as grounds for divorce.[68] This one piece of legislation managed to tie together a series of Socialist platforms and present them in the name of public health reform. The tactic was brilliant and, even though it was never completely implemented, sensitized the Argentine public to such matters, and eventually a series of public health measures were approved.

Throughout the 1920s and 1930s Socialists worked with others to promote greater state control of the economy and public health, so the idea of a venereal disease law was not unrealistic. Nevertheless, it was not until 1934 that Argentine politicians allied with the military began to formulate their stance on the issue. The opportunity arose in May when Deputy Tiburcio Padilla, a prominent physician who claimed he was apolitical, offered a national venereal disease law that excluded sex education and made no mention of prostitution or divorce. Then in June 1935 Padilla introduced another sex education bill. His version specified in which grades sex education should be offered and made it obligatory for bars, hotels, and other sites of assignation to sell prophylactic devices. He also insisted that bachelors over twenty-five pay a 3 to 5 percent tax to encourage them to get married.[69]

Eventually a Commission of Hygiene and Social Assistance was formed in the Chamber of Deputies to help Padilla and Giménez work out a compromise that would resolve differences. The final version of this legislation was passed in December 1936. It included provisions to close all bordellos and create a national program of mandatory prenuptial exams for men (women were exempted).[70]

Organized prostitution had become such an embarrassment for Buenos Aires and other Argentine cities that the 1936 Law of Social Prophylaxis was enacted, with the hope that rings of pimps and madams would disappear once and for all. Unfortunately they were only the tip of the social and political iceberg that tolerated and often benefited from sexual commerce. The success of these groups had been due not only to legalized prostitution, but also to the impact of unpredictable reform efforts, the Argentine economy, the ever diminishing supply of eastern European prostitutes, and the corruptibility of local constabularies and public officials. Attitudes toward prostitution and gender relations thus mirrored other power structures in the Argentine polity, and this could be clearly seen in the relation of prostitution to women's work in factories.

After 1914 the increased participation of women in the industrial labor force, rather than in commerce, contributed to gender tensions in the capital city. Men became concerned that less expensive female labor would take jobs away from them. They also feared the increased freedom of women who were not economically dependent. At the same time that protective laws were defending the rights of husbands and fathers to supervise family labor, other legislation restricted the rights of men to select their wives' and children's occupations and appropriate their salaries. Moral reformers, both male and female, worried that women who worked in factories would damage their childbearing capacity and that their morality would be endangered as well. Eventually such fears translated into the belief that women factory workers suffered more diseases than women who stayed at home. In this way, as it became obvious that legalized prostitution would eventually disappear, the symbolic debate over the dangerous woman ultimately shifted from the bordello to the factory.

World War I precipitated the expansion of porteño industry by cutting off traditional sources of imported manufactured goods. Increased factory activity during the war did not improve economic conditions for the entire urban working class. A general study of salaries in Buenos Aires between 1914 and 1917 revealed that the wages of men had decreased by 3 percent, while women's wages had declined by 5 percent. Yet those employed in textile production seemed to hold their own after the war. In 1919 they were among the best paid. Female employees also benefited from this situation even though they still were paid less than men.[71] By 1935 21,000 women composed 57.3 percent of the textile work force in large establishments. The expansion of textile production meant that women could compete with men in the industrial workplace.[72]

The passage of the Palacios antipimping law in 1913 should be seen as an early government reaction to women in the workplace. By criminalizing the sexual commerce of wives and daughters, the Argentine Congress had defined the moral boundaries of family labor. In 1924 labor law 11.317 finally established boundaries for labor performed in the home. It applied to all children under twelve and to rural as well as urban labor. Yet once again, women who worked for relatives or were domestic servants were exempted from most restrictions. Thus as late as 1924 any type of family employment except sexual commerce remained overseen by family heads.[73]

While legislators regulated women's work in public factories and guaranteed unsupervised family labor, Socialist-inspired 1926 civil code revisions struck another symbolic blow to patriarchal authority. Among the new provisions was the right of married women to seek work freely, whether or not they had permission from their husbands.[74] Thus even though it might be desirable for married women not to work, or to work only under family supervision, those women still had the right to select their own jobs. This meant that the Argentine government would not defend husbands and fathers in family disputes over work.

Prostitution and women's work were linked by additional factors. Medical fears about unhealthful factory conditions were also related to reforms of prostitution ordinances. To replace bordellos in 1919, Socialist-inspired municipal ordinances directed the city to establish venereal disease treatment clinics in working-class neighborhoods. The intent of this law was to ensure that poor people could obtain medical treatment, regardless of their work schedule and their ability to pay. Yet at the same time, this meant that Socialists targeted the working class as more prone to venereal disease than other sectors of the city's population. And since women were still seen as the source of contagion and were entering factories more rapidly than men, it is clear that monitoring the health of prostitutes was slowly being redesigned to include female factory employees.

In 1921 city councilmen were asked to subsidize the operation of a school to teach women how to weave on nonmechanized looms, so as to enable poor women to find acceptable employment without having to work with machines or in a factory. Although there is no evidence to verify that the factory was actually opened, the municipal council promised to invest a maximum of 15,000 pesos to construct looms, purchase raw materials, and hire teachers so that a former restaurant in the Parque de los Patricios, a working-class neighborhood on the southern edge of the city, could be converted into a weaving school. Upon graduation, the best students would be presented with hand looms and cotton or wool.[75]

Two years later the intendente felt it necessary to protect not only women who might seek factory jobs, but those who already worked there. To that end in 1923 Intendente Noel amended the 1919 prostitution ordinances by decreeing that no woman could register at the Dispensario if she worked on the same block as a school, religious institution, or factory employing women.[76] By the time the Argentine Congress outlawed bordellos in 1936 as part of an anti–venereal disease program, the factory was clearly defined as a potential target for the new laws. According to article 5 of the Law of Social Prophylaxis, any business or institution that employed more than fifty people could be ordered by the national Prophylaxis Institute to provide free venereal disease treatment and set up information programs. Textile factories were soon pressured to provide these services, and in June 1939 the *Gaceta Textil*, a publication representing factory owners, contained an article by Dr. Carlos Silvestre defending their refusal to comply with the law.[77]

In general, the increased numbers of women working in factories, along with those who taught school or were secretaries or telephone operators, represented a threat to family hierarchy. Even though their income might have been crucial to family survival, industrial employment was still viewed as a dangerous occupation for women. Nevertheless, the national government of the 1920s, dominated by the Radical party and influenced by Socialists, passed laws freeing women from family hierarchy so they could become a mainstay of the industrial work force.

Opposition to women's employment, particularly in factories, therefore became a key platform of conservative politicians throughout the 1930s. The Legión Cívica (Civic Legion), a paramilitary organization that supported the military dictatorship of General Uriburu (1930–32), strongly advocated the traditional family and, along with it, women's retreat into the home. Its attitude was shared by Instituto Alejandro E. Bunge, which in 1945 published a study of Argentine economic and social problems. Among the conclusions offered was a strong recommendation that women withdraw from the labor force: "We believe the essential problem is that women who abandon the home to work at tasks inappropriate for women and who compete successfully for these jobs with men because they accept lower wages, also change the hierarchy of the family, reduce the acquisitive power of the family, and defy their patriotic and social duties of motherhood."[78]

Once again female gender roles were inextricably linked to family and nation. Good women stayed home and performed their "patriotic and social duties." In contrast, working women were as deviant as prostitutes had been. Both evaded marital responsibilities and contributed to social and political disorder.

Efforts to outlaw prostitution in Buenos Aires, along with the crackdown on rings of white slavers, helped promote the idea that it was possible to resolve the problem of dangerous women and immoral families. Socialist reformers like Giménez, as well intentioned as they might have been, used the prostitution issue to attract political support by arguing that the abolition of legalized prostitution, added to changes in the civil rights of women, would deter immorality among immigrants and the native-born. Increased female employment and economic independence, however, dampened much of the enthusiasm generated by moral reformers. For many Argentine men, regardless of class, all independent working women essentially destroyed male authority and family life. Until they relinquished their freedom and submitted to authority, just as prostitutes had done in the past, all women were potential victims of sexual slavery and needed to be protected. Hence the white slavery controversy raged on.

Needlework was one of the many poorly paid sources of women's income—and one that often drove them to become prostitutes. Courtesy Archivo General de la Nación, Argentina.

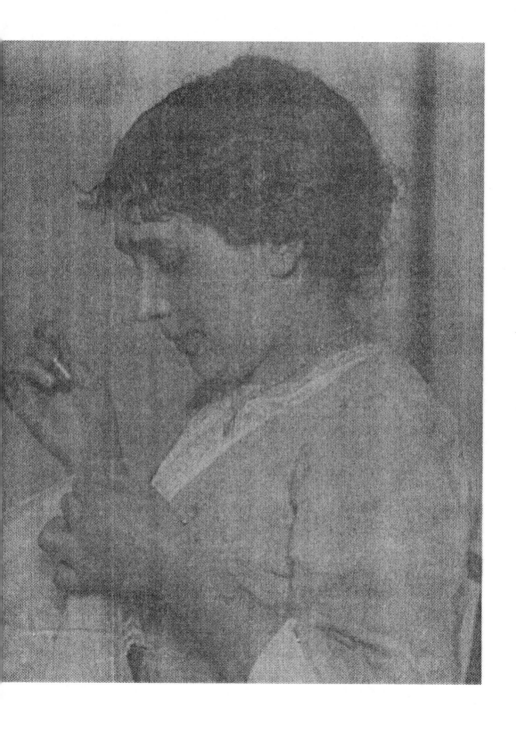

Doing laundry, another female occupation, also provided too little income to
deter poor women from engaging in
prostitution. Courtesy Archivo General
de la Nación, Argentina.

These photographs of French pimps were
sent to the United States Immigration
and Naturalization Service by Argentine
authorities in 1932. These men had left
Argentina in the wake of the Zwi Migdal
incident. Courtesy National Archives and
Records Service, Washington, D.C.

5

Tango, Gender, and
Politics

Out of sight but never out of mind. No laws enclosing prostitutes could ever remove the fear of female sexual danger from the male imagination. The battle to control prostitution was not limited to political debates in municipal and congressional chambers. Nor was it simply a concern of elite leaders. Men of other classes, expressing themselves in a variety of ways, discussed the implications of women's independence and sexuality by invoking the theme of prostitution in songs, plays, and novels. Occasionally the female voice was heard, but it was often men speaking through women singers and actors. Because prostitution was a recurring theme in Argentine popular culture, the activity that city officials tried so hard to hide became one of the liveliest and most frequently discussed topics in late nineteenth- and early twentieth-century Argentina.

Invariably male writers perceived prostitutes as symbolizing various aspects of the problematic immigrant or urban woman. To some, women were dangerous—vectors of disease and immorality. Others characterized them as passive victims of white slavery or abusive family members. Several authors believed female prostitution represented the choice between immorality and poverty or between traditional modes of production and industrial capitalism. From 1900 onward, however, prostitutes were also linked symbolically and sexually to the most dangerous group of men in Argentina, the anarchists. Some anarchists wrote about prostitutes. To them, prostitutes were victims of authoritarian families, corrupt political structures, or their own greed. Other writers, ranging from ardent Catholics to leftist social reformers, also sympathized with the plight of women doomed by economic, social, or personal circumstances. Nevertheless, they still believed prostitutes were dangerous and expressed this concern through plots involving the sexual and political union of anarchists and prostitutes. While these writers imagined that social or political revolution might result, their real fear was linked to the belief that women were stronger than men.

As anarchism became less threatening in Argentina, men wrote about prostitutes who freed themselves by taking responsibility for their lives and actions. Independence strengthened women's resolve at the same time as their men became less assertive. Debates about the consequences of inverse male/female power relations allowed Argentine popular culture to explore social anxieties mediated through portrayals of unacceptable people and dysfunctional families.

One form of popular expression that permeated all others was the Argentine tango. This dance has been called a paradigm of national popular culture: "Nothing expresses it [Argentine popular culture] better than the invention of the tango in the Río de la Plata. Paralleling migratory movements, both internal and external, . . . the tango was forged in suburban bordellos and within twenty years was accepted in the salons of the middle classes."[1]

The tango conveyed all the ambiguities of gender relations. To dance it was an act of courage. Like the waltz, the tango encouraged close embraces, but it could be described more as clutching that led to total female domination by the male dancer. Legs were used not only for movement, but also for the man to kick his partner in ritual fashion.[2]

According to traditional accounts, at first men danced with each other because the tango was too erotic for women. What passed for virile activity, however, could also be seen as entertainment for weak men. After all, if they could find no female partners, what kind of men were they? Eventually men were discouraged from dancing with each other, and the first hints of questioned male virility thus surfaced in Argentine popular culture.[3]

Prostitutes were the first women to dance the tango. Mixed tango dancing evolved in the bordellos and music halls in the waterfront areas of Buenos Aires and in Montevideo, Uruguay, from the 1860s to the 1930s. Based on rhythms and dancing styles of African, Spanish, and Italian origins, the tango often served as a prelude to commercial sex. By the 1870s men frequented urban establishments where female companionship was available for a price. Music halls, romerías (marquees set up on holidays), and even the circus were sites of tangos and sexual assignations. In all these places poor soldiers and immigrant laborers mingled with youthful upper-class swells (niños bien) and found opportunities for drinking, mischief making, and commercial sex.

Before soccer became a mass spectator sport in the 1930s, drinking and dancing were particularly popular forms of male recreation but were anathema to decent women. Whoever could afford to buy a piano or hire a band and serve fiery beverages would be assured an extensive male clientele, as well as a reputation for immorality. Music halls, cafés with entertainment, nightclubs, and private clubs sprang up all over the city. An 1881 newspaper article described such spots: "One of the neighborhoods filled with bars and coffee shops can be found near the Plaza del Parque. It is well known that . . . entire blocks are filled with music spots, often next to houses of prostitution. The principal business that takes place in these establishments is dancing. They hire a number of women and a musician, and for every dance a man has to pay one peso".[4] Beneath the veneer of the dance hall lay the true business: commercial sex. The real function of the dancer was to excite clients sexually so they would return for more.

In these establishments rural cowboys in town for a visit, sailors and soldiers, and *compadritos* (young men who fancied themselves daring) danced with waitresses who were usually considered clandestine prostitutes. The popularity of the tango helped fill the antechambers of bawdy houses and halls with men looking to dance—and perhaps something more. By 1897 Buenos Aires police chief Francisco J. Beazley had become so concerned about the disreputable nature of city entertainment that he informed the minister of interior that "small bars that serve tables on the street as well as the fancy café with lavish scenery, orchestra, and indoor service, are driving the legal bordellos out of business. . . . Every night, because no efforts are taken to stop it, young girls who are barely fifteen, exhibit themselves . . . for the lubricious entertainment of the dense crowds attracted by the female waitresses who drink with the audience".[5]

By 1915, fears of rowdy public entertainment shifted from the bordello to the cabaret and from prostitution to the tango. That year the Buenos Aires municipal council identified dance halls as dangerous places. A new law threatened closure and a 500 peso fine for cabarets, bars, restaurants, and cafés whose entertainment encouraged scandalous activity. Subsequent accusations led to permanent closing.[6]

Buenos Aires was not the only Argentine city to regulate cabarets, the new form of nightclub that became popular in Argentina after 1910. In 1925 Rosario officials enacted ordinances to deal with the presumed medical consequences of urban entertainment. Instead of relying solely on police to defend the social order, the Rosario Asistencia Pública insisted that all female cabaret employees obtain venereal disease health certificates every three months. This ordinance was justified by the belief that these employees regularly engaged in clandestine prostitution, and most physicians involved in the program advocated even more frequent exams.[7]

Tango dancing was entertainment for men and work for poor, morally dubious, and potentially infected women. In such circumstances, women of virtue could not dance in public. They had to find more private leisure pursuits until the tango could escape its unsavory reputation. The cabaret attempted to provide that opportunity, but it never fully succeeded.

Most tango historians divide the evolution of the dance into three phases. The first could be called the bordello era, roughly from 1870 to 1918. It was characterized by an emphasis upon dance rather than verse. The second phase, often called the *época de oro* (the golden era), lasted from 1918, and Carlos Gardel's first recording, until 1935 and his tragic death in a plane crash. The third phase, from 1935 to the present, has been characterized by a return to an emphasis on dancing and experimentation with music rather than lyrics. Significantly, without denying Gardel's incredible contribution to tango singing, these same periods also correspond to the tango's bordello era, its era of cabaret and theater, and its era of lyrical co-optation and suppression.

During the years when the tango was linked to prostitution and the bordello, few lyrics were written, but the earliest set of verses proudly identified the dance's origins. In 1888 "Dame la lata" was written. The title referred to the metal tokens customers gave to both prostitutes and dance hall girls as proof they had paid for their privilege.[8] It was one of several songs that dealt with a wide range of social types encountered in lower-class porteño neighborhoods. Of those composed before 1918, many were as sympathetic to prostitutes, famous bordellos, madams, and female tango singers as they were to mothers, laundresses, and the *percal*, the humbly dressed working-class woman. They also referred proudly to black Argentines who were renowned musicians and madams, themes less commonly treated in later songs.[9]

Although the bordello and its habitués were popular topics of the primitive sung tango, their commentaries on sexuality, family relations, and the personal dilemma of the author or singer were the true links between the early verses and the more polished *tango-canción* (sung tango) of subsequent years. The role of gender anxiety and family relations also helps explain the significance of prostitution to other aspects of Argentine popular culture.

Argentine tango lyrics, before they were suppressed by public authorities in the 1930s, shared a common gender concern: men doubted their ability to control their fiancées or female family members. An example of this can be found in "Señor Comisario," first composed in 1880. Over the years several sets of lyrics were written, including one sung from a female perspective and another from that of a witness to female adultery, presumable male. Each questioned whether husbands satisfied the sexual demands of their wives:

> Señor Comisario, give me another husband;
> because the one I have won't sleep with me.
>
> Señor Comisario, I have been a witness when that scoundrel,
> when that pig of a woman, deceived her husband.[10]

Even more important, both versions questioned male authority and virility within the home, not the bordello. Thus, instead of supporting efforts to define women's morality through the medically supervised bordello, these early tango lyrics, written mostly by lower-class men, urged greater dominance by male heads of households over supposedly virtuous women. They also criticized impotent or irresponsible men who evaded their marital obligations.[11]

In the decade between 1910 and 1920 the tango underwent a major transformation that enabled it to enter a new phase. The process began when the dance was discovered by Parisian nightclub aficionados, and soon it was the rage of Europe and the United States. A new word, *tangomania*, was coined to describe the frenzied acceptance of the music by people who cared little about its origins, moral implications, or lyrical message. By 1913, "bishops, cardinals, even Pope Pius X himself pronounced against the dance as lubricious and immoral; the emperors of Austria-Hungary and Germany prohibited their soldiers to dance it when in uniform . . . the tango triumphed over all such obstacles."[12]

Back home in Buenos Aires, middle- and upper-class men and women who relied on French tastes to determine Argentine chic found it difficult to accept Parisian tangomania. One reason was the tango's origin in prostitution. Another was that over a period of twenty years, the tango had become more sexually explicit. The introduction in the 1890s of the *bandoneón*, a German accordion made by the Band Union Company, reputedly caused the change, because pioneer musicians had insufficient technical skills to keep up with the traditional piano, flute, guitar, and violin.[13] In this acci-

dental way, the tango had changed from a spirited dance with limited physical contact to a slow, languorous, stylized erotic art form where couples
embraced in a scandalous manner.

There were several ways to deal with the tango's eroticism and its allu-
sions to the bordello. One was to sanitize the dance so that proper men and
women could enjoy it. This was the method employed in the United States
by the famous cabaret dancing duet of Irene and Vernon Castle: "In the
tango they envisioned grace rather than fiery passion. 'It should be practiced frequently, so as to make it smooth,' they said. The Castles also mod-
erated the dips that revealed too much of the woman's leg, brought wom-
en's pelvic regions dangerously close to male bodies, and placed women in a
sexually suggestive position."[14] The Castles made up their own history of
the tango. At times they claimed it was European rather than Argentine.
When forced to admit the dance had Latin origins, Vernon Castle insisted
that an Argentine diplomat had introduced the tango at Maxim's, thereby
inferring that it was an elite dance form.[15]

The Argentine middle and upper classes sanitized the tango in their own
way. First of all, unlike the North Americans and Europeans who changed
the dance, Argentines made the tango safer by moving it out of the bordello. In 1910 the Centenario Café, in a central spot along the Avenida de
Mayo, was one of the first "decent" establishments to hire a tango orchestra. Soon others followed. In 1912 the Baron Demarchi, an Italian who had
made Argentina his home, gave a huge party in a downtown Buenos Aires
restaurant and hired tango dancers as entertainment. Gradually tango musicians and "tango professors" were sought after in the posh establishments
of the city.[16]

The middle class introduced the tango into the home as an acceptable
family activity. Patio dances, organized by local neighborhoods, allowed
men and women to tango without moral ambivalence. The availability of
sheet music, as well as the musical skills of family members, were critical to
this process. Finally, after World War I, the development of the Argentine
radio and record industry made the tango accessible to all.

For all these reasons, at the same time that the tango began to be separated from its bordello origins, Argentine tango dancing was soon linked to
European formal evening attire. Originally tango dancers dressed according to their class or origin, and many of the early Argentines who danced or
sang in Europe were requested to dress in gaucho, or cowboy, clothing.
For Argentines back at home, gaucho clothing implied a lack of manners
and civilization. In 1910 *Caras y Caretas*, the principal bourgeois Argentine

magazine, published a short story about a local tango dance. Accompanied by a drawing of a gaucho asking a woman to dance, the brief story-conversation told of a woman's initial refusal to dance with a man who did not wash with the proper brand of soap![17]

Three years later *Caras y Caretas* published a series of photographs that documented tangomania in Europe. In Paris evening gowns and tuxedos had become de rigueur tango costumes for the Europeans; unlike the gaucho performers, Parisians did not tango in any other clothing. The contrasting uniform of the Argentine dancer Bernabé Limarra and his Spanish partner María la Bella clearly showed that Argentines had to change their dress in order to civilize the tango.[18]

Although *Caras y Caretas* continued to publish photographs of elite Parisians dancing, the magazine went out of its way to encourage Argentine pride. In late 1913 José María Salaverría sent a short piece from Paris describing his attendance at a tango tea. In it he criticized the way foreigners had tamed the Argentine dance: "How could Paris and half of Europe become impassioned [by such a graceless way to dance]? Could it be that in other places it is danced better? . . . It was left to me, perhaps the least qualified, worst dancer, barely a tango devotee, to become indignant by what I saw. It transformed me into a tango fan. Oh, poor tango, how you have been ill treated in Paris, shorn of all your passion, all your rare and plebeian elegance!"[19]

The second way Argentines sanitized the tango was to turn it into a more passive, spectator activity by emphasizing lyrics over dance. This second possibility was more frequently explored by Argentine than United States audiences. *Caras y Caretas* aided this transition when it published its first facsimile of tango sheet music in 1912.[20]

Lyrics became even more important after Argentines began to record tangos, a process accelerated by the spectacular popularity of Carlos Gardel. In late 1917 Gardel excited theater patrons with renditions of one of his most famous tangos, "Mi noche triste" (My Saddest Night). Written by Pablo Contursi, it dramatized the lament of a man rejected by his mistress. Unable to forget her ("I can find no consolation"), the man turned to alcohol to dull his agony. "Mi noche triste" not only became a popular recording in 1918, it was also incorporated into an Argentine play, thereby linking the tango to the theater.[21]

Gardel's career had begun several years earlier. In 1914 the French immigrant had been offered his first full-time job as a cabaret performer. The schedule that led to his job offer typified the nightclub scene in Buenos

Aires just as the cabarets became popular. The evening began in a downtown café. Later Gardel and his friends, some of whom were politicians, moved on to a nearby private club and clandestine bawdy house operated by Madame Jeanne, an Italian posing as a Frenchwoman. In the early morning hours Gardel and his friends went on to the Armenonville, a new cabaret named after a Parisian bistro in the Bois de Boulogne, where the management asked Gardel and his partner to return as regular performers.[22]

In all the places Gardel attended, few respectable women were present. Instead, dubious nightclub waitresses, dancers, and entertainers were available to provide companionship for upper- and lower-class men. His final stop, however, was the kind of place that tried to separate itself from the bawdy house. Cabarets like these benefited greatly from Gardel's popularity, and they became one of the urban institutions often alluded to in tangos that dealt with gender relations.

These new bistros offered an urban place for men and women to tango that was more acceptable than the bordello. Nevertheless, to dance in a cabaret was still dangerous for professional female dancers, let alone respectable middle-class women. At the turn of the century European moral reformers expanded their anti–white slavery campaign after discovering that female dancing troupes and dancers were being recruited for work in Buenos Aires. As early as 1899 the National Vigilance Anti–White Slavery Congress noted:

> Certain classes of situations are specially dangerous, and might be subjected to special precautions. For example, it might be enacted that no foreign girls under 21 should be employed in a coffee-house, café chantant, or other places of public entertainment, nor in any place where wines and spirits are sold, without the leave of her own consul, who would himself be responsible for seeing that the consent of the girl's parents or guardians was obtained, and would send her home on her or their request.[23]

Before the cabaret developed, music halls where foreign troupes entertained porteño crowds were particularly suspect. In 1913 Samuel Cohen went to the Royal Theater, a typical music hall. There he found clandestine prostitution rampant among independent women as well as music hall employees:

> Prostitutes are, in some of them, allowed to walk freely about and

solicit prostitution, and they are even encouraged to do so. In one, the Royal, there is a gallery where I was refused permission to sit down on the seats, as I was told they were reserved for these women. In this Music Hall, there is also a restaurant, at special prices, which continues after the entertainment is over, and in which all the young actresses are expected to attend after their performance, to "entertain" the men who are present. It is, I am told, one of the clauses of their contracts.[24]

Reports of theatrical troupes forced into white slavery persisted. Yet observant moral reformers chose to distinguish the degree of depravity that existed among the diverse groups of entertainers in the city. Rosalie Lighton Robinson, the British social worker, commented in 1914 that there were vast moral distinctions between actresses and cabaret employees, and she called those who worked in *cafés chantants* (cafés where singers performed) "girls who have forgotten themselves."[25]

Moral reformers perpetuated the belief that immorality awaited women who danced professionally in Argentina. A 1927 report noted:

A man was arrested at Florence who was about to take eighteen girls to Buenos Ayres, where they were engaged to dance. This man was the brother of a brothel-keeper at Buenos Ayres.

The girls who belong to these troupes have to dance and sing in low-class music-halls or theatres; in nearly all cases they are obliged to associate with the audience, to drink with the men, and to incite the men to drink. They are paid absurdly low wages. It is quite impossible for them to live on what they earn in their capacity of "artiste"; they have to try to supplement their earnings by commissions which they receive on drinks sold, and by practicing prostitution.[26]

Rumors that illicit drugs were available at cabarets, along with clandestine prostitution, alarmed Europeans and Argentines alike. After 1910 cocaine and other drugs appeared to become popular among those who frequented nightclubs and music spots. In 1914 a play entitled *El cabaret* opened in Buenos Aires. Its characters included an "artiste" who was addicted to cocaine. This theme was expanded in 1922 when *Los dopados* (The Drug Fiends) told the tale of evil men who seduced a woman by drugging her champagne with cocaine.[27]

Carlos Gardel immortalized the introduction of drugs into porteño nightlife when he recorded "Tiempos viejos" (The Old Times). Gardel recalled that the halcyon years had been "when other men, better men than we, knew neither cocaine nor morphine," when "women of great courage each defended their lover in fights at Laura's." Drugs, weak men, and the cabaret had replaced the freewheeling years before state-regulated prostitution. In contrast to the independence of men and women in the past, "modern"—that is, weak—men needed drugs, and strong women betrayed their men. Thus Gardel linked the nostalgic drug-free past with the era of bordello-based musical entertainment and more traditional gender relations.[28]

Fears of white slavery accompanied drugs. In May 1920 the British Actors' Association received a letter warning the organization to be wary of white slavers who used drugs to take advantage of theatrical or cabaret workers in Buenos Aires: "At the Hotel the waiter drugs the food, or has a duplicate key of the bedroom—of course many other methods are used, but they eventually abduct the girl, she is then interned in one of their numerous houses, from which she is quite unable to escape."[29] When the Foreign Office was asked to verify the matter, it claimed that though similar reports had not been received before, "There is no reason to disbelieve the report."

In contrast, after years of working in Buenos Aires, Lighton Robinson was still campaigning to distinguish the bad reputation of café workers from that of more bourgeois nightclub life in the Argentine capital city. Consequently, in 1928 the *Vigilance Record* openly criticized an alarmist article that claimed that any young girl who signed on for work in South American cabarets had "no kick if she finds the place is not a bed of roses." As the *Vigilance Record* put it, "We . . . [question] the inevitableness of the . . . low-class cabarets where the girls are expected to supplement their salary by selling drinks and by practicing prostitution."[30]

The association of prostitution with the tango and the cabaret continued to make it difficult for habitués to take along their wives, fiancés, or daughters. Women who showed up alone were certain to have suspicious morals. Yet gradually the tango and the nightclub could be enjoyed by some daring but respectable women. In Argentina, unlike the United States, the dance remained scandalous, but fewer middle-class people were actually dancing in public. Instead they were listening to notable tango singers.

The lyrics finally sanitized the tango for Argentine audiences because they mocked the sexual prowess of the male singer and warned against women who were too independent. Again Gardel was the vocalist principally responsible for accomplishing this task. One of the most prolific recorders of tango songs, in his own lyrics and his renditions of others Gardel tended to envision women who were good because they were mothers. Submissive and kept at home, they were no threat to men. Women were evil or prone to seduction by false values if they left the house. They were also viewed as prostitutes or as evil if they abandoned or betrayed the man singing. For the same reason, immoral women were reproached if they had deceived the singer but were more sympathetically portrayed if others had seduced them.

Gardel and almost all the tango lyricists of the 1920s and 1930s were men who came from lower-class backgrounds, and most had worked in trades while they developed their skills as composers, singers, or performers. The early tango composer Angel Villoldo (d. 1919) had been a type-setter. Roberto Firpo had been a metalworker, and several others were railroad men. In addition to their working-class origins, a number of them were anarchists, and their class and ideology helped account for their disillusion and bitterness about the change in personal and gender values they perceived in modernizing Argentina.[31]

Anarchism became very popular among the lower classes in Buenos Aires. Although the movement was divided over organizational tactics, there was a strong belief that personal relationships between men and women, untainted by the coercive forces of civil or religious marriage, were the foundations of a truly free society and the ideal family. Anarchists decried the hierarchy and authoritarianism of the traditional family, but anarchist men were also uncomfortable about the prospect of women's gaining the ascendancy.[32]

Anarchist ambivalence about male authority permeated tango lyrics. Darío Cantón's study of the lyrics sung by Carlos Gardel reveals the depths of discontent and anxiety expressed in his most popular tangos. Out of seventy-seven songs, 54 percent (forty-two) dealt with love and hate. Of these forty-two songs, thirty described a love that had ended—in twenty-five of them by female initiative. When the singer felt betrayed, three of the women were killed by the singer, one had her face cut, and two male lovers were murdered. When he merely felt abandoned by his love (fourteen songs), he expressed sadness in 50 percent of the songs and was pleased by her actions in only two cases. This song portrait of porteño men clearly demonstrated that many felt they were not in control when it came to affective relationships, and it contrasts sharply with the more pleasant recollections of their childhood (fifteen songs).[33]

Some of the most famous tango verses sung by Gardel and others reinforced the tension and conflicting messages conveyed by words that mocked the dance. Despite the control men exhibited in dancing, the singer informed them of their true status: men wanted to be in charge instead of women. José Bohr lamented that "women used to be feminine, but now fashion has ruined everything. . . . Today all the girls look like men, smoke, drink whisky, and wear pants." Pascual Contursi's "La Cumparsita" expressed cynical joy that an oppressive woman had finally left and liberated the man so that her absence was noted only while he slept *despatarrao*— abandoned. Rodolfo Schiamarella, in "No te perdono más" (I'll Never Forgive You Again), proclaimed that life would be fair only if the woman who had abandoned the singer because of her *orgullos de mujer* (female pride), suffered the same fate as he: sadness and tears. Sometimes the only recourse left to men was revenge. Armando Tagini's tango title "Buey manso" (Tamed Castrated Bull) directly challenged the statement that if the singer met the woman again, only blood would quench his thirst for revenge.[34]

Tangos that specifically referred to prostitutes who had not personally betrayed the singer were more sympathetic. Samuel Linning's "Milonguita," one of the most famous of all tangos and another that became as famous in the theater as in the cabaret, told the story of a dance hall girl who became a prostitute. In this way Esthercita, the working-class girl, had become Milonguita, the whore. Despite her success, the author claimed that Milonguita would have given her soul to be able to dress in her humble but respectable clothing once again. In this case the singer did not express personal anger at Esthercita and thus could see the tragedy of her situation. Nevertheless "Milonguita" had its message for young women. This song, like many others, berated women for the desire for conspicuous consumption that allowed men to lead them into lives of degradation.[35]

For tango lyricists, it mattered little whether prostitutes were legal or clandestine, native-born or foreign. They used the street argot of Buenos Aires (*lunfardo*) to convey the complexities of victimization—women seduced and abandoned by *bacanes*, *apaches*, and *cafishios* (rich lovers, gangsters, and pimps) or betrayed by their own desires. Writers were also deeply concerned about men betrayed or abandoned by their female lovers. They could forgive prostitutes who had been seduced by others but could never accept the infidelity of their mates.

Women who abandoned their spouses or fiancés for a life of illusion and glitter were also accused of leaving their mothers behind, or of forcing men to do so. Margot, a prostitute once known as Margarita, was supported in a luxurious apartment by her *bacán* (rich lover) while her mother did laundry and lived in a tenement building. In "Te odio" (I Hate You) a former lover forced the male singer to abandon his mother "sick, alone, with nowhere to live and no bread to eat."[36]

One of the few songs that specifically referred to white slavery was sympathetic to women degraded by men other than the singer. Horacio Pettorossi's "Esclavas Blancas" (White Slaves) described these women as *almitas torturadas* (tortured souls), infertile women, automatons of vice. While they were trying to forget their sorrows in champagne, they should think of the children who might have called them mother. Pettorossi encouraged them to "Pensá cinco minutos, en esa criatura de manecitas blancas, que en este mismo instante . . . tal vez a una extraña la llamará mamá!" (Just spend five minutes thinking about that little one with white hands who at this very moment might be calling another woman "mamá!")[37]

The message that this generation of tango music conveyed to the Argentine public—fears of independent working women; empowered female sexuality and male impotence; the desire to return to a simpler life (adolescence) and the old neighborhood; the breakdown of parental authority (fathers are rarely mentioned; women are driving sons away from their mothers or are abandoning motherhood)—had resonance for all urban dwellers, not just the lower classes. Upper- and middle-class men might have been more concerned about nationality and white slavery, but they were equally fearful about the destruction of the traditional family. For these reasons tango themes in their mature phase between 1918 and 1935 made the tango much more acceptable to the Argentine public because they dealt with anxieties and frustrations that cut across class lines.[38]

Eventually many middle- and upper-class men and some women went to Argentine nightclubs and cabarets to listen and to dance the tango. Nevertheless, many still disapproved of women's tango dancing. In 1933 Ezequiel Martínez Estrada, one of Argentina's most important essayists and a man deeply troubled by the changing nature of gender and politics, described the cabaret as a place where "women carry out a task that does not amuse them: they gain their bread by dancing and drinking."[39] He then went on to describe the movement of the tango:

> It is danced from the hips to the feet. From the waist upward, the body does not dance: it is rigid, as if the lively legs carried two bodies asleep in an embrace. . . . It is a monotonous and expressionless dance, with the stylized rhythm of coupling.
>
> The dance was prestigious in the bawdyhouses. It was music only, a lascivious music without the lyrics that would appear only after sev-

eral years, when the masses found their popular poet. The chords could be heard from the brothel like a vapor through the always closed jalousies. . . . It clandestinely infiltrated a world that denied it access. It reached the cities under disguise and triumphantly entered into the parlors and homes.[40]

For this Argentine essayist, the tango and the cabaret were still so disreputable that women who left their houses at night to frequent these bistros risked sexual advances from male passersby. "The honest women who retire early implicate those who do not. The open doors proclaim the chastity of closed doors."[41]

Martínez Estrada shrewdly noted that even though the tango initiated sexual encounters where men were supposed to be dominant, the dance did not signify male strength, but rather reflected men's weakness. To him the dance was devoid of sensuality, since it had "the seriousness of the human during copulation because it seems to engender without pleasure." Furthermore he bitterly proclaimed that the tango humiliated women not because it demonstrated their sexual subordination, but rather because they were dominated by men "as passive and as bound" as themselves.[42]

Although this author clearly disapproved of cabarets, he noted that the "decent" middle class could enjoy the dance within their own homes. This transition, however, complicated the process of identifying an immoral woman. Lyrics in the 1920s showed that the bordello had already been displaced by love nests, music halls, and nightclubs. Women's immorality, like the tango, was no longer associated solely with commercial sex. All independent women were potential prostitutes because they symbolized social decay and the loss of social and personal virtues.

Perhaps no other set of lyrics more clearly conveyed this attitude than verses composed by Enrique Santos Discépolo. Discépolo wrote "Yira, Yira" in 1930, the year the Argentine military deposed Yrigoyen. Known for his pessimism and emphasis on unfulfilled human relationships, Discépolo chose to express his dismay over the condition of Argentine society by comparing it to a streetwalker, a *yiranta*, who lives by selling herself to anyone who will pay. Why not sell oneself? He points out:

> You'll see that everything is a lie,
> You'll see that love is nothing,
> The world cares nothing
> Yira! . . . Yira!
> Even though you kill yourself

Even though pain eats you up
You can never expect any help,
Not an outstretched hand or a favor.[43]

In a January 1931 interview for *La Nación*, Discépolo explained why he wrote "Yira, Yira." He said that in 1927 he found himself penniless and without much success in his musical endeavors. At that time his spirits were so low that he began to think about a tango to express his disillusion. The song was finally composed three years later. "Yira, Yira, was born in the streets . . . Buenos Aires. [It was] the man of Buenos Aires, the rage of Buenos Aires. . . . The universal solitude of man confronted by his problems." Was it a coincidence that he used the image of the immoral female to denote the political and economic corruption facing men? Not at all.[44]

For Discépolo and Martínez Estrada as well as the anarchists, the source of immorality was corrupt society. In these circumstances there were few options for individuals, men or women: their behavior was merely a response to the available opportunities. Thus the prostitute who walked the streets in search of customers was no more or less moral than the rest of society; she became a metaphor for society as a whole. In this way the nation as well as its inhabitants had become as marginalized as the least acceptable woman.

Female singers were rarely heard performing tangos. Even fewer inspired writers—male or female—to compose tango lyrics specifically for them. Furthermore, when women sang tangos professionally, they rarely made their reputations in the cabarets, but appeared in theatrical performances or sang on the radio, which became an important medium in the 1920s.

Among the few women acknowledged by the public for tango singing was Azucena Maizani. Her June 1923 debut took place not in a cabaret, but rather in the Teatro Nacional, and her song, "Padre nuestro" (Our Father), was written especially for her by Enrique Delfino. Significantly, this tango did not deal with her relationship with a man, but rather concerned a father's affair with another woman. Clearly this type of morality tale was more appropriate for a female singer than many of those that Gardel sang. When women did sing songs composed for men, they often wore glamorous tuxedos. By dressing as elite men they claimed the right to sing men's songs.[45]

Maizani and Rosita Quiroga, another female tango singer of the 1920s, soon gained fame on the radio, where their physical presence would not interfere with the message they transmitted. These women provided the only acceptable female voice to counterbalance the male vision of the tango. By the 1930s they were joined by Libertad Lamarque, Anita Palermo, Mercedes Carné, and Marta de los Ríos.[46]

Women could sing the tangos that extolled the old neighborhood or adolescence, but when it came to tangos with love themes, they had to be more selective. One favorite of female singers was "Julian," the story of a woman abandoned by her tango-dancing lover. Left with a child and her tears, the woman still hoped that Julian would return. This song, which told of abandonment and betrayal by a man, implied that the woman would forgive him—something rarely expressed when the gender roles were reversed—and was quite popular with singers both male and female. Even Gardel recorded it.[47] Other songs had to have inappropriate lyrics changed. Such was the case when Lola Candales wanted to sing "La Morocha" (The Lively Woman).[48]

Because of the strong misogynist themes of its lyrics, the tango was truly the expression of a male vision of Argentine society. Yet women insisted on their right to sing, even if they had to do it on the radio or dressed in men's clothing. In this way they provided a female presence, if not a female voice. Their popularity was also a factor that led to the improved reputation of the tango. And when Argentines began making sound films in the 1930s, the tango was the first subject, and female tango singers like Libertad Lamarque became important actresses.

Besides the radio, theater offered another opportunity for women to express themselves, but this form of employment was considered as immoral as working in cabarets or music halls. After the successful production of the gaucho crime drama *Juan Moreira* in the 1880s, local theater came into its own and expanded the demand for actors and actresses. *Juan Moreira* was first presented as a circus production. In the 1880s circuses were neutral territory for people of all classes, men and women, who wanted to enjoy a public form of entertainment. Whether it was the famous English clown Frank Brown or the acrobatics of the Podesta and Scotti families, regardless whether the performers were male or female, circuses were considered decent entertainment even though lower-class individuals mingled in the audience with the niños bien.[49]

Before the introduction of theater into the circus, plays had been an integral part of elite culture in Buenos Aires. The advent of the Spanish *sainete*, a one-act burlesque comic farce, soon changed this. After 1884 these sainetes were performed all over the city and in the countryside, initially by circus performers who were later hired to act in regular theaters. The vaudeville-like plays often had musical accompaniment and required a large cadre of talented native-born men and women.

Although female circus performers were relatively well thought of, linking the theater to the circus tended to encourage the denigration of female entertainers as immoral. The independent life of the actress, as well as the dangers of work that involved public entertainment, had always made that profession somewhat disreputable for women. In Argentina this problem was exacerbated by the purported links between white slavery and the theater. Nevertheless, the possibility of gaining fame and fortune by becoming a star was a powerful magnet for many young women, European and Argentine, who made their way to Buenos Aires looking for work.

By the 1890s Argentine sainetes had become so popular that several porteño theaters began to highlight them instead of the more traditional Spanish version. Once local plays were produced at a profit in a fixed theater, many authors began to turn their attention to them. Writing plays had many advantages over writing newspaper articles or books. First of all, you did not need a literate audience. Second, selling a play was usually more profitable than publishing a book. And finally, a play offered an immediate emotional connection between the playwright and the audience.

All these factors encouraged sainete writers to deal with issues that were familiar to audiences consisting of workers and people of means, men and women. If the subject was linked to a particular class, sainetes usually offered explanatory comments for those who might not understand what was happening. They also included discussions of pressing contemporary issues. As with the tango, authors used lunfardo to convey that the play's characters really lived in Argentina. Once the geographic location was established, family relations, sexual perversion, economic conditions, rural life, political corruption, disease, love, death, gang violence, and social life were all discussed within an Argentine context. Writers were particularly attracted to themes that involved the local demimonde: the criminal, the prostitute, and the dandy.

The Argentine sainete came into its own by the early twentieth century. In 1895 Enrique de María's *A vuelo de pájaro* (The Bird's Flight) was put on by a Spanish company. The play involved a creole pimp, "El Nene," and his prostitute, Manuela. To convey that they were locals, one actor played an out-of-town visitor who asked what kind of language they were speaking and was told it was lunfardo, the "dialect . . . of the lower classes." Sainetes also introduced strikers, pimps, tenement family life, and even public health campaigns of the Asistencia Pública to the audience.[50]

The plight of working-class women, prostitutes or not, was central to the sainete, offering an opportunity to discuss gender and class relations while creating a demand for local actresses. Women in these plays were often symbols of social, economic, and political tyranny. A very early example of this was a one-act play by Miguel Ocampo, *Otra revista* (Another Review). The subject of the play was the political revolt of 1890, but there was also a scene where a policeman arrested two young women for walking on Florida Street. He claimed it was a municipal ordinance. The women responded in unison:

> I don't understand
> Why we should be kept from strolling.
> It is an abuse of authority.
> An attempt to rob us of liberty.[51]

The sympathetic officer suggested they stroll on another street. The plight of these women was similar to the situation of prostitutes in downtown Buenos Aires in the 1880s when Torcuato de Alvear was beautifying the city by banning prostitutes.

A few years later Uruguayan playwright Florencio Sánchez's sainetes became very popular in Buenos Aires, and they continued the tradition of linking politics to gender relations. An anarchist, Sánchez was deeply concerned about the moral deterioration of the working-class family as a result of the stresses due to immigration, difficult economic circumstances, and insensitive governments. In *Canillita* (Newspaper Boy), a mother and her son supported the male head of the family. *El desalojo* (The Eviction), a play first put on in 1906, showed the insensitivity of landlords when a worker was hospitalized and his family was threatened with starvation and eviction. The following year *La pobre gente* (Poor People) was produced. In this sainete a mother and her younger children had to deal with her husband's demand that the oldest daughter engage in prostitution.[52]

The common thread in all these plays was that immoral societies and family heads victimized women. This did not mean that Sánchez and other sainete writers did not believe women were immoral. Indeed, another favorite theme was that women often spurned opportunities for rehabilitation. If redemption ensured their poverty, women often preferred a more comfortable life of vice. A classic example of this theme was Vicente Martínez Cutiño's 1912 *El malón blanco* (White Men's Raid). In this play Regina was forced by her father to marry El Chervo, a man who turned out to be a pimp. Though her impoverished former boyfriend Chiquin tried to save her by taking her to his abode, she preferred white slavery to poverty. Carlos Pacheco's 1922 *El otro mundo* (The Other Life) had a similar theme.[53]

Even though these plays portrayed women either as victims or as responsible for their own decisions, they shared a common belief that men often forced women into exploitative relationships. One daring and controversial play about bisexual men dwelled on this theme. In 1914 anarchist José González Castillo's *Los invertidos* (The Homosexuals) opened in Buenos Aires. Its central theme was how a wife and mother discovered that both her husband and her would-be lover were bisexuals. She was close to giving in to the advances of her paramour when his transvestite friends barged in. After discovering that her husband too was bisexual, she confronted both men. She shot her would-be lover, handed the gun to her husband, and insisted that he kill himself to save his son from his bad example.[54]

This play demonstrated anarchist ambivalence toward homosexuality. Having accepted contemporary medical "evidence" that homosexuality was an acquired trait, the mother defended her son so that he would not "acquire" his father's unacceptable habits. The theme of the woman who rescues the rest of the family by saving them from homosexuality was not unique to anarchist ideology, and its use in 1914 foreshadowed the rationale that justified the reopening of bordellos by the Peronist government in 1955.

Perhaps the best expression of anarchist awareness of male culpability in family abuse—and inability to deal with it—came from Eduardo G. López's 1910 *El pescador* (The Fisherman). In this play an urban dandy had the audacity to chant anarchist slogans at the same time as he oppressed his wife. When confronted with the contradiction, the man excused himself by claiming that it was the uncontrollable male "beast" in him that caused him to treat her so miserably.[55] His attitude resembled the feminist-anarchists' critique of their male counterparts.

Plays were very popular in Buenos Aires, and people of all classes continued to go to them. Attendance in theaters and movies had doubled between 1900 and 1909. By 1909, more performances of local sainetes were offered in porteño theaters than foreign offerings in Spanish, French, and Italian. Only movies drew greater attendance than sainete performances.[56]

Just as the national sainete was used as a vehicle for anarchist gender attitudes, it also incorporated the tango as a cultural icon. As early as 1897, a sainete by Ezequiel Soria (*Vida nacional* [National Life]) included a parade of contemporary dances that ended with the tango. In 1908 Eduardo López's *Garras* (In the Clutches) had a character dance a strange tango while an onlooker prophetically assured the audience that "The tango . . . used to be danced by lower-class dandies to guitars and accordions; now it has grown up, and we must put on a tuxedo and white gloves."[57]

The tango reached its first critical theatrical success in 1918 when José González Castillo and Alberto Weisbach's sainete *Los dientes del perro* (The Dog's Teeth) became a smash hit by substituting a tango sung by Manolita Poli for the Gardel hit "Mi noche triste." Thereafter it became almost obligatory to create sainetes incorporating the popular tango. In that way, according to Domingo Casadevall, sainetes began to lose their significance as a literary genre as they became slaves to the dance.[58]

In contrast to tango lyrics, the themes of the early sainete were explicitly political rather than personal. Within the sainete, a woman victimized by a rich lover was not alone in her plight, and a man whose lover had abandoned him for a life of glitter and decadence was told that his personal tragedy resulted from social and political conditions. Gradually, however, the political aspect of the sainete disappeared. As the thematic content was sacrificed for tango profits, yet another theatrical genre appeared and continued the political discourse on gender and the family—the theater of the grotesque (*teatro grotesco*).

This new kind of play continued the sainete's tradition of debating the causes of family disintegration, but it tended to emphasize economic and technological causes as well as political ones. Typical of this genre was Armando Discépolo's *Mateo*. The play was named for a family man unable to provide for his wife and children, but Mateo's problem was not moral. Economic conditions rather than personal conduct accounted for the family's dilemma.[59] The advent of grotesco plays opened a new discourse on the problems of Buenos Aires society. Prostitution was still rife, but social conditions were complicated by the advances of industrial capitalism, particularly the growth of the factory, which tended to take work away from men and expose women to new dangers. There seemed to be no escape for the working-class family.

At the same time that Argentine theater produced grotesco plays, tangos reflected this pessimistic vision of society in the tango. A series of Discépolo tangos, augmented by the productions of other lyricists, heralded the era of *mishiadura*—of poverty and disgrace. Once again the tango was deeply intertwined in the evolution of Argentine drama.

The development of the novel paralleled that of legalized prostitution, the tango, and the sainete. Although Argentines began to write novels from the 1840s onward, the reading public remained limited. Only with mass education after 1860 and technological advances in printing did the novel expand its audience in the 1880s. In early Argentine novels, prostitutes appeared as vectors of disease and immorality or as passive victims. Eugenio Cambaceres' 1884 novel *Música sentimental*, for example, linked female prostitution to syphilis and death. And Silverio Domínguez's two novels published in 1886 linked prostitution to moral decay.[60]

Eduardo López Bagó wrote *Carne importada* (Imported Flesh), about the turn of the century. Although López Bagó was probably Spanish, his novel is important because it was published in Buenos Aires and introduced the white slavery issue to Argentine readers. *Carne importada* told of a beautiful Spanish orphan who sailed to Buenos Aires in search of a position as governess. During the voyage she was befriended by an elegant German who turned out to be the leader of immigrant Jewish traffickers. Unknown to her, he arranged for her seduction by the son of a powerful Argentine politician, an act that forced her into a legal bordello and eventually drove her to her death.[61]

By the early twentieth century, Argentine novels began to portray the prostitution theme within a new context. They viewed prostitutes as strong women linked to anarchists. Three novelists, Francisco Sicardi, Manuel Gálvez, and Roberto Arlt, maintained a particularly compelling discourse about the relation of prostitution and gender to political revolution. Their novels, when linked to a 1920s poetry hoax perpetrated by Israel Zeitlin (pseudonym César Tiempo), elevated the political discussions found in the sainete to a new level, marked by recognition that only a return to authoritarianism would relieve the middle class's fears of women and of lower-class political radicals.

The first novel of this genre was written by Dr. Francisco A. Sicardi (1856–1927). Although he was a liberal higienista, he relied on literature to deal with issues he believed were beyond the reach of science and medicine. Sicardi was the first novelist to contemplate the prospect that a prostitute could transform herself from a victim to a revolutionary and ally herself with the anarchist cause. Sicardi wrote five novels between 1895 and 1902, which were eventually united under the title *Libro extraño* (Strange Book). Effusive in language, colorful in its descriptions of the porteño urban landscape, and romantic in its literary excesses, *Libro extraño* also relied on naturalist techniques to examine the life of the poor, the revolutionary, and the criminal element in the Argentine capital city.[62]

The last novel of the series, *Hacia la justicia* (The Battle for Justice), imagined how the conflict between good and evil might be resolved. Armageddon was a fight between a corrupt Argentine government linked to evil capitalists and the working poor of Buenos Aires. Unfortunately, from Sicardi's perspective, laborers were divided by ideology. Anarchists, led by Germán Valverde, were committed to class war and to crime. Prostitutes had joined them in their battle, along with working women, all led by Goga—bordello owner, procuress, and Germán's mistress.

Catholic organizers, represented by Ricardo Méndez and Dolores Del Río, also aspired to lead the workers. They were committed to pacifism, prayer, and the destruction of anarchism. Between the anarchists and the Catholics stood the "free laborers," workers who wanted change without engaging in criminal activities or being linked to a religious hierarchy. They were led by Elbio Errécar, a committed higienista (like Sicardi) and an idealistic positivist reformer.

The revolution was about to begin with an anarchist attack on a tobacco factory where men, women, and children were being poisoned by noxious chemicals and fumes. Goga and Germán led the contingent of angry workers, inciting them first to burn the factory, then to attack Catholics. The revolution would have spread out of control had Goga not had a change of heart at the last moment. Inexplicably, Goga discovered God and spirituality by recalling Dolores' earlier kindness toward her. Goga decided to protect Dolores against the crowd's wrath, and in so doing the prostitute incurred the rage of her lover. Germán ended up killing Goga with a knife. The horror of the incident took the momentum out of the revolution, thereby allowing moderate free workers led by Elbio to advocate a government-sanctioned workers' tribunal to solve the problems caused by industrial capitalism.[63]

The novel both shocked and fascinated the Argentine reading public. They were not used to characters like Goga who, after Dolores asked her to adopt a young orphan, proudly proclaimed: "Me be a mother? How ridiculous! I who have always aborted!" Shortly thereafter, Goga began a diatribe that blamed insensitive men for the terrible dilemma confronting pregnant, unmarried women forced to abort, thereby identifying her own situation with those of white slaves.[64] If Argentines did not want to hear about abortion, they certainly did not want to imagine hordes of women workers and prostitutes supposedly marching in unison with anarchists, but with Goga chanting:

> Don't undress! Don't undress!
> Cover your bosom. The men are watching.
> They are beasts!
> Guard your roses!
> Men are worms;
> They leave their drivel all over the meadow's flowers
> That turn bloody, full of wrinkles, and die![65]

The public may have been shocked and reluctant to purchase such a novel, but José Ingenieros, a colleague of Sicardi's, was so impressed by the message of *Hacia la justicia* that he wrote a long critique praising the work and encouraging physicians to convey their understanding of social problems by writing novels. As Ingenieros explained:

> Few readers have been able to appreciate its originality. Many critics confess that they don't understand [*Hacia la justicia*]; some, without meaning to be ironic, confess that they understand it only too well.
> . . .
>
> Psychologists and sociologists cannot remain indifferent to this novel. It describes the type of people who become agitators and join in crowds to participate in social conflicts [and] . . . the entire series of novels within *Libro extraño* describes the disturbing and emotion-filled life of our city of Buenos Aires.[66]

Ingenieros was deeply concerned with crowd psychology. He believed that Goga and Germán's plot to burn down the factory was an accurate description of how unorganized crowds evolve into rebellious mobs (*multitude rebelde*). Nevertheless, he criticized Sicardi's belief that the working class could be so easily divided by ideology and so quickly pacified with just a workers' tribunal. Instead, Ingenieros argued that Argentina needed extensive institutional reforms.[67]

The appearance of *Hacia la justicia* was a critical juncture in the discourse about prostitution within the Argentine novel. Its publication coincided with an era of violent strikes by anarchists and with the real fear that anarchism would become the dominant working-class ideology. An anarchist assassination attempt against President Julio Roca in 1902 resulted in the passage of the Ley de Residencia (Law of Residence) that allowed the Argentine government to deport immigrant anarchists as well as revoke their citizenship.[68] By the time the next major novel to debate this subject appeared in 1919, another antianarchist measure, the Social Defense Law, had been enacted in 1910, as well as the Palacios antipimping law in 1913. By 1919 most Argentines considered neither anarchists nor foreign pimps to be major political or social threats.

In the midst of these political developments, one of the few people who read Sicardi's novels and contemplated the white slavery issue was Manuel Gálvez (1882–1962). One of Argentina's most important conservative Catholic novelists of the early twentieth century, he published thirty novels, nine political biographies, and essays and poetry, including two novels about prostitution, *Nacha Regules* (1919) and *Historia de arrabal* (History of the Slums) (1923). In addition to these works, he also left a multivolume set of memoirs, *Recuerdos de la vida literaria* (Recollections of My Literary Life).[69]

Gálvez's decision to write about prostitutes in Buenos Aires was not an accident. As a young student in 1903 he wrote a play, *La hija de Atenor* (Atenor's Daughter), which became the basis for *Historia de arrabal*. His 1905 law thesis examined the international white slave trade and its repercussions in Buenos Aires. In 1910 he wrote an essay on the causes of unemployment in Buenos Aires as part of his duties as delegate to an international unemployment conference in Paris. These early writings all prepared him for the task of turning the reality of lower-class working women into realistic fiction.[70]

Gálvez had selected white slavery as his thesis topic because he believed it helped him link the profession selected by his parents, law, with his true vocation, writing. His research provided additional evidence for moral reformers because he carefully documented the existence of foreign traffickers and their ability to bribe porteño authorities to look the other way. He recounted tragic stories of deception and cruelty toward foreign women forced to engage in prostitution in Argentina. His vignettes came from local newspapers and his statistics from the Dispensario de Salubridad.[71]

For many years thereafter, Gálvez's thesis was cited by researchers fascinated by the history of white slavery in Argentina. Yet the author himself scorned the work as bad literature and never again approached the theme of involuntary female sexual commerce from the same perspective. When he wrote about prostitutes in his novels they were principally native-born, not foreign, and when he described how they got involved in that business, he rarely mentioned the legal bordellos or foreign pimps.

Had Gálvez rejected white slavery and legalized prostitution as principal causes of prostitution in Buenos Aires? It seems likely. After all, he could have written a novel like *Carne importada*. Instead Gálvez wrote *Nacha Regules*, with a cast of native-born Argentines and with clandestine prostitution as the setting.[72]

Nacha Regules began in a cabaret in 1910, thereby linking clandestine prostitution to tango dancing and the new type of nightclub. There, according to his description, "young upper-class men, their mistresses, the curious, and some fast women [*muchachas 'de la vida'*] who arrive unaccompanied," tangoed and drank champagne. Nacha Regules was one of the kept women sitting with a group of influential men. She was being humiliated by her protector, and Fernando Monsalvat, a well-intentioned reformer, tried to rescue her.[73]

Unlike the typical white slavery story, the villain of *Nacha Regules* was Dalmacio "Pampa" Arnedo, an evil Argentine with influential friends. Ignacia "Nacha" Regules, an Argentine woman, was the victim of a love affair, not of white slavery. The man who tried to save Nacha, Monsalvat, was also creole. Fernando Monsalvat fervently believed he could improve living conditions in Buenos Aires through social reform. Instead he lost his inheritance and his health. He was labeled a dangerous anarchist by upper-class Catholic friends, who soon avoided him. In response to Monsalvat's vain efforts, Nacha found out that help would come only from her personal spiritual salvation and self-abnegation. Once she understood this, Nacha repented of her sins and was saved.

Four years after *Nacha Regules* appeared, Gálvez published *Historia de arrabal*. This second novel again emphasized the critical role that women's religion played in moral salvation. This time, instead of a strong woman, Gálvez wrote about one who was unable to save herself. The protagonist was a native-born woman, Rosalinda "Linda" Corrales, the victim of rape by her stepbrother and eventual pimp, "El Chino." The man who wanted to save Linda was Daniel Forti, a bricklayer and self-identified anarchist.[74]

Unlike Nacha, Linda was a weak-willed person caught in the grip of a Rasputin. Every time El Chino looked at her, she lost all willpower. Daniel could not help Linda because he was too preoccupied with his own life. Although a committed labor organizer and a fervent follower of Bakunin and other anarchist revolutionaries, he refused to risk discomfort and possible embarrassment to help the woman he loved. After Linda told him she had been raped by her stepbrother, Daniel was reluctant to live up to his promise to take her home. He was embarrassed to introduce a nonvirgin to his mother. Later Daniel postponed saving Linda from the clutches of El Chino, who had forced her to walk the streets in search of customers. This time Daniel hesitated because he had not terminated a relationship with another woman. Linda's lack of self-control and Daniel's indecision resulted in a tragic conclusion when Linda was forced by her evil stepbrother to plunge a dagger into Daniel's heart, just as Germán had killed Goga.

The connections between *Nacha Regules*, *Historia de arrabal*, and *Hacia la justicia* were more than casual. In Gálvez's memoirs he acknowledged his intellectual debt to Sicardi. Had he not read *Libro extraño*, Gálvez admitted, he probably would never have written either *Nacha Regules* or *Historia de arrabal*.[75] Sicardi's preoccupation with the revolutionary implications of "*el problema social*," the great class questions confronting Argentine politics, deeply influenced the works of Gálvez and others.[76]

In *Nacha Regules*, as in *Hacia la justicia*, there were anarchists, prostitutes, and social reformers. Basic ideological differences between Sicardi and Gálvez, however, prevented Gálvez from precipitating the same kind of revolution, even in fiction. Sicardi had great faith in reasoned solutions to social and political conflict as well as an abiding pride in the rationality of socially conscious physicians like Elbio. Gálvez did not. In *Nacha Regules*, Gálvez's physician, Amilcar Torres (a police doctor and specialist on white slavery), denied the practicality of social reform and implied that revolution was impossible.[77]

For Gálvez, anarchist threats were more symbolic than real, and social revolution seemed less probable than at the time *Hacia la justicia* was written. Even though *Nacha Regules* was published the same year as the *Semana Trágica*, the real threat of anarchism had already been replaced by that of communism and socialism. Furthermore, the strikes had shown that the forces of repression were stronger than any anarchist threat, and this was clear in both *Nacha Regules* and *Historia de arrabal*.

Gálvez's Catholic faith further separated him from Sicardi. Personal religious commitment offered strength for Nacha and would have saved Linda had she been stronger. Yet Gálvez's depiction of Catholic reformers led to sharp criticism. In contrast to the way Sicardi portrayed Catholic reformers, in *Nacha Regules* Gálvez depicted them as petty upper-class women interested only in charity, not reform. In fact Gálvez had such unkind words for Catholic reformers that the Socialist newspaper *La Vanguardia* published the novel in serial form. Although *Nacha Regules* was harshly reviewed by Catholic intellectuals, Gálvez claimed it was the most Catholic work he ever wrote because it showed that personal spiritual salvation, rather than revolution or charity, was the only solution to social problems.[78]

Gálvez's commitment to Catholicism was clearly seen in his attitude toward abortion. Nacha, unlike Goga, refused to have an abortion after her love affair left her pregnant. As she told Monsalvat: "Oh, how I suffered when the man who dishonored me wanted me to abort my little child, my only security, the only person who would have enabled me to draw closer to my mother and forced me to be honest."[79] Nacha eventually had a stillborn baby, but at least she ended up married and honorable.

Capitalism, as well as religion, took on a different perspective in 1919. In Sicardi's *Libro extraño* the factory was the site of female conflict, the source of female destruction. In Gálvez's *Historia de arrabal* the factory was a refuge for poor women, a place where Linda could earn enough money to satisfy her stepbrother and thereby avoid streetwalking until he got her fired. In *Nacha Regules*, commercial capitalism in the department store, rather than in the factory, exploited females. Nacha got a job in a department store to avoid prostitution, but she was forced to carry a heavy mannequin down the stairs. She was fined so much money for breaking it that she went back out on the streets.

Gálvez was totally committed to constructing an accurate portrait of contemporary poverty. As he put it, "In order to write a social realist novel, documentation is as necessary as it would be for a historical novel."[80] While writing *Nacha Regules* he consulted with Socialist Carolina Muzilli. Nacha's department store experience was taken from an incident reported in Muzilli's 1913 study of female employment.[81]

In his quest for authenticity, Gálvez also visited some of the worst neighborhoods of Buenos Aires in order to place the action of *Nacha Regules* and *Historia de arrabal* in the appropriate environment. He made his first visit to a cabaret, suitably chaperoned by more worldly friends, so that he could describe the type of people who frequented them. Gálvez deliberately sought out a notorious clandestine bordello where Pampa Arnedo would take Nacha.

Despite this close attention to physical environment, it was clear that Gálvez relied on his own religious, economic, and gender beliefs to construct the plots of his two novels. This was clearly seen in Nacha's changing attitudes toward fate. At the beginning she believed that "everything was the work of destiny. An implacable premonition had pushed her toward the evil life. It was impossible to defend herself against this force. Evil was more powerful than the will of a poor woman."[82] During her last effort to escape from the grasp of Pampa Arnedo, a compassionate lawyer (like Gálvez) criticized her sense of helplessness: "Your fate? This word has no meaning. Each person creates his own fate."[83] Nacha finally realized this when she decided to back out of a loveless marriage to a wealthy rancher and marry the man who truly loved her. Her marriage to Fernando would force her to suffer purifying poverty, because he had recently lost his vision. Nacha believed this sacrificial marriage would allow her to be "pardoned by God for her former life, by love for having offended its sensibilities, and by myself. I need to forgive myself."[84] Since Linda could not repent, she died.

One more difference distinguished Gálvez's novels from those of his predecessor. In *Libro extraño* Goga had a passionate love affair with Germán. Nacha refused such love because she felt unworthy of Monsalvat and remained chaste with him until she repented and they married. Linda was not given the opportunity because El Chino always prevented her union with Daniel. This difference is critical, since it was the key to understanding changing gender relations in twentieth-century Argentina.

When men were strong enough to direct the revolution, a writer like Sicardi could contemplate the sexual union of prostitutes and anarchists. When women were believed to be more powerful than men, both revolution and carnal union of the strong prostitute and weak anarchist were too dangerous to consummate. Sexual intercourse would empower the women, and they would gain political power. Therefore Gálvez used a variety of obstacles to keep the potential lovers apart.

By the time Roberto Arlt published *Los siete locos* (The Seven Madmen) in 1929 and *Los lanzallamas* (The Flame Throwers) in 1931, the separation of prostitute and anarchist was even more imperative. The two novels are directly linked in that *Los lanzallamas* finished the story begun in *Los siete locos*. In these novels the principal anarchist and revolutionary was castrated and the prostitute was frigid. The two could never share a procreative sexual experience, nor could they consummate the revolution. *Los lanzallamas* ended with the prostitute and anarchist running away. The revolution never occurred.[85]

The world that Roberto Arlt (1900–1942) wrote about was quite different from that described by Gálvez a decade earlier. Recognizing this, Arlt openly criticized Gálvez both personally and politically in biting newspaper columns. His outspoken animosity toward a writer he disdained for his upper-class views led some to question whether the young writer had ever read *Nacha Regules*.[86]

Clearly Arlt had read the novel, since his two works dealt with similar gender issues. Nevertheless, Arlt viewed life in Buenos Aires from a different vantage point. Unlike Gálvez, who came from an established family from the Argentine interior, Arlt was the son of an immigrant. Although thrown out of school at age eight, Arlt wrote well enough to obtain work later as a newspaper reporter. He also wrote novels and plays.

In the lower-class world that Arlt wrote about, religion provided neither comfort nor the prospect of salvation. Buenos Aires was a terribly bleak and harsh place where men extorted money, took drugs, abused women and children, yet still felt helpless. His characters were sexually adolescent, preferring masturbation to sexual encounters with women. They contemplated revolution, but without defining whether it would be anarchist, fascist, or communist. Reality was so difficult to deal with that Arlt relied heavily upon irony, the absurd, and techniques of criminal investigation to question and reconstruct it.

The plot of *Los siete locos* related the meeting of Remo Erdosain, a petty embezzler, and a secret society run by the Astrologer, the revolutionary. The Astrologer's revolution was supposed to be financed by the operation of a string of bordellos. The woman later selected to be at his side during the revolution, Hipólita, was a frigid prostitute who had had seven abortions, and the Astrologer was impotent as the result of an accident. Under these circumstances the prostitute and the anarchist were equals. When Hipólita first met the Astrologer, she tried to put him in his place; but as with Linda's experience, Hipólita felt the Astrologer was dominating her.[87] When she declared her attraction to him, he informed her of his accidental castration. Hipólita, upon finding out he was incapable of procreative physical love, said "What, you, too? . . . what a tragedy. . . . You see, we're equals. I too have never felt anything with any man . . . and you . . . you would have been the only hope. What a life!"[88]

The Astrologer enlisted Erdosain, a petty embezzler, to raise money through kidnapping, extortion, and murder. The revolution, however, appeared to be a figment of the Astrologer's imagination, and the supposed murder never occurred. Neither did the revolution. The sequel to *Los siete locos*, entitled *Los lanzallamas*, indicated that war was imminent, but in it the revolution was postponed once again. Instead the novel dealt principally with the story of Hipólita and the Astrologer and of Erdosain's murder of his mistress, La Bizca.

In her study of the Argentine political novel since 1930, Kathleen Newman suggested that changing gender relations in Argentine society have been mediated in Argentine novels and popular magazines since World War I. To accomplish this goal, a number of novels discussed relationships that were described as love with an impossible woman:

> The impossible woman, the best of all women, can only exist as a rupture with all the social rules governing sexuality. The gender system in the West is predicated on the exchange of women between family groups to insure social reproduction. . . . It is interesting to note that this moment of rupture in the discourse on women, the appearance of the impossible woman, occurs at moments of State crisis: the 1919 Semana Trágica. . . . [and] in 1928 . . . [shortly before] Yrigoyen was ousted by the military on September 6, 1930.[89]

For most Argentine novelists during the era of legalized prostitution, unrepentant prostitutes were always impossible women, and anarchists were impossible men. From this perspective it is clear that the ruptures began to appear at the height of anarchist activity in 1902, rather than in 1919, and reappeared in 1928.

The prostitutes described by Sicardi, Gálvez, and Arlt shared common characteristics. All were Argentines and clandestines who worked outside a formal bordello. All were considered immoral. Most had contemplated abortion, and only the inherently "good" Nacha had been able to resist killing her unborn child. All resented the lives they were forced to lead.

To the liberal Sicardi, the conservative Gálvez, and the leftist Arlt, the changing status of women in Argentina was potentially more threatening than anarchism. Sicardi believed that independent women would no longer bear children. Female subordination and self-sacrifice, to Gálvez, were the mainstays of the traditional Catholic family, and the future of society depended on maintaining religion, hierarchy, and family. Even to a leftist like Arlt, female empowerment was intolerable at a time when religion was useless and there appeared to be no hope for men. If prostitutes were as strong as male revolutionaries, traditional marriage served no useful purpose. Therefore equality could be achieved only in a nonphysical relationship, through self-gratification, or by homoeroticism.

Despite their differences, the authors shared certain similarities. All used prostitutes as the dangerous women and anarchists as their male counterparts. All brought up the subject of abortion—the quintessential form of female control—as an issue within the story plot. All discussed ways that male-female relationships were unequal and unacceptable in contemporary Argentine society. Although political ideology may have divided the three

authors, their male fears of female domination and their concern for immoral and dysfunctional families brought a certain cohesiveness to their
discourse.

To explain the implications of changing gender relations in Argentina,
these writers had to abandon the theme of white slavery—involuntary female sexual servitude—and concentrate on the dangers of male weakness
within Argentina. The linkage of gender relations to thwarted revolution
suggested that authoritarian structures were necessary to restore men and
women to their proper relationships. In these circumstances, the belief that
prostitutes were passive white slaves, unable to control their destinies, ran
contrary to the agenda of many male Argentine writers of the 1920s.

The need to abandon the theme of white slavery became clear in an incident involving yet another writer, the poet César Tiempo (Israel Zeitlin),
in the 1920s. A young writer and associate within the Boedo group of writers that included Roberto Arlt, Tiempo decided to play a "practical joke"
on his peers by creating poetry that had supposedly been written by a
Ukrainian white slave named Clara Beter (for bitter). The poetry was published first in journals and later as a compilation with an introduction written by Elías Castelnuovo, another popular novelist of the Boedo group.

"Clara" told the tragic story of a woman's life. Snatched from a happy
childhood, she had become a white slave in Argentina, forced to walk the
streets. Nevertheless, Clara had remarkable humility. She considered her
own degradation inconsequential compared with the plight of the poor. As
she put it in "Mi dolor" (My Suffering):

> At times it shames me when I cry,
> Because my suffering is but a minor problem
> Compared with universal suffering.
>
> What does the life of a sad streetwalker matter,
> Compared with those who have no bread?[90]

The image Tiempo created through Clara Beter was particularly compelling because piety and humility characterized her verses. In many ways she
was an ideal woman. As Castelnuovo, one of the principal anarchist spokes-
men of his era, wrote in his introduction to "her" collected poems, suitably
entitled *Versos de una . . .* : "Clara Beter is the voice of anguish that comes
from the bordello. Her verses vindicate all infamous women . . . because
[her poetry] brings a new element to our literature: piety. . . . Clara Beter
. . . does not protest: the people who look at her protest. She fell and has

arisen and now recounts the history of her descent. . . . This woman distinguishes herself completely from other women who write because she is incredibly sincere."[91] Clara Beter might cause a revolution, but she would never actively participate in it. The true role of women was to set examples, not break rules.

The poems were a smashing success because men like Castelnuovo really wanted to believe that a woman would still be passive and humble in the face of humiliation and degradation. They wanted to meet her, to save her. The only problem with all this was that Clara was the product of César Tiempo's imagination. He continued the hoax by establishing a residence for Clara in Rosario, Santa Fe, so that she could receive fan mail.

Finally, under pressure from literary friends like Castelnuovo who were eager to meet this ideal woman, Tiempo was forced to admit there was no Clara Beter. His friends were infuriated and exposed him as a fraud. Tiempo's final comment on the matter was: "That prostitute created a male prostitute. I was that male prostitute." The incident was the literary scandal of the 1920s.[92]

The prostitute who suffered but did not protest existed only in Tiempo's imagination. As long as he did not confess, it had been comforting to believe that women would not rebel. When the public found out about the hoax, it was clear that youthful male pranks had created a fantasy. Hence Arlt was compelled to pursue his anxieties without relying on white slavery as a dominant literary device, and prostitutes and anarchists were again identified as dangerous women and men.

In 1935 a young woman from the provincial town of Junín arrived in Buenos Aires. Impoverished, resentful of her illegitimacy, she sought escape in fame and fortune. She was as much a dreamer as any migrant in the bustling capital city, but she had good survival instincts. Gradually, awkwardly, she learned the ropes in the theater and the radio business and discovered how to find powerful male friends and protectors. Within a decade this woman achieved the impossible: she became a famous radio star and wife of the president of Argentina. Before her death from cancer in 1952, she almost became vice president. She was Eva Duarte de Perón, "Evita."

To many she was a saint, a feminist, a revolutionary, a woman devoted to her leader and husband, Juan Perón, and to her country. To her detractors and enemies she was a vindictive and evil woman, but most of all a whore who had capitalized on her sexuality to achieve success. Some accused her outright of having been a prostitute. Her critics arrived at this conclusion because of prevailing sexual myths:

The idea that prostitutes, far from being exploited, possessed some mysterious power over men, was widely adhered to. Because they were not emotionally engaged in their sexual activities, prostitutes were supposed to be able to enthrall their victims and hold them powerless. Wives were restrained by the marriage vows from such behavior, and anyhow no decent woman would use such wiles and devices—the predatory prostitute was, of course, taken to be lower-class. This set of assumptions was readily applied to Evita, the more so because it seemed to validate the contempt and fear Perón inspired, particularly among the Argentine wealthy.[93]

Just as myths surrounded Evita Duarte de Perón, they enveloped her husband. Being childless, he was accused of being less than virile. His later dalliance with a young schoolgirl, Nellie Rivas, resulted in morals charges and accusations of sexual perversion. Like the Astrologer, he was a political maverick who was difficult to describe. He was accused of being a fascist, a revolutionary, and a counterrevolutionary.[94]

Much of the class anger directed at Evita and Juan Perón in the 1940s and 1950s derived from the same value systems that had generated the lively debates about prostitution and popular culture before 1936. That same fear of female independence, of lower-class and dubious women's taking control over their lives, of their joining with society's most dangerous men in a social revolution, all came true within the context of the Peronist years, 1943–55, and in this way fiction became a reality.

To those who opposed Peronism, Juan and Evita Perón embodied the political and gender alliances novelists had feared. During the years of Perón's first administration, politically motivated cultural repression prevented the publication of novels and lyrics that might have directly linked the Peróns to literary and musical discourse. Censorship could muzzle the press but not the imagination.

The marriage of these two dangerous people reaffirmed Arlt's contention that heterosexual union no longer served to promote the ideal Argentine citizen. The Peróns' inability to produce children might have calmed the anxieties of some while heightening fears others had that the future of the nation was in jeopardy. After Evita's death in 1952, however, unlike the predictions that anarchists would weaken as women took over, the Peronist scenario was quite different. Perón became stronger because he was alone, but he was less in control of politics and economics. Men disunited from women were as dangerous as the antithesis. Hence Peronist mobilization of men in mass political parties, labor unions, and demonstrations without the moderating influence of a female presence, no matter how dangerous the women, fueled new anxieties about political marginality. Ultimately, prostitutes were called upon to perform a patriotic duty by saving men from themselves.

UNA DELICIOSA LECHERA

El reparto a domicilio está lleno de sorpresas...

These photographs of women from the Buenos Aires demimondaine are taken from the December 17, 1929, issue of a weekly entitled *Vida Nocturna* (Night Life). Some maintain the fiction that the women are singers, dancers, or artists' models; others contain frankly sexual double entendres that work as well in English as in Spanish. From the author's collection.

El formidable TRIO BROT — Maruja, Matilde y Conchita — cuyo arte, juventud y alegría se destacan en las fiestas nocturnas del popular dancing.

LAS CHICAS DEL AMERICAN

La deliciosa pareja de danza s modernas MARY-CONDE, de larga y brillante actuación en el con- currido dancing de la calle Paraná.

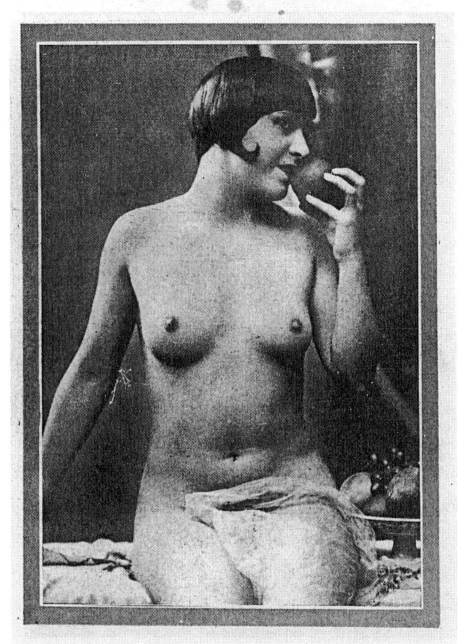

Una golosa

Carlos Gardel
became one of
Argentina's most
famous tango
singers. Courtesy
Abel Malvestiti,
Amigos del Tango
en New York.

6

Patriotic Prostitutes and
Dangerous Men

In late December 1954 the Buenos Aires federal police began rounding up presumed sexual deviants, mostly male homosexuals identified in the press as *amorales*. On December 28 *La Prensa* announced that one hundred amorales had been arrested in different parts of the city as part of a campaign to "end once and for all the dangerous deviations that these people present to society." Not coincidentally, the antihomosexual police campaign took place just as a group of government higienistas were meeting at a national public health conference. Two days later Dr. Oscar A. Camaño, chief of public health for Buenos Aires and the Littoral, urged physicians to support revisions of the Law of Social Prophylaxis to reduce the incidence of venereal disease and "crimes against decency" (*delitos contra la honestidad*). Without specifying exactly which type of crimes offended decency or how they were related to venereal disease, he advocated the return to legalized prostitution and directly linked the arrest of "sexual perverts" to adverse consequences of the bordellos' being closed since 1936. That same day fifty more people were arrested and accused of being amorales.[1]

Despite the absence of data that confirmed increased incidents of public homosexual behavior, President Juan Perón responded to the carefully orchestrated outcries for bordello reform with an alacrity that shocked most observers, national and foreign. On the evening of December 30 he authorized the Ministry of Justice and the Interior to allow provincial and territorial governments, including the municipality of Buenos Aires, "to permit the installation of those establishments referred to by the Law of Social Prophylaxis." The words bordello and prostitution were never mentioned, but everyone knew what the decree implied.[2]

The Argentine newspaper *La Prensa*, directly controlled by the Peronist government, praised the measure. The absence of houses of prostitution had perverted people, causing them to have "damaged characters" (*formación de carácteres dañados en sus intimidades*). Perón's decree promised to allow human behavior to return to normal instead of fomenting profound social malaise (*profundos malestares sociales*). In contrast, the London *Times* was dismayed by the haste and nature of the decree and entitled its report "New Argentine Rebuff to Catholics": "This step has been taken even more quickly than the recent divorce law. . . . The purpose of such haste is apparently to give the Roman Catholic ecclesiastical authorities no time to protest." The British newspaper had been caught off guard by this development in Argentina because it believed the Peronist government had carried out the 1936 bordello ban "inflexibly, and suppressed open prostitution to an extent unequalled elsewhere. His [Perón's] motives were understood to be to obtain the good will of the Church."[3]

The *New York Times* also interpreted the Peronist decree as an attack against the Roman Catholic church. It reported that the church totally opposed reopening bordellos and that the decree was one more step in a concerted effort to limit church influence in Argentina. "The Government of President Perón already is embroiled in a feud with the church, charging some of its clergy with attempting to upset the regime. Earlier this month President Perón pushed through a law legalizing divorce despite strong protests of the church."[4]

Despite the public's perception that Perón was using legalized prostitution to attack the church, his goals and motives were quite the opposite. The principal goal of the decree was to defend family, society, and nation through medically supervised municipal bordellos. In the past, licensed bawdy houses had been linked to Catholic, if not Vatican, approval, and municipal governments had defended their laws by arguing that legalized prostitution protected society from dread diseases. Yet this time, after years of the government's suppressing all information about prostitution and closing the houses, the public knew little about the history of legalized prostitution in Argentina or about the earlier acquiescence of the church. They were also unaware that supporters of the measure still quoted Saint Thomas Aquinas and Saint Augustine to justify their actions.

The new advocates of licensed bordellos did have a different set of motives than their earlier counterparts, but few understood the new rationale. In the past the relation between religion and prostitution had justified monitoring women. This time the same medical and religious authorities were used to monitor deviant men. The only problem with Peronist strategy was that the government's own efforts to censor all discussions of class and sexuality undermined the need to explain its actions.

That Perón wanted to open the bawdy houses to save men from homosexuality gave a clear indication that something had happened to Argentine society, politics, and culture after 1936, and the Law of Social Prophylaxis had been identified as the source of the problem. Men had changed their habits and customs, and their new behavior troubled politicians and higienistas. Without the bordello, men rather than women became sources of social danger. Deprived of sexual commerce, men found other amusements, potentially more dangerous than sex and tango dancing.

Sports and politics soon replaced drinking, dancing, and prostitution. By the 1940s the rising strength of organized labor, principally male, vied for popularity with male sports, particularly soccer. Men did not seek female companionship as openly as they had in earlier years, and sexual segregation in public and private life became increasingly common.

Neo-Victorian prudery accompanied the abolition of legalized prostitution. Men spent less leisure time with women, and they were told by public authorities that discussion and viewing of women and heterosexual sex should be suppressed. Instead of monitoring dubious women, public authorities censored movies, theater, and lyrics. It was no longer proper to hear about the profligate life, since it was supposed to have disappeared with the bordello. As prudery increased, so did homophobia, the fear of homosexuality. Rather than acknowledge that heterosexual values were being suppressed, many believed the changed emphasis was the result of increased homosexuality caused by the closed bordellos. By the 1950s the disappearance of the bordello, added to homophobic anxieties, led many to recollect the days of legalized prostitution with nostalgia.

Physicians too changed their minds about the viability of medically supervised female prostitution. In 1936 most higienistas opposed mandatory medical exams. By 1950 medical technology had changed drastically, and this caused many public health physicians to reconsider. It was easier to detect and—even more important—simpler to cure venereal disease. Penicillin, the new drug that could cure both syphilis and gonorrhea with just one injection, became readily available. Armed with syringes, in the 1950s Peronist public health physicians advocated opening "safe" and "hygienic" houses. Peronist efforts to return to legalized prostitution clearly showed that attitudes toward female sexual commerce, women's work, and sexual mores in general had undergone a major transformation since the 1930s.

Homosexuals and independent men, rather than prostitutes and independent women, became the outcasts and the medically dangerous within the body politic.

An Argentine cultural critic suggested that the ban on legalized prostitution, rather than the 1935 death of Carlos Gardel, marked the end of the golden era of Argentine popular culture:

> The closing of the bordellos ended an era in our country. . . . Local art, realist and naturalist, was always inspired by daily life, the profligate life. . . . With the removal of the stimulus [i.e., the bordello], art was affected, and many artists . . . lost the source of their inspiration. To date no one has analyzed the parallel development of the bordello and popular art, nor have they linked the abrupt end of popular art with law no. 12.331 [Law of Social Prophylaxis].[5]

The relation between the demise of the tango and other cultural manifestations of the 1930s was more complex than the supposed absence of "profligate life." Tango writers, poets, and artists were not dependent upon the bordello for inspiration. What they needed was freedom to express themselves. Instead, they were attacked and censored by the same groups that had earlier supported abolishing legalized prostitution. Popular culture was sanitized and ultimately suppressed by moral reformers, and in the process gender relations were restructured to focus on males.

The tango and other manifestations of popular culture were beset by campaigns to improve the moral fiber of Argentine society. In the name of decency, reformers criticized cabarets, movies, radio, theater, and other forms of entertainment where music was played and lower-class values were extolled. Censorship was justified by the principles of the anti–white slavery organization, the International Abolitionist Federation, which supported the "fight against profligacy and pornography." To promote these goals, federation members throughout the world urged municipalities to monitor all "public spectacles," prohibit cafés with female singers, and fight alcoholism.[6]

In Argentina, Angel Giménez pursued the federation's policies as vigorously as possible within his socialist strategy. As part of his January 1919 antibordello campaign in Buenos Aires, he recommended that cabarets and obscene movies be suppressed. He rejected the idea that the cabaret was a musical institution transplanted from France. To him it was "a coarse bordello, typical of those found in the countryside, with its dance hall and suffocating atmosphere."[7]

Rosalie Lighton Robinson kept European reformers informed of the censorship campaign in Buenos Aires. In late 1923 she sent two clippings from porteño newspapers to document the war against obscenity. The *Buenos Aires Herald* clipping, dated October 26, 1923, commented on plans contemplated by the Buenos Aires municipal council "to combat the exhibition of immoral pictures in cinemas, the production of suggestive plays in the theatres, and the sale of pornographic literature." The other Anglo-Argentine newspaper, the *Standard*, reported on November 9, 1923, that the French minister in Buenos Aires was fearful that his country's reputation would be tarnished by the showing of the French movie *La Garçonne*. He therefore warned the Argentine minister for foreign affairs that the movie had been banned in France. Copies of the letter were sent to government officials throughout Argentina, and the municipality of Buenos Aires used the letter to justify banning the movie.[8]

In 1925 Giménez introduced his own municipal legislation to revise ordinances that monitored immoral plays, pornographic literature, and establishments dispensing alcoholic beverages. In his accompanying message, the Socialist criticized Argentine theater, deploring the popular sainetes and the "completely depressing absence of good taste and degeneration of dramatic standards that began with 'Juan Moreira.' "[9]

Radio became the object of repressive strategies as well. Enrique Santos Discépolo was one of the first tango lyricists whose tunes were banned. In 1929 a decree of the Ministerio de Marina (Naval Ministry) prohibited radio transmission of three of his songs. According to the navy, his lunfardo lyrics constituted improper Spanish.[10]

During the early years of the censorship campaign, Socialists attempted to rid society of immoral influences through public discussion. They might have wanted to repress popular culture, but they did it within the context of democratic politics and a public education campaign. Legislators in the 1920s, however, failed to delineate the limits of municipal censorship rights because most Socialist regulations were never implemented.

New groups entered the censorship debate after 1930. They tended to be more authoritarian and conservative than the Socialists and, like the Naval Ministry, emphasized purity of language and political ideology rather than morality of thought. Furthermore, conservatives were more willing to force the Argentine public to conform to moral virtues.

Throughout the 1930s the Argentine Senate was inundated with censorship bills. Conservative senator Benjamín Villafañe periodically introduced legislation to create a national cinema censorship commission. Based upon a 1929 proposal suggested by Radical deputy Leopoldo Bard to protect minors from inappropriate movies, Villafañe's unsuccessful proposals of 1932, 1934, 1936, and 1939 were much more extensive and included provisions to ban antipatriotic and antireligious works.[11]

Although the military-backed governments of the 1930s could not agree on national cinema censorship legislation, Buenos Aires governments were more successful. A 1910 municipal ordinance had authorized creation of a censorship board, and in December 1933 this group was invested with more power. By 1940 the censorship board (Comisión Honorario Asesora de Control Cinematográfico) classified movies in the following way: without restrictions; children's movies; parental guidance suggested for minors under sixteen; adult movies—minors under sixteen not admitted; and banned movies. For "scientific" movies, additional categories were created: suitable for sexually mixed audiences; and suitable only for sexually segregated audiences.[12]

Municipal deliberations on censorship continued in a debate that cropped up intermittently between 1938 and 1941. Dr. Carlos Ibaguren, a leader of right-wing conservatism, periodically sent notes to the council. As president of the Academia Argentina de Letras (Argentine Academy of Letters), a society dedicated to preserving correct traditional Spanish, Ibaguren informed city officials: "The Academia has considered the social problem confronting the nation caused by the distribution of immoral and pornographic literature disguised as artistic themes, hygiene, etc. . . . There was unanimous agreement that we should study ways to prevent the diffusion of works that offend morality and custom."[13]

Unable to reach consensus on censorship through the democratic process, Argentine governments increasingly sought more arbitrary and authoritarian ways to control popular culture. By the 1940s military dictators (1943–46) allied themselves with civilian cultural repressors like Ibaguren and Monsignor Gustavo Francesechi. During the rule of General Pedro Ramírez (June 1943 to March 1944), a series of decrees restricted ownership of radio stations to Argentines, limited the amount of foreign music transmitted, and insisted that lyrics be linguistically pure.

For many years conservatives had been intolerant of the language and message of the tango. Despite efforts to rehabilitate the dance before 1935, its connections to the lower class and to the bordello still troubled many Argentines. Tango historian José Sebastian Tallón noted that his family "has been split on the issue of the tango since 1910. To this day my father cannot accept the tango because it was a dance that came from the lower classes. . . . The tango wasn't just music, a song, or a popular dance of the moment. It was something derived from the dregs of society, from the bordello."[14] Military decrees backed this viewpoint by objecting to vulgar tango lyrics and asserted the government's right to promote good language on the radio. The Dirección General de Correos y Telégrafos (Postal and Telegraph Service), charged with surveillance of the mass media, in 1943 warned radio stations that it would not tolerate colloquial expressions. This edict was applied with a vengeance to lunfardo tango lyrics. The result was to censor the songs' philosophical content and replace it with a more acceptable social image.[15]

At the same time that tangos were criticized for their vulgarity, folk music was extolled as truly national. Rather than listen to urban tangos, Argentine city dwellers were supposed to feel more patriotic hearing songs about sugarcane fields, burros, and the glory of rural life. Evidently the language of the pristine countryside, as well as the message of folk music, was more clearly Argentine and therefore more acceptable.

The anti–popular culture campaign was paralleled by a medical and legal campaign against the cabaret. By the 1940s cabarets had become morally offensive to public authorities. This too was presumably linked to the 1936 Law of Social Prophylaxis. Once bordellos became illegal in 1936, it remained unclear whether individual acts of prostitution were also violations of the national law. Cabarets were considered centers of clandestine prostitution, and public authorities took various measures to deal with women hired there. If the cabaret was considered a bordello, it could be closed and the women arrested. If not, city officials wanted to devise some way to protect public health and monitor the clandestine prostitutes who worked there.

Legal experts were divided on how to interpret the 1936 law. Between 1936 and 1944 a number of conflicting legal opinions were offered. Some courts decided that all acts of prostitution violated the bordello ban. Others insisted that the law did not criminalize prostitution, only bordellos. In 1939, for example, the Buenos Aires (city) Appeals Court ruled that any woman accused of engaging in a criminal act in a room that was owned or rented could also be charged with operating a bordello. At the same time, provincial courts in the Argentine interior came to the opposite conclusion and allowed clandestine prostitution to go unpunished.

Legal specialist Dr. Enrique Aftalión accused the Buenos Aires courts of creating their own prostitution law by interpreting rather than implementing the bordello ban. Nevertheless, in 1940 a higher court reaffirmed the

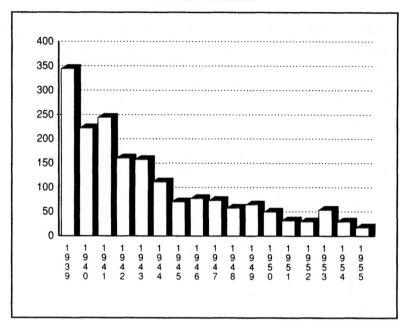

Arrests for violating Article 17

Source: José León Pagano, Jr., *Criminalidad argentina* (Buenos Aires: Depalma, 1964), p. 136.

Buenos Aires ruling. In contrast to the court, Aftalión believed that the Law of Social Prophylaxis was primarily a health measure. Insofar as it dealt with prostitution, its bordello ban referred to organized commercial sex. The activities of individual women should therefore be exempt from prosecution by provisions in articles 15 and 17.[16]

While the courts and legal specialists haggled over how to interpret the national ban on bordellos, prostitutes in Buenos Aires were subject to arrest and harassment if they used any lodging to carry on their business. In addition to those arrested for inciting scandalous behavior in the streets, within the city of Buenos Aires hundreds of women were arrested each year until 1944 for violating the Law of Social Prophylaxis by engaging in commercial sex in their bedrooms.

To evade arrest, many prostitutes sought work in the seamier music halls and cabarets. Soon it became a matter of public knowledge that women were openly soliciting in entertainment spots. The move to the cabaret occurred in Buenos Aires as soon as the municipality banned bordellos after 1934. Less than a year later, three porteño physicians wrote that the local bordello ban was a complete disaster. They estimated that there were more than 25,000 clandestine prostitutes plying their trade all over the city. Almost half (12,000) held other jobs. Among the professionals 7,000 were called "low class" (*gruesa*), 3,000 were "middle class" (*media*), and 3,500 were "high class" (*fina*). The low-class prostitutes worked the streets. The middle- and upper-class women worked out of cabarets, nightclubs, and dance halls that catered to a variety of tastes.[17].

At first porteño physicians argued that night spots had to be medically and legally supervised just like bordellos. Among the suggestions they offered were creation of ordinances to deter sexual acts within such businesses; application of new codes of moral conduct and decency; and medical surveillance of suspicious businesses. Even with these measures, the doctors believed that only a national venereal disease control law would control these women.[18]

The passage of the national Law of Social Prophylaxis, however, did little to deter prostitutes from working in cabarets. In Rosario, the passage of the 1936 law made little difference because cabaret employees were already under medical surveillance. Rather than rely on the vague national law, Rosario officials continued their 1920s strategy of forcing female dancers to have periodic venereal disease examinations. Consequently on June 21, 1938, the intendente of Rosario decreed that all dance hall employees, male and female, had to carry identity cards and have periodic medical examinations (every three months for women, every six months for men) as a condition of employment. This law marked the first time in Argentina that males were identified as a source of venereal disease worthy of medical inspection.[19]

Although the Rosario law was specifically designed to examine women, male employees were included. Given the infrequent and distinct intervals when men and women were to have mandatory inspections, it was clear that the law was designed not to oversee female prostitutes per se, but rather to impose medical vigilance in a particular work environment where women were still considered more infectious than their male counterparts. The law assured the public that many more women, along with a few men, would carry medical identity cards than in earlier years. By 1942 physicians in Rosario argued that the new decree had been a success. They attributed the drop in new cases of syphilis and gonorrhea to the dance hall decree.[20]

The male quest for clandestine prostitutes, along with the absence of legal ones, supposedly made the search for commercial sex much more visible than it had been before 1936. In response to the demand, and to avoid prosecution for luring men into houses, streetwalkers abounded. Women scouted for clients on the streets as well as in porteño cabarets in the downtown area of Reconquista, 25 de Mayo, and Leandro M. Alem (formerly Paseo de Julio) Streets. Female prostitution remained, but there were no legal prostitutes. Without the cloak of political protection, prostitution finally became visible to moral reformers. Once again women defied the efforts of public officials to make them invisible.[21]

Furnished rooms replaced the bawdy house. For those who could not afford their own love nests (*bulín*), lodging became available by the hour. In this way the *alojamiento* (short-term hotel) was created as a new service to meet the needs of commercial sex. By the 1960s and the sexual revolution, these hotels also provided privacy for young lovers and couples pursuing affairs as well as for prostitutes.

Even though clandestine prostitution became more public, the most important consequence attributed to the Law of Social Prophylaxis was a supposed increase in homosexuality. Before the 1930s there seemed to be little preoccupation with homoerotic behavior. Despite the writings of hygienists, the 1914 play about bisexual men, and descriptions of masturbation in writings by Roberto Arlt and several other authors in the 1920s, homosexuality among adults, male or female, did not constitute a criminal act. Men were rarely arrested unless they procured young boys or offended other men by wearing women's clothes. Nevertheless, although homosexuality remained legal and was deemed medically safe, official attitudes began to change in response to fears that groups of men excited by sports or politics might transform latent homophobic fears into violence.

From the 1920s to the 1940s neo-Victorian sexual prudery was imposed on Argentine males by military as well as civilian moral reformers. With the bordellos closed, and with the media and, after 1930, politics censored, the level of sexual anxiety rose. Unfortunately, rather than recognize the amount of sexual and cultural repression in Argentina, contemporary writers, according to Juan José Sebreli, simply blamed a perceived increase in homosexuality on frustrations brought on by the Law of Social Prophylaxis.[22]

Sports, according to Victorian reformers, should have diverted men from unclean thoughts. In 1916 Dr. Ernesto J. J. Bott, an ardent anti–white slavery moral reformer and disciple of Baron Robert Baden-Powell, suggested that sports would have a salutary effect on the hormones of young Argentine men. In place of frequenting bordellos, Bott believed that a visit to the countryside or the distraction of sports were healthier leisure pursuits. At that time spectator sports were not well developed in Argentina. Between 1916 and the 1950s, however, sports became big business and developed a fanatic following. By 1934 Argentina even had its own soccer federation. Nevertheless, the popularity of soccer did not guarantee the maintenance of social order, nor did it solve the problems supposedly caused by the absence of houses of prostitution.[23]

The introduction of soccer in Argentina—characterized by sexually segregated crowds or ones with few females—seemed to accentuate homophobic anxieties along with inspiring genuine enjoyment of the game. Sports became the principal male leisure activity in the 1930s and 1940s. Private clubs offered facilities for golf, tennis, and soccer. In addition to engaging in sports directly, men of all classes became extremely fond of spectator events, particularly soccer. Rather then frequenting bars and whorehouses, men started to go to the *cancha* (soccer stadium). Initially they went with women, but eventually it became a male pastime. Many fans developed a lifelong affection for a soccer club that in many ways defined their class and social status.

Observers of contemporary Argentine culture detected political, economic, and social aspects of soccer. In 1929 Roberto Arlt wrote about the first soccer game he attended. Dismayed that fans threw rotten oranges and men urinated from the middle-class grandstands into the working-class crowds below, Arlt also noted that such behavior was defended by participants as part of their constitutional rights. Ezequiel Martínez Estrada commented on soccer's political implications in 1933: "The demagogue knows that the electoral forces are in the stadium and that politics cannot run counter to the natural technique of the masses."[24]

Sexual aspects of fans' behavior were also noticed. Freud had been translated into Spanish in 1923, and thereafter other works of noted psychiatrists also became available. By the 1930s both the soccer game and its fans became the subject of psychological scrutiny that continues to characterize the study of Argentine soccer. Thus Martínez Estrada suggested that men were drawn to the soccer stadium not only because they enjoyed the game, but also because they could not find love at home. It was a form of sexual sublimation, one of many that helped foment "perhaps greater evils."[25]

Martínez Estrada made these observations because he detected the latent, but always repressed, fear of homosexuality among soccer fanatics. In deed, what happened in the Argentine soccer stadium probably would have horrified Dr. Bott and other believers in spectator sports as a healthy and safe form of leisure. In the stadium men stayed away from women and alcohol, the two targets of moral reformers. But freed from the preoccupations of heterosexual relations and unaffected by drink, Argentine soccer fans developed their own set of rituals that helped define them as true men.

As in other Latin American countries from the 1930s to the present, soccer in Argentina became a male spectator sport. Unlike other countries, however, chanting songs to support a team became an explicit process of constructing male sexual identity. In many ways the identification of the fan with a particular team became as important to Argentine men as their first sexual experience in a bordello: both implied and reinforced their sense of maleness.

To maintain their sense of virility, soccer spectators began to judge the game not only by the outcome, but also by evaluating the maleness of the players. When a game was played poorly or the visiting team lost, fans shouted aggressive homosexual taunts. These *cantitos* (songs) often accused the visitors of being passive partners in homosexual relationships or of playing son—a family subordinate—to the home team's father. Such chants were seized on by the crowds and repeated until spectators worked themselves into a frenzy. Sometimes they had political as well as sexual implications, and often the tension that arose within the crowds could barely contain the implicit violence produced by strong emotions.

In the soccer stadium where players thrilled the audience by demonstrating their macho qualities, Argentine spectators, according to Eduardo Archetti, created their own drama. The audience reacted to soccer in a symbolic way that challenged established patterns of social hierarchy and control. Rather than accept a poorly played game or even the victory of their home team, fans reacted by shouting that the visiting team had been rendered subordinate and passive—just like children, women, and the submissive partner of a homosexual encounter: "The songs are part of the drama associated with masculinity and gender relations. Sexuality is what is being discussed, and the play deals with machismo, virility, and the ability to distinguish 'real men' from the others—'the men disguised as men,' i.e. the homosexuals."[26] No longer was it feared that prostitutes could pass for good women; rather, the anxiety was that sexually dubious males were "disguised as men."

Soccer did not encourage homosexual behavior. On the contrary, it reinforced an angry contempt for men who challenged the local team, with all its barrio, work, and political connections. No wonder politicians sought to serve on boards of important teams and psychologists and public health physicians became concerned about the stability of the fans. Tension within the soccer stadium needed to be tightly controlled or it would result in violence. The last thing authoritarian politicians of the 1930s and 1940s wanted was uncontrolled emotions fomenting political anarchy. Consequently politicians had to learn how to control the crowds in the soccer stadium for the same reasons that Sicardi and Ingenieros studied the mass psychology of anarchist strikers.[27]

Before Perón came to power, politicians dealt with soccer crowds by injecting political patronage into clubs, in the same way that politicians used to congregate in particular bordellos. Each barrio had its own club, or else residents devotedly followed one of the larger clubs that were identified with ethnic groups, such as River and Boca Juniors. In addition to the neighborhood links, clubs were sponsored by Socialist, Conservative, and Radical politicians. The Argentine Football Federation (AFA), created in 1934, recognized the significance of national politics by electing as its president relatives or political allies of Argentine presidents. After the 1943 coup, a member of the controlling military clique, the GOU (Grupo Obra de Unificación—Group Devoted to Unification), was elected. Eventually Peronist physicians tried to lure men away from the stadium by encouraging legalized prostitution and healthier forms of sports.[28]

While municipal authorities in the 1930s and 1940s struggled with medical and police complaints that stemmed from the Law of Social Prophylaxis, Argentine military authorities decided to open bordellos near army bases and to decriminalize female prostitution elsewhere. Decree 10.638 of April 1944, signed by military president Edelmiro Farrell (as well as by future president Juan Perón), amended the two clauses of the 1936 Law of Social Prophylaxis that banned prostitution and bordellos. Revised article 15 authorized the Dirección Nacional de Salud Pública (National Public Health Agency), in consultation with the Ministry of the Interior, to allow some houses of prostitution to operate, provided women submit to medical supervision.

The 1944 decree also amended article 17. The new version stated categorically that women employed in authorized bordellos committed no crime. Furthermore, any other female who, uncoerced and living alone, decided to sell her sexual services would also be exempt from criminal prosecution. After 1944 it was no longer necessary for prostitutes to seek customers in dance halls and cabarets. They could lure men into their homes without fear of prosecution. Streetwalkers, as long as they did not engage in scandalous acts, could not be arrested for propositioning a potential client.[29]

The 1944 decree had two objectives. First, military officials wanted to provide female entertainment for soldiers stationed at remote bases, particularly in the south. Rather than risk increased incidents of homosexuality or cope with unruly men, they preferred to make prostitutes available. They also wanted to use medically inspected bordellos to reduce the likelihood of venereal disease. It was clear that authorized bordellos would not be found in major metropolitan areas, where their presence would provoke national and international criticism.

The military's desire to establish bordellos was partly a result of the efforts of the Liga Argentina de Profilaxis Social to educate the military about the dangers of venereal disease. As early as 1923 Dr. Prudencio Plaza, the head of sanitation for the Argentine army, presented his design for a national venereal disease control law to a sanitation conference in Buenos Aires. He argued that the work of the League, though laudable, was insufficient. Prophylactic pomades for men should be available in bordellos. In an effort to lower the incidence of venereal disease among troops, the army had begun to open its own bordellos, but this had been too difficult for the navy. The military therefore supported the passage of a national law to monitor all bordellos as well as to establish venereal disease clinics throughout the nation that would provide free and compulsory treatment.[30]

The 1944 decree was an effort not only to implement the 1923 plan, but also to deal with homosexuality. Shortly before the 1943 coup, a sex scandal embarrassed military officials. Students at the Colegio Militar (Military College) were accused of having participated in homosexual orgies. In October 1942 thirty-two young men were charged in the matter after one of their classmates formally accused them of impropriety. Significantly, they were charged with the same crime as the Zwi Migdal—illicit association. Most of the young men fled to Uruguay. Two committed suicide.[31]

In 1944, the same year the military decreed the amendments to the Law of Social Prophylaxis, another homosexual incident occurred. This time the individual was a civilian, a famous Spanish entertainer. He was arrested along with all his fellow actors and the entire theater audience. The entertainer was deported. The 1942 and 1944 incidents had clearly sensitized the armed forces to be wary of homosexuals.[32]

Juan Perón, president of Argentina from 1946 until 1955, legalized municipal bordellos shortly before he was overthrown by a military coup. At the time he issued his December 30, 1954, decree, it seemed out of character and part of his last-minute attack against the church. In retrospect, his decision marked the culmination of cultural, medical, and military politics since 1936. Long before he was elected president in 1946, Perón had been involved in several incidents that linked him to debate about the Law of Social Prophylaxis. These early measures, combined with an extensive public health program, prepared him to accept the inevitability of legalized prostitution.

Perón had been one of the leaders of the GOU, the military clique that seized power in 1943. As secretary of labor and social welfare within the military government, Colonel Perón met with a group of tango lyricists protesting the criticism of lunfardo words. Even though Perón probably did nothing to deter the repressive campaign, the interview allowed him to meet a number of tango poets and convey his ideas about the need for social reform. Several of them, including Enrique Santos Discépolo, eventually became defenders of Peronist cultural politics.

This meeting with tango lyricists was important because it showed that Perón was aware of how easily the media could consciously suppress or manipulate popular culture. In the future, whether Perón's friends or foes, lyricists had to alter first the lyrics and then the social content of their tangos. If they wanted to lament social relations or economic conditions, they had to deal with incidents in the past. The Peronist present and future, with all their legislated social advances, denied that the working class had anything to complain about.[33]

Perón must also have been aware of military efforts to turn the cinema into an agent of government propaganda. On December 31, 1943, the military government decreed that eight minutes of national news, defined as "national propaganda," be shown in Argentine theaters. It was a simple way to garner patriotic support for government efforts, and these newsreels have remained an important feature of Argentine cinema presentations.[34]

The following year the military government took the side of Argentine movie producers against foreign movies. An August 1944 decree insisted that film exhibitors establish guidelines for showing national movies. Thereafter theaters in the national capital reluctantly showed more Argentine films instead of the more popular North American or European movies.[35]

Perón built on this controversial policy by sending Congress more extensive legislation for the movie business. According to the new law enacted in August 1947, all movie theaters except those in downtown Buenos Aires were to show Argentine feature movies for two weeks out of every five. Furthermore, that same year the municipal government sent national filmmakers a long list of moral guidelines and invited them to monitor their productions to avoid censorship problems. In this way Perón and his supporters limited the number of foreign films shown at the same time that they encouraged censorship of those produced in Argentina.[36]

Perón was also aware of the new places that men were congregating. Once the military came to power in 1943, the young colonel set about to win the support of organized labor. By promising more government support for the working class, Perón eventually turned the labor confederation into his base of civilian support. Eventually Evita Perón helped him with this project and also organized women by forming a separate women's political party. The sexual segregation of political parties at the very time when women finally received the vote and were supposed to receive equal pay reinforced rather than abolished gender segregation within the labor movement.[37]

Perón also curried favor with male sports fans. An athletics enthusiast himself, Perón continued the tradition of sponsoring sports events as part of his political strategy. He and Evita often attended boxing matches. Although personally not fond of soccer, Perón recognized how important it was to be seen with successful teams and to be identified with their fans.

> He quickly saw how important it was for his government to officially support sports . . . for clear and defined political objectives. He knew that the same groups that chanted his name also cheered on soccer players or boxers each week. To promote those sports promised to multiply the occasions when this would occur. . . . It was preferable for fanatics to fight about sports rather than politics, for the nation to be divided by clubs rather than political parties. In this way the restrictions Perón placed on politics were compensated for by solid support of sports.[38]

Perón initially supported soccer through the personal efforts of Ramón A. Cerijo, minister of finance and fan of the Racing soccer team, and other Peronist officials. Perón's director of the post office and telegraphs was elected president of the national soccer federation, the AFA. Government funds helped construct new stadia and increase attendance at local games.

Under Peronist guidance, mass sports became even more popular and were thoroughly politicized.[39]

In addition to cultivating support among possible voters, both men and women, Perón's decision to reopen bordellos in 1954 was a direct result of his government's efforts to rescind the 1936 Law of Social Prophylaxis. Although he was one of the signers of the 1944 decree, most people did not know the army had allowed new houses of prostitution to open near military bases. Nevertheless, even if the public had been fully cognizant of Perón's involvement in the creation of military bordellos, it would have been difficult to predict that he would reopen bawdy houses in Buenos Aires. Only a careful examination of Peronist venereal disease control programs, buried deep within official reports and medical journals, provided the eventual rationale.

Just before Perón took office as president, he elevated public health from a minor department to a secretariat. In 1949 it became a ministry. During both phases Dr. Ramón Carrillo, a dedicated higienista, was named head. Carrillo won the confidence of the new president in the same way he had captured the attention and support of Evita Perón with his plans to improve medical treatment all over Argentina.[40]

Once in office, Perón announced that venereal disease control would be an important aspect of his national health policy. To promote that goal, in September 1946 he issued decree 9.863 to bolster provisions of the Law of Social Prophylaxis. It introduced measures designed to lower the incidence of venereal disease, which after years of decline supposedly had begun to increase after 1940. The September decree stated that Perón had been informed of the unfavorable rate. To deal with this problem, he declared it mandatory to report cases of venereal disease. Specific penalties were imposed for all, including physicians, who ignored the law. The decree established new agencies to collect statistics and reinforced the 1936 law's mandate to provide sex education. The costs of the new services were to be covered by revenues obtained from casinos in Mar del Plata, Miramar, and Necochea. The proceeds from other sins would help combat the medical consequences of venereal disease.[41]

Perón's decree also dealt specifically with venereal disease among prostitutes. Article 8 declared that all women who engaged in commercial sex, "independently and individually," were by definition sources of contamination. This meant that municipal and police officials could insist on medical supervision of prostitutes. Despite that right, no medical official could issue

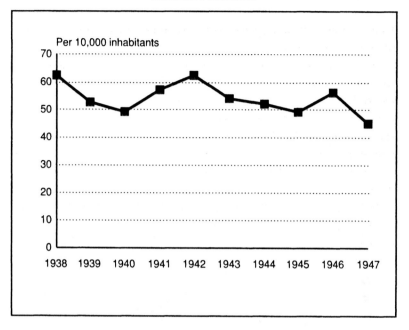

Reported cases of veneral disease, Argentina
Source: Study conducted by the Secretariat of Public Health, published in 1948
and reprinted in Carrillo, *Política sanitaria argentina*, 2:342.

a health certificate guaranteeing a woman was free of disease, so she would always be obligated to return for additional exams.[42]

Two months later Perón announced his plans for public health reform in Argentina. In it he compared physicians to the army and insisted that they needed to address public health measures in a collective rather than individual fashion. The Secretariat of Public Health would enable this new army to combat *males colectivos* (group illness), and the state would provide free treatment for those unable to pay.[43]

In January 1947 the Secretaría de Salud Pública published an article by Dr. Alejandro Dicovsky. It was the outcome of a 1946 venereal disease conference held in Buenos Aires and dealt with the medical inspection of immigrants. A preliminary statement made it clear that Dicovsky's recommendations were supported by Carrillo and his associates.[44]

Dicovsky noted that increased incidence of venereal disease since 1944 did not represent uniform regional trends. Instead, it appeared that port and frontier cities reported more cases of new infections than anywhere else in the republic. To remedy this situation, the physician urged government officials to implement more comprehensive medical surveillance of border areas. This could be accomplished by creating a group of *agentes sanitarios*, a corps of paramedics, to ferret out unhealthy visitors and immigrants. Infected individuals would be kept at the border until they were no longer contagious.[45]

In addition to the port of Buenos Aires, many other frontier areas needed health agents. The border with Bolivia, for example, consisted of land, not water, and there were various crossing points. A similar situation existed along the frontier with Chile. In all these areas health officials needed facilities for physical exams and blood tests as well as a place to store penicillin, the only drug that could make such a system practical.[46]

The following year two more articles on venereal disease control were published by the secretariat. Instead of focusing on immigrants, all three were directed at female prostitutes. The first, titled "El abolicionismo no excluye la policía sanitaria" (Abolitionism Does Not Preclude Medical Vigilance), argued that the brothel ban had been fundamentally altered since 1944. Originally it was a prohibitionist measure designed to eradicate all forms of prostitution. Subsequent modifications, however, left Argentina partly in the camp of those who tolerated houses of prostitution and partly in the camp of the abolitionists — those who banned bordellos but did not punish prostitutes. The Secretariat of Public Health argued that Argentina should also join neoregulationist groups, those who did not license prostitution but still insisted that prostitutes be monitored by health officials.

Significantly, the agency suggested that Argentina reexamine its bordello policies for another reason. According to the secretariat, "There is always another problem that remains latent, that is, what one refers to as the social pathology of sexual abstainers, and especially those impulsive persons whose crimes have multiplied. Many of those who argue that it is necessary to return to the primitive state of legalized prostitution do so because they are aware of police reports that demonstrate that sexual aberrations, and the crimes they provoke, have multiplied."[47]

This editorial proceeded to review all extant legislation on venereal disease control. It stressed legal clauses that empowered the national government to combat venereal diseases but were frustrated by an inability to monitor prostitutes overtly. Rather than argue about the immorality of bordellos, the secretariat urged its readers to recognize the moral validity of its argument and consider the issue an integral aspect of the Peronist revolution. The editorial closed by observing that the decriminalization of prostitution meant that "as soon as prostitutes find out they can practice their disgraceful profession without courting arrest, when they have the security that their own health will be overseen medically without fear of harassment from other authorities, we will then return to the earlier system. At that time any man will be able to deal with his impulses without having to go to . . . vile places. He will be assured that the national constitution will guard his right to privacy, and only divine authority will be able to judge him."[48]

The second article consisted of an extensive study of international and national opinions concerning prostitution. Prepared by a subdepartment of the secretariat under Carrillo's direction, it reinforced earlier opinions through more extensive analysis of a vast amount of historical, statistical, and legislative material. As part of the contemporary evidence, it analyzed the conclusions of a 1943 Buenos Aires survey. Among those who sought treatment in venereal disease centers were female prostitutes and women detained for scandalous behavior. This group had a 19.34 percent incidence rate for syphilis, and 31 percent were infected with gonorrhea. The data, according to the authors, justified the most aggressive public health measures possible.[49]

It was one thing to suggest a broad public health campaign to reduce the incidence of venereal disease. It was quite another to suggest that bordellos be allowed to operate again. The 1936 Argentine law had been greeted with enthusiasm by national and foreign observers alike. The League of Nations had been firmly critical of countries that continued to tolerate bordellos, particularly if they contained foreigners, and the United Nations eventually reaffirmed this policy. Nevertheless, physicians in the Secretariat of Public Health went out of their way to justify their desire to monitor prostitutes.

The final article attempted to provide a religious rationale. Written by Dr. Nicolás V. Greco, it offered a moral rather than a medical justification. Greco argued that both civil and religious law identified marriage as the basis of family and home. Nevertheless, other forms of sexuality existed. The 1936 ban on bordellos had inhibited men from pursuing sexual relations, forcing them to seek "clandestine female prostitutes, when available. Otherwise they seek artificial methods such as masturbation or sexual perversions, that is, homosexuality or pederasty in men or Tribadism or Saphism in women, who also need an outlet when they have no access to men. Other sexual perversions like the kissing of genitalia or bestiality lead, as with homosexuality and masturbation, to organic and mental debility in both men and women."[50]

When Argentina had allowed bordellos to operate, claimed Greco, they prevented pleasure seekers from engaging in sexual perversions. Since they encouraged traditional heterosexuality, bordellos reinforced the institution of marriage and the family. Without providing a shred of evidence or one corroborative statistic, Greco claimed that the Law of Social Prophylaxis had contributed to fragmenting, rather than augmenting, families.[51]

Since there was no way Greco could substantiate a single claim he made, he retreated to Catholic authority. Just as nineteenth-century municipal legislators had relied on medieval thought to justify modern forms of gendered medical control, so did Dr. Greco. He cited Thomas Aquinas and Augustine and pointed out how the April 1944 amendment to the Law of Social Prophylaxis approximated religious counsel.[52]

The full details of Perón's first five-year public health campaign were published in two volumes in 1947. One entire chapter was devoted to the treatment of venereal disease. Prostitutes were identified as the group most likely to harbor infection, followed distantly by prisoners (overwhelmingly male), railroad workers (political opponents to Peronism), and beggars. The Peronist government argued that all forms of social prophylaxis would be justified, because "son los menos los que están en condiciones de perjudicar a los demás" (the few endanger the majority).[53]

The government made several policy suggestions. First of all, it insisted that brides as well as grooms be tested for syphilis as a patriotic gesture. Second, it argued that more extensive public education was needed to explain venereal disease transmission. Finally, it argued that a mass treatment campaign was feasible given recent medical advances that made it possible to cure infected individuals within one week.[54]

The Secretariat of Public Health vigorously attacked the 1936 bordello ban as a justification for Peronist health policy. After all, the earlier law had only led to increased clandestine prostitution and venereal disease in many Argentine cities, while the infection rate among the military had decreased owing to access to bordellos and effective sex education. The city of Buenos Aires shared a similar decrease, at least until 1940, although officials there noted that the law made it difficult to control the activities of cabaret and bar employees.[55]

The head of the Tucumán Venereal Disease Institute (Instituto Antiluético de Tucumán) reaffirmed the position of the Secretariat of Public Health. Initially, reported cases in that province declined. The reduced numbers were misleading, however. According to the Tucumán expert, ill people avoided medical doctors and instead sought healers (*curanderos*).

Even more serious, clandestine prostitution was on the increase. Therefore the physician used medical evidence to reaffirm the provincial stance that it was safer to have legal bordellos than clandestine ones.[56]

The secretariat also offered several strategies to improve venereal disease control nationally. One was to allow mass screenings of schools and of factories and other places of work. Another was to combat charlatans so that people received effective treatment. A third was to find new ways to rehabilitate prostitutes and deter other women from sexual commerce.[57]

The Argentine Congress could aid this campaign by enacting several new laws. One would be a national vagrancy law. The second would make transmitting venereal disease a crime. The third would allocate money for medical inspection of cabaret employees. The fourth would insist on prenuptial medical exams for women as well as men.

The last suggested reform, and the most important for this discussion, advocated reopening bordellos nationally. There prostitutes would have exams two or three times each week, and booths would be constructed so that male nurses could inspect customers beforehand and teach men how to apply pomades after intercourse. As part of this final law the Secretariat of Public Health also envisioned free mass testing of all new soldiers, workers, and students.[58]

The legislative process suggested by the 1947 report began even before the document was made available to the public. On November 20, 1946, Deputy Humberto Messina introduced new health legislation in Congress. It authorized the formation of the Instituto de Higiene Social (Social Hygiene Institute) within the Secretariat of Public Health to coordinate venereal disease control programs, monitor sex education, and oversee the national production of medicine. The bill also mandated the opening of "scientifically monitored" bordellos "in large population centers within special districts." Messina justified reopening bordellos as part of an effort to correct deficiencies in the Law of Social Prophylaxis. He believed that the increased number of new cases of venereal disease justified municipally operated houses near factories and military barracks.[59]

Messina's proposal was buried in committee. In September 1947 Deputy Vicente Bagnasco tried to force the Chamber of Deputies to create a commission that would report on the 1946 bill by April 30, 1948. His efforts were criticized by other deputies, who believed a new committee was unnecessary. Furthermore, according to Deputy Reynaldo Pastor of San Luis province, the real issue had nothing to do with health matters, but rather was moral. No reforms of law 12.331 would be possible until links between bordellos and organized crime were eradicated: "No one in this country is unaware of the special interests involved with the type of activities that were prohibited by this law [the Law of Social Prophylaxis]. No one can ignore how these interests could influence the actions of legislators. The truth of the matter is that this Gordian knot must be cut so that we can reform this law in a way that is satisfactory to all."[60]

Peronist legislators made one more attempt to legalize prostitution through congressional reform of the Law of Social Prophylaxis. In July 1951 Messina introduced a shortened version of his original bill. The new proposal was designed to modify three articles of the 1936 law. Article 13, which made prenuptial exams for men mandatory, was extended to women except under specified conditions. Article 15, which banned bordellos, was modified to enable the Ministry of Public Health to reopen them. Finally, article 17, which defined the crime of bordello operations, would henceforth exclude state-run houses. Once again the legislation was buried in committee.[61]

In the midst of these congressional debates *Criterio* magazine, directly linked to powerful church prelates, responded to the purported health reforms that would once again legalize prostitution. In June 1950 Guillermo F. Frugoni Rey, president of the Catholic Workers' Circle of Our Lady of Balvanera, stated:

> Our position is clear and reflects reality, as well as moral, legal, and hygienic norms. We recognize the absolute impossibility that prostitution . . . can disappear completely . . . but we cannot, in any circumstances, condone . . . the legalization of prostitution. . . . And it cannot be claimed that Saint Augustine and Saint Thomas offer arguments to promote legalization . . . because none of the saints mentioned explicitly deal with the issue [state-regulated bordellos] in the way that is often cited.[62]

Two years later another article, this time written by one Luis María Baliña, reinforced the views expressed by Frugoni Rey. This time the author admitted that Saint Augustine might have supported proponents of legalized prostitution, but those views "were expressed before he was baptized." As for Saint Thomas, once again only one time did the saint admit that it was acceptable to tolerate a minor evil in order to prevent one even worse. In any case, Baliña believed that more responsible parents and better public education on the subject would bring a decrease in venereal disease. These were the only two articles on the subject published by the journal during the Perón era.[63]

Even though Peronists failed to marshal sufficient support to relegalize prostitution through congressional legislation, they continued to explore public health reforms. If they could not be obtained by democratic means, authoritarian measures were warranted. This was the way the national production of penicillin was secured.

At the time the 1947 report was written, penicillin was unavailable for mass use in Argentina. It was not locally produced, and during the war supplies had been limited. Perón took measures to ensure that future supplies would be made available, and in April 1947 he granted the United States firm Squibb and Company the right to build a local penicillin factory. The contract was announced just as Perón embarked on a public campaign to promote economic independence from foreign companies, and he was soundly criticized for this inconsistency. Dr. Carrillo came to his defense at a series of press conferences by arguing that the cheap penicillin was critical to Argentina's future. Furthermore, the three-year monopoly that accompanied the contract promised to prevent local competition for only a limited period.[64]

The penicillin factory opened two years later. After 1949 it was possible to expand venereal disease control in new and significant ways. Unlike Salvarsan and earlier treatments, penicillin was considered the surest cure for both syphilis and gonorrhea. More important, treatment could be accomplished through a single injection.

In 1950, in an effort to control venereal disease among rural migrants who had settled along the outskirts of Buenos Aires, 6,010 people were arrested. All of them were young female migrants, and none were eventually charged. Before they left detention centers, however, they all received penicillin injections. The penicillin factory had become an accomplice to a policy of authoritarian public health control, one that would soon be redirected toward men.[65]

Four years later, in the midst of a battle for political survival, Perón authorized the reopening of bordellos. It is quite possible that physicians had convinced him such a plan not only was necessary but also would be received with great enthusiasm by the male population. Women would have fewer objections to such a system because prostitutes would be serving a patriotic purpose under conditions where their own participation was clearly welcomed and decriminalized. The only catch to the whole scheme was that it had been designed in relative secrecy and without the multiclass male support that typified the earlier program. When most Argentines heard about the December decree, they were frankly shocked and unwilling to support Perón in this new endeavor. Given the public outcry, it is understandable that the government retreated into censorship to delay publication of the decree and supplementary ordinances.

Few if any bordellos opened up in Buenos Aires. The whole idea apparently backfired, and the government of Juan Perón did not survive the combined stresses of economic stagnation, increased political opposition, and the disintegration of Peronist support. Eight months after Perón tried to reopen houses of prostitution, his government was overthrown by a military coup.

After 1955 the new military dictatorship maintained most of the original provisions of the Law of Social Prophylaxis, although it neither closed down military bordellos authorized in 1944 nor recriminalized prostitution. A new law in June 1965, law 16.666, finally annulled the April 1944 decree. Since that time female prostitution, as well as bordellos, has been subject to the original provisions of the Law of Social Prophylaxis. Legal bordellos have not been a major social, medical, or political preoccupation in Argentina since 1955.[66]

Traditionally the Peronist bordello decree has been seen as part of an attack against the Catholic church. Enacted at the same time as anticlerical legislation, this particular measure had its origins in the homophobic debate of the 1940s as well as in the public health program drawn up by the Ministry of Public Health. Although his decree antagonized the hierarchy of the Catholic church, it was compatible with earlier Catholic attitudes toward prostitution. Thus the Peronist experiment with legalized prostitution was not an aberrant effort to harass the church, but rather another politically motivated effort to impose government control over sexually unacceptable women and men. Its failure reflected the changes that had reshaped Argentine culture and society since the nineteenth century, ones that challenged the right of the state to define family, nation, and social acceptability on the basis of sexual behavior.

Conclusion

For more than eighty years Argentines debated the merits of medically supervised prostitution in licensed bordellos. Originally conceived as a source of municipal revenue and a public health measure to protect families from venereal disease, the 1875 Buenos Aires ordinance also defined the status of women in Argentine society in terms of their medical danger, sexuality, and economic function. This system was explicitly associated with women, since no male prostitutes ever experienced similar restrictions. Once implemented, legalized female prostitution created a series of dilemmas that caused politicians, higienistas, and writers to explore the essence of gender, class, and Argentine nationality.

Gender and nation combined in inextricable ways. After all, who was an Argentine? To answer this question, moral and medical criteria combined in a gendered way to explore the limits of civil rights and led to curtailing prostitutes' right to work and to move about freely. Prostitution laws, in turn, provoked additional debate about the right of the Argentine nation to exploit foreign women.

Class combined not only with gender and nationality issues, but also with the future of the Argentine family. Most women engaged in sexual commerce because they were poor, but men of all classes sought out prostitutes. Consequently, Argentine families of all classes were threatened by the spread of venereal disease. Socialist efforts to shut down bordellos led to venereal disease clinics set up in poor neighborhoods and within factories. By implication, venereal disease continued to be perceived as a class problem.

Writers of novels and tango lyrics reinforced the relation of prostitution to class and family. They set their stories in working-class neighborhoods where young women lost their innocence because of the wiles of rich men, the desire for fine clothing, or family pressure to earn money quickly. Their tales conformed to earlier accounts of involuntary prostitution forced on women by husbands, fathers, and mothers. Only occasionally did they concern themselves with nationality issues.

Political pressure within and outside Argentina by diplomats, socialists, feminists, and public health physicians, as well as prostitutes, combined to reform national and local laws between 1880 and 1936. During the same period, increased industrial activity in Buenos Aires demanded greater freedom for women to work. The results were legal reforms. Initially local prostitution ordinances were modified, but eventually modification of national penal and civil codes resulted in significant changes in the legal status of prostitutes and married women.

By the 1930s debates about white slavery in Argentina began to diminish, and in one respect they changed dramatically. It became difficult to criticize Argentine laws and customs after Argentine women were discovered to be ensnared in European bordellos. In 1932 Francisco Ciccotti lambasted League of Nations efforts to portray Argentina as a haven for white slavers. He argued that European nations were responsible because traffickers and prostitutes all embarked from European ports. Even more important, the traffic had changed its direction. In March 1932 a block of buildings collapsed in Lyons, France. In the wreckage, drug paraphernalia and the bodies of five nude women were found. All the women were of Latin American origin, and two were Argentine. The women had been imported to meet the desire of Europeans for "exotic" skin color. They had traveled in innocence to France, believing they had dancing and acting contracts to make a movie. Among those implicated was a former justice of the peace of Marseilles, a man who admitted during the trial that he had imported sixteen Latin American women within six months and sold them for 10,000 francs each. European white women were no longer the only victims.[1]

As debates about white slavery and the appropriateness of women's working began to abate, the rise of censorship and authoritarian governments led to a reexamination of women's role in Argentine society. Women became less of a political concern, but groups of potentially dangerous men now disturbed public officials. Men left to their own devices in labor unions, soccer matches, and political parties soon endangered family, class, and nation.

The rise of Juan Perón as a dominant political figure marked the moment in modern Argentine history when family, class, and nation had to be reexamined. Emerging as a popularly elected president after years of author-itarian rule, Perón promised a new political role for the working class and, through female suffrage and Evita Perón's efforts to organize the Women's Peronist party, a new role for women as well. He also enacted a new con-stitution in 1949, redefining the rights and responsibilities of Argentine families and citizens.

Family played a central role in the formation of the new Peronist Argen-tina. Class tensions were diminished by a redistribution of wealth by Peron-ist labor reforms, and the family rather than one's class became the domi-nant economic and social unit. Henceforth, according to Perón's last laws and decrees, legal divorce, if necessary, would ensure the right of Argen-tines to form legal family units. Even if couples did not marry, illegitimate children were assured of inheritance rights. All of these reforms, however, hinged on men's willingness to form new families. To deter them from al-ternative sexual life-styles, government-licensed bordellos were supposed to open. There patriotic prostitutes would serve the nation by stimulating het-erosexual desires among errant men.

Perón's overthrow marked the definitive end of legalized prostitution and municipally regulated bordellos in Argentina. His 1954 decree was clearly a decision arrived at in a moment of crisis. Yet at the same time it was the culmination of a public health campaign that had been discussed for many years by higienistas. Perón's homophobia was also a reflection of more than thirty years of military concern about the relation of prostitution to homosexuality.

Whereas homophobia stemmed from anxieties within the Argentine military and male sports, concern about female prostitution was deeply rooted within Argentine traditions of liberalism. Public health physicians from Coni to Camaño used medical theory to support laws they knew le-gitimated discriminatory health policies based on a gendered construction of politics and medicine. Despite the evolution of medical science since the 1870s, physicians in the 1950s were still arguing that prostitutes' health should be monitored to ensure the health of everyone else, including the homosexuals targeted by the 1954 decree. What had changed over time was which group was perceived as dangerous.

By the time of the 1954 decree, female prostitution was no longer a wea-thervane of female economic opportunity. Evita Perón had dignified work for women, just as she helped make it acceptable for women to vote. Whether in the factory or in the voting booth, like Evita, women were sup-posed to remain devoted to Perón. Thus, even for prostitutes it was neither immoral nor inappropriate for women to work outside the home, so long as the home itself was both moral and Peronist.

Even the tango had disappeared as a significant cultural influence associated with female sexual commerce. Most cabarets in Buenos Aires had closed by the 1950s, replaced by nightclubs offering foreign music or Argentine folk music. Sports rather than dancing had become the major pastime. Here too the Peronist experiment with legalized prostitution was quite different from its earlier version.

Despite all these variations, Perón's plans derived much of their logic from the system of legalized prostitution before 1936. The national Ministry of Public Health planned to cure Argentina of its various maladies in the same way that municipal hygienists of Emilio Coni's generation had attempted to control endemic and pandemic diseases. Both relied on a combination of gendered medicine, behavior modification, coercion, and drugs.

As prophylactic medicine became more effective, physicians demanded more authority to impose their cures. It was as arbitrary for nineteenth-century Dispensario regulations to declare an unruly prostitute unwell as it was for doctors to forcibly inoculate thousands of women in the 1950s without testing them for infection. The only difference between the two actions was that the former was sanctioned by national policy and could be conducted on a larger scale, while the latter was the outcome of a municipal campaign.

The history of legalized prostitution in Argentina reveals complex relations between politics, culture, gender, and medicine. It shows that there are tendencies within Argentine democratic traditions that justify the systematic restriction of civil rights on the basis of gender, class, and health. Although an open discussion of these issues has been one of the cornerstones of Argentine literature and popular culture, the same political traditions that allowed such discourse to flourish also created the rationale for its suppression.

The politics of moral reform in Argentina have failed to address authoritarian aspects of its agenda. Whether one considers proponents of anti–white slavery legislation, temperance, or an antihomosexual campaign, many of their assumptions were as arbitrary as the behavior they intended to suppress. Furthermore, most reform campaigns have paid attention only to the symptoms, not the root causes, of so-called unacceptable behavior. If military governments have tended to be even more extreme in their zeal, once again the difference between their tactics and those of police forces of nonmilitary governments are not great. The history of legalized prostitution suggests that the roots of authoritarian behavior are found in gendered structures within democratic societies, not just within the overtly antidemocratic military.

At the same time that governments, physicians, moral reformers, and police have historically attempted to coerce women into or out of bordellos, women have consistently resisted. They have worked without medical certificates, refused to pay municipal fees, run away from pimps, and spoken out against their potential oppressors. Women entertainers have dressed like men to be able to sing about victimization. These facts, long hidden but implicitly feared by many male intellectuals, are testimony that people, male and female, resist oppression in ways that are not easily discerned but still exist. Female prostitutes who resisted arbitrary authority in earlier years are therefore the predecessors of those who today, openly or covertly, resist gendered injustice.

The history of legalized prostitution in Argentina is of concern not only to students of gender issues but to those interested in Latin American history. The roots of Latin American authoritarianism are deep within gender relations and the politics of social control, and the civil liberties of even the most socially unacceptable men, women, and children must be protected lest their civil incapacity be extended to other members of the population. Decisions to round up prostitutes and anarchists, to evict independent businesswomen by labeling them prostitutes, and to inject poor women with pencillin on the presumption that they were syphilitic were predecessors of later schemes to rid Argentina of terrorists. Authoritarian politics of social control thus began with efforts to define the ideal family by isolating people who did not conform to political, medical, or social standards, and they led to municipal and national laws that threatened social and political marginals with loss of economic freedom, *patria potestad* (parental authority), or citizenship. The leap from social control to social destruction was one of degree rather than an essential change in philosophy or attitude. The presumption that authoritarianism can be best understood by examining institutions such as the military, national elections, and dictatorship is challenged by the rich documentation offered by social and municipal history.

On an international scale, the history of Argentine venereal disease control is also a modern parable of medicomoral tyranny and its futility. The belief that sexually promiscuous women were more medically dangerous than their male counterparts meant venereal disease was linked to gender. The identification of prostitutes as medically dangerous resulted in unjust treatment strategies. Men continued to infect others, while women were hospitalized and unable to work. In response to harsh treatment, social censure, and the absence of a guaranteed cure, most prostitutes refused to seek medical help. And this parable should remind us that public understanding and tolerance, as well as universal sex and hygiene education, are as important in the age of AIDS as they were during the scourge of syphilis.

Notes

INTRODUCTION

1. Joan W. Scott, "Gender: A Useful Category of Historical Analysis," *American Historical Review* 91, 5 (December 1986): 1070.

2. Constitution of 1853, part 1, article 14, including reforms of September 23, 1860. Arturo Enrique Sampay, comp., *Las constituciones de la Argentina (1810–1972)* (Buenos Aires: EUDEBA, 1975); law no. 346, Ley de Ciudadanía, October 1, 1866, found in Argentine Republic, Cámara de Diputados, *Diario de Sesiones*, 1869, pp. 478–79.

3. Benedict R. O. Anderson, *Imagined Communities: Reflections on the Origin and Spread of Nationalism* (London: Verso, 1983), pp. 16, 131.

4. Nira Yuval-Davies and Flora Anthias, eds., *Woman—Nation—State* (London: Macmillan, 1989), pp. 4, 7.

5. Argentine Republic, *Código civil* (Buenos Aires: Pablo E. Coni, 1874).

6. Michel Foucault, *Discipline and Punish: The Birth of the Prison*, trans. Alan Sheridan (New York: Random House, 1979); idem, *Madness and Civilization: A History of Insanity in the Age of Reason*, trans. Richard Howard (New York: Vintage Books, 1973); idem, *The Birth of the Clinic: An Archeology of Medical Perception*, trans. A. M. Sheridan Smith (New York: Vintage Books, 1975).

7. Jacques Donzelot, *The Policing of Families*, trans. Robert Hurley (New York: Pantheon Books, 1977), p. 94.

CHAPTER 1

1. *In the Grip of the White Slave Trader* [by the author of *The White Slave Traffic*] (London: MAP, n.d.), p. 77. Edward J. Bristow, *Prostitution and Prejudice: The Jewish Fight against White Slavery, 1870–1939* (Oxford: Clarendon Press, 1982), p. 110.

2. Bristow, *Prostitution and Prejudice*, p. 112.

3. Ibid., p. 113.

4. *Le Bulletin Continental* 14, 10 (October 15, 1889): 86.

5. *Vigilance Record*, November 1890, n.p. See also *Vigilance Record*, May 1890, p. 39; August 1890, n.p.; *Le Bulletin Continental* 21, 4 (1896): 31–37; 22 (1897): 11; 23, 3 (1898): 19.

6. National Vigilance Association, *Congress of the White Slave Traffic* (London: National Vigilance Association, 1899), p. 86.

7. *Vigilance Record*, February 1890, p. 10.

8. Ibid., pp. 44–45; Kathleen Barry, *Female Sexual Slavery* (New York: Avon, 1979), pp. 14–38.

9. Sander L. Gilman, *Jewish Self-Hatred: Anti-Semitism and the Hidden Language of the Jews* (Baltimore: Johns Hopkins University Press, 1986).

10. Marion A. Kaplan, *The Jewish Feminist Movement in Germany: The Campaigns of the Jüdischer Frauenbund, 1904–1938* (Westport, Conn.: Greenwood Press, 1979), p. 119.

11. Quoted in Bristow, *Prostitution and Prejudice*, p. 111.

12. Ibid., p. 116.

13. Kaplan, *Jewish Feminist Movement in Germany*, p. 115.

14. Marcus Braun Report, Berlin, June 18, 1909. National Archives of the United States of America, Record Group 85, file 52484/D; Bristow, *Prostitution and Prejudice*, especially chap. 4.

15. National Vigilance Association, *Fourth Annual Report of the Executive Committee, November 26, 1889* (London, 1889), p. 26.

16. National Vigilance Association, *Fifth Annual Report of the Executive Committee, November 26, 1890* (London, 1890), p. 35. In the earlier report of this incident in the August 1890 *Vigilance Record*, the women were identified as Jewish and the man as German.

17. Kaplan, *Jewish Feminist Movement in Germany*, pp. 108–9. *Vigilance Record*, March 1907, p. 22.

18. *The Fifth International Congress for the Suppression of the White Slave Traffic* (London: National Vigilance Association, 1913), p. 119.

19. National Vigilance Association, *Fourth Annual Report of the Executive Committee*, p. 27.

20. Frances Korn, *Buenos Aires: Los huéspedes del 20* (Buenos Aires: Editorial Sudamericana, 1974), pp. 91–92; Edward J. Bristow, *Vice and Vigilance: Purity Movements in Britain since 1700* (Dublin: Gill and Macmillan, 1977), p. 178.

21. Jill Harsin, *Policing Prostitution in Nineteenth-Century Paris* (Princeton: Princeton University Press, 1985), p. 324. Bristow, *Vice and Vigilance*, chap. 7.

22. Jewish Association for the Protection of Girls and Women (hereafter referred to as JAPGW), *Official Report of the Jewish International Conference on the Suppression of the Traffic in Girls and Women: Private and Confidential Report* (London: JAPGW, 1910), p. 67.

23. For a background on the British purity movement see Bristow, *Vice and Vigilance*. As he notes on p. 175, it was the British National Vigilance Association that began the campaign for an international treaty to prevent white slavery. On the role of social purity in the anti–white slavery movements in the United States see Carroll Smith-Rosenberg, "Beauty, the Beast, and the Militant Woman: A Case Study in Sex Roles and Social Stress in Jacksonian America," in *Disorderly Conduct: Visions of Gender in Victorian America* (New York: Alfred A. Knopf, 1985), pp. 109–28.

24. Vern L. Bullough and James A. Brundage, eds., *Sexual Practices and the Medieval Church* (Buffalo, N.Y.: Prometheus Books, 1982), p. 36.

25. Ibid.

26. For interpretations of Augustinian and Thomist views of prostitution see Jacques Rossiaud, *Medieval Prostitution*, trans. Lydia G. Cochrane (London: Basil Blackwell, 1988), pp. 73–75. Argentine resistance to official policy was similar to the general Italian attitude toward prostitution. See Mary Gibson, *Prostitution and the State in Italy, 1860–1915* (New Brunswick, N.J.: Rutgers University Press, 1986), p. 14.

27. In France, where the Protestant/Catholic split strongly influenced political attitudes, both feminism and the campaign against legalized prostitution were clearly anti-Catholic and anticlerical and worked to weaken the influence of the Catholic church in French law and society. See Harsin, *Policing Prostitution in Nineteenth-Century Paris*, p. 326.

28. Gunilla Johansson, "Life Chances: Prostitutes in the Swedish Reglamentation System, 1850–1915," paper presented at the seventh Berkshire Conference on the History of Women, Wellesley College, June 20, 1987.

29. Juan María Méndez Avellaneda, "El motín de la 'Lady Shore,'" *Todo Es Historia* 265 (July 1989): 12. See chapter 2 for an examination of 1869 census data.

30. *La Nación*, March 20, 1875.

31. Bristow, *Prostitution and Prejudice*, p. 113.

32. *La Tribuna*, September 20, 1877.

33. *El Puente de los Suspiros* 1, 8 (April 26, 1878): 1–2.

34. Ibid. *El Puente de los Suspiros* was published from April to June 1878. In his issue of May 2, Guerrero included a drawing of five men, three of whom he identified as white slavers. *El Puente de los Suspiros*, April

26, 1878; May 2, 1878, p. 2. The municipal council of Buenos Aires was outraged by the newspaper and made diligent efforts to suppress this publication as well as another known as *La Matraca*. Finally the council authorized the police to prevent their distribution and to imprison and fine the publishers. Buenos Aires Municipality, Comisión Municipal de la Ciudad de Buenos Aires, *Actas de la Comisión Municipal de la Ciudad de Buenos Aires* (hereafter Buenos Aires Municipality, *Actas*), June 25, 1878, p. 240. A review of the court case that identified both *La Matraca* and *El Puente de los Suspiros* as newspapers operated by pimps can be found in Buenos Aires Municipality, *Sentencias y resoluciones judiciales en asuntos de carácter municipal*, 3 vols. (Buenos Aires: Imprenta de la Lotería Nacional, 1895), 1:6.

35. *La Pampa*, October 6, 1881, p. 1; December 14, 1881, p. 1.

36. Statistics enclosed in reply of Jacinte Fernández, Judge of the Political Division, Buenos Aires Police, to League of Nations inquiry, August 27, 1924, National Vigilance Association Executive Minutes, Fawcett Library, NVA International Bureau, (hereafter NVA), box 111; *La Vanguardia*, May 26, 1919, p. 3; Ernesto M. Pareja, *La prostitución en Buenos Aires* (Buenos Aires: Tor, 1936); League of Nations, *Report of the Special Body of Experts on Traffic in Women and Children*, 2 parts (Geneva, 1927), 2:19.

37. According to Adolfo Batiz, a Buenos Aires policeman who wrote a book about his experiences, there was more than one organization, and their members included other foreign-born pimps besides Polish

Jews. Adolfo Batiz, *Buenos Aires, la ribera y los prostíbulos en 1880* (Buenos Aires: AGA-TAURA, n.d.), p. 79. In contrast, *El Diario* first mentioned El Club de los 40 in 1893. *El Diario*, August 30, September 9 and 12, 1893.

38. The history of the JAPGW and its affiliates in Argentina can be found in its report to the NVA, December 3, 1934, box 111, file 3. The letter to rabbis was written in December 1898 and reprinted in JAPGW, *Official Report of the Jewish International Conference*, pp. 156–57.

39. Quoted in Bristow, *Prostitution and Prejudice*, p. 116.

40. JAPGW, *Annual Report*, 1904, p. 25; *Annual Report*, 1907, p. 33.

41. Eugene Franklin Sofer, "From Pale to Pampa: Eastern European Jewish Social Mobility in Gran Buenos Aires, 1890–1945" (Ph.D. diss., University of California, Los Angeles, 1976), pp. 126, 228–29.

42. Quoted in Haim Avni, *Argentina y la historia de la inmigración judía (1810–1930)* (Jerusalem: Universitaria Magnes, Universidad Hebrea de Jerusalem, 1983), p. 248.

43. Ibid., p. 257.

44. JAPGW, *Official Report of the Jewish International Conference*, pp. 33–34.

45. Quoted in Kaplan, *Jewish Feminist Movement in Germany*, p. 109.

46. Sofer, "From Pale to Pampa," p. 126.

47. Manuel Gálvez, *La trata de blancas: Tesis para optar al grado de doctor en jurisprudencia* (Buenos Aires: José Tragant, 1905); his recollections of this incident can be found in idem, *Recuerdos de la vida literaria*, 4 vols. (Buenos Aires: Hachette, 1961), 1:160.

48. Quoted in Victor A. Mirelman, "The Jews in Argentina (1890–1930): As-

similation and Particularism" Ph.D. diss., Columbia University, 1973), p. 77.

49. JAPGW *Annual Report* 1907, pp. 35–37.

50. Ibid., 1912, pp. 52–54.

51. Ibid., 1911, p. 38.

52. Samuel Cohen, *Report of the Secretary on His Visit to South America in 1913* (Oxford, Jewish Association for the Protection of Girls and Women, 1913), pp. 11–12; 14–15, 16.

53. Ibid., p. 31.

54. Gerardo Bra, *La organización negra: La increíble historia de la Zwi Migdal* (Buenos Aires: Corregidor, 1982), pp. 25, 52–53.

55. Héctor Nicolás Zinni, *El Rosario de satanás: Historia triste de la mala vida* (Rosario: Centauro, 1980), p. 105.

56. Albert Londres, *The Road to Buenos Ayres*, trans. Eric Sutton (New York: Blue Ribbon Books, 1928), pp. 104–7.

57. NVA, Executive Minutes, June 4, 1912, p. 227; July 16, 1912, p. 237; September 30, 1913, pp. 332–33, box 192.

58. *Vigilance Record* 2 (February 1917): 14.

59. NVA Executive Minutes, April 4, 1913, 2: 34–35, box 192.

60. *Fifth International Congress for the Suppression of the White Slave Traffic*, p. 42.

61. *Women in a Changing World: The Dynamic Story of the International Council of Women since 1888* (London: Routledge and Kegan Paul, 1966), pp. 178–79.

62. Bristow, *Prostitution and Prejudice*, p. 36.

63. League of Nations, *Report of the Special Body of Experts on Traffic in Women and Children*, 2, 4: 197–98.

64. Report of Major Wagener, in Troisième Congrès International, *Compte rendu du Troisième Congrès International* (Paris: S.A. de Publications Périodiques, 1907), pp. 399–411.

65. Fédération Abolitionniste Internationale, *Dixième Congrès tenu à Genève, le 7–11 septembre 1908* (Geneva: Secrétariat Générale de la Fédération, 1909), pp. 264–65.

66. Asociación Nacional Argentina contra la Trata de Blancas, *Memoria*, 1904–5, p. 7.

67. *El Diario*, September 13, 1893.

68. Asociación Nacional Argentina contra la Trata de Blancas, *Memoria*, 1902–3, pp. 3–9. Letter of Arturo Condomí to William A. Coote, November 1903, NVA Minutes, COIB, box 111, letter 1721.

69. Asociación Nacional Argentina contra la Trata de Blancas, *Memoria*, 1902–3, pp. 12–15.

70. Ibid., 1904–5, pp. 13–15.

71. Ibid., 1906–8, p. 3. Letters of Arturo Condomí to William A. Coote, August 8, 1905, December 22, 1905, September 18, 1908, NVA Correspondence COIB, box 111. Letter from the Comité Argentino de Moralidad Pública to William A. Coote, secretary of the International Association against White Slavery, July 17, 1913, NVA Correspondence COIE, box 112.

72. Cohen, *Report of the Secretary on His Visit to South America in 1913*, p. 13.

73. Donna J. Guy, "White Slavery, Public Health, and the Socialist Position on Legalized Prostitution in Argentina, 1913–1936," *Latin American Research Review* 23, 3 (1988): 60–80; Argentine Republic, Cámara de Diputados, *Diario de Sesiones*, September 20, 1907, pp. 1240–41.

74. Argentine Republic, Cámara de Diputados, *Diario de Sesiones*, August 8, 1913, pp. 838–39.

75. Ibid., pp. 838–42.

76. Ibid, September 17, 1913, pp. 321–22.

77. Speech of Arturo Bas, ibid.

78. Ibid., pp. 329–31.

79. *Vigilance Record* 11 (November 1913): 91.

80. Teresa Billington-Grieg, "The Truth about White Slavery," *English Review*, June 1913, p. 438.

81. Ibid., pp. 434–35.

82. Ibid., p. 446.

83. Cohen, *Report of the Secretary of His Visit to South America*, p. 11.

84. *In the Grip of the White Slave Trader*, pp. 76, 83–84.

85. Letter from J. J. Jameson Grant to Sir Reginald Tower, undated letter, ca. July 1914, Public Record Office (hereafter PRO), Foreign Office Papers (FO) 371/2817, 34817; Letter from Sir Reginald Tower to Mr. Spicer, July 29, 1914, PRO FO371/2817, 34817.

86. *Vigilance Record* 3 (March 1915): 22; report of Rosalie Lighton Robinson, ibid., 4 (March 1916): 19.

87. Speech of Right Reverend Bishop Ryle, dean of Westminster, February 15, 1916, ibid., p. 17.

88. Report of Rosalie Lighton Robinson, *Vigilance Record* 4 (March, 1916): 18.

89. Ibid.

90. Ibid., p. 19.

91. Ibid., p. 20.

92. Anna Macías, *Against All Odds: The Feminist Movement in Mexico to 1940* (Westport, Conn.: Greenwood Press, 1982), p. 44.

93. Bristow, *Prostitution and Prejudice*, pp. 111–13. See Gilberto Freyre, *Ordem e progresso*, 2 vols. (Rio de Ja-

neiro: José Olympio, 1959), for the role of foreign women in Rio bordellos.

94. *La Patria Argentina*, November 2, 4, 10, 12, 1879; *La República*, November 4, 1879. The diplomatic documents relating to Argentina's commitment to the first international treaty can be found in Asociación Nacional Argentina contra la Trata de Blancas, *Memoria*, 1904–5, pp. 8–12.

95. Charles van Onselen, *Studies in the Social and Economic History of the Witwatersrand, 1886–1914*, vol. 1, *New Babylon* (New York: Longman, 1982), pp. 103–62, recounts the rise of commercial sex and changing social relations brought about by rapid capitalist development in the Transvaal.

CHAPTER 2

1. Mark D. Szuchman, "Disorder and Social Control in Buenos Aires, 1810–1860," *Journal of Interdisciplinary History* 15, 1 (Summer 1984): 108.

2. Richard W. Slatta, *Gauchos and the Vanishing Frontier* (Lincoln: University of Nebraska Press, 1983), p. 66.

3. María Sáenz Quesada, *El estado rebelde, Buenos Aires entre 1850/1860* (Buenos Aires: Belgrano, 1982), pp. 201, 246.

4. Slatta, *Gauchos and the Vanishing Frontier*, p. 122.

5. Argentine Republic, *Primer censo de la República Argentina verificado en los días 15, 16 y 17 de septiembre de 1869.* (Buenos Aires: Imprenta de Porvenir, 1872), pp. 64–75, 506–12. The 1869 census failed to distinguish employment by sex, so the real statistics were somewhat lower, since males did work at these tasks, though

they were a distinct minority. Inland Argentine cities had a long tradition of female artisan labor compared with Buenos Aires. Donna J. Guy, "Women, Peonage and Industrialization: Argentina, 1810–1914," *Latin American Research Review* 16, 3 (Fall 1981): 65–89.

6. Ibid., pp. xlvii, 64–65, 118–25, 506–12.

7. Ibid., p. xlvii.

8. Argentine Republic, Comisión Directiva del censo, *Tercer censo nacional de la República Argentina* (Buenos Aires: L. J. Rosso, 1917–19), 2:421 (hereafter *Tercer censo*). Adults were those age fifteen or older.

9. Richard J. Evans, "Prostitution, State and Society in Imperial Germany," *Past and Present* 70 (1976): 115; Slatta, *Gauchos and the Vanishing Frontier*, pp. 57–59.

10. On abandoned children in 1840 see Mark D. Szuchman, "Continuity and Conflict in Buenos Aires: Comments on the Historical City," in *Buenos Aires: Four Hundred Years*, ed. Stanley R. Ross and Thomas F. McGann (Austin: University of Texas Press, 1982), p. 58. Statistics for 1887 can be found in Buenos Aires Municipality, *Censo general de población, edificación, comercio e industrias de la ciudad de Buenos Aires*, 2 vols. (Buenos Aires: Cía. Sud-Americana de Billetes de Banco, 1889), 2:95, 442 (hereafter *Censo general*, 1887). Levillier made his remarks in an essay on delinquency: Roberto Levillier, "La delincuencia en Buenos Aires," in *Censo general de la población, edificación, comercio e industrias de la ciudad de Buenos Aires*, ed. Alberto B. Martínez, 3 vols. (Buenos Aires: Cía. Sud-Americana de Billetes de Banco, 1910), 3:395–420. (hereafter Martí-

nez, *Censo general*, 1910). Illegitimate births had increased from 13.89 percent in 1890–99 to 14.15 percent for 1900–1909. Martínez, *Censo general*, 1910, 2:viii.

11. Argentine Republic, *Código civil*, passim. The amendments to the civil code that made pimping by family heads a crime were the result of the Ley Palacios.

12. Donna J. Guy, "Lower-Class Families, Women and the Law in Nineteenth-Century Argentina," *Journal of Family History* 10, 3 (Fall 1985): 318–30.

13. Argentine Republic, Comisión Directiva del Censo, *Segundo censo de la república Argentina*, 3 vols. (Buenos Aires: Penitenciaria Nacional, 1898) 2:cxlii–cxliii (hereafter *Segundo censo*). Buenos Aires Municipality, *Anuario estadístico de la ciudad de Buenos Aires*, 1900, p. 225. See also Catalina H. Wainerman and Marysa Navarro, *El trabajo de la mujer en la Argentina: Un análisis preliminar de las ideas dominantes en las primeras décadas del siglo XX*, Cuadernos de CENEP 7 (Buenos Aires: CENEP, 1979), pp. 15, 31.

14. Blas Matamoro, *La ciudad del tango: Tango histórico y sociedad*, 2d. ed. (Buenos Aires: Galerna, 1982), pp. 33–35; for information on multifamily dwellings see Juan Suriano, *La huelga de inquilinos de 1907* (Buenos Aires: Centro Editor de América Latina, 1983), pp. 13, 21–22.

15. Judith R. Walkowitz, *Prostitution and Victorian Society: Women, Class and the State* (Cambridge: Cambridge University Press, 1980), pp. 14–15, 22. See also p. 36 for an analysis of why nineteenth-century Parisian women turned to prostitution.

16. Matamoro, *Ciudad del tango*, pp. 27–28; Pareja, *Prostitución en Buenos Aires*, p. 160.

17. Matamoro, *Ciudad del tango*, p. 53; Enrique Horacio Puccia, *El Buenos Aires de Angel G. Villoldo (1860 . . . 1919)* (Buenos Aires, 1976), p. 80.

18. Batiz, *Buenos Aires, la ribera y los prostíbulos en 1880*, pp. 43–45.

19. Blas Matamoro, "Orígines musicales," in *La historia del tango*, vol. 1, *Sus origines*, ed. Manuel Pampín (Buenos Aires: Corregidor, 1976), p. 70; León Benarós, "El tango y los lugares y casas de baile," in Pampín, *Historia del tango*, 2:232. See also José Sebastián Tallón, *El tango en sus etapas de música prohibida*, 2d ed. (Buenos Aires: Instituto Amigos del Libro Argentino, 1964). On literary salons see Lily Sosa de Newton, *Las argentinas de ayer a hoy* (Buenos Aires: L. V. Zanetti, 1967), pp. 64–70; 112–15.

20. In 1642 the Buenos Aires Cabildo ordered all women of low repute (*mal opinadas*) to reside in lodgings apart from respectable society (*casas honestas y principales*), but the neighborhood was never established. R. de Lafuente Machain, *Buenos Aires en el siglo XVII* (Buenos Aires: EMECE, 1944), p. 76.

21. Archivo General de la Nación Argentina (hereafter AGN), 1869 census, book 1, section 1, book 2, section 2, book 17, section 6, book 28, section 13. I thank Hugo Vainikoff for helping with this data.

22. Buenos Aires Police, *Memoria de la Policía de Buenos Aires* (hereafter Buenos Aires Police, *Memoria*), 1867, p. 564; 1873, p. 484.

23. Bristow, *Vice and Vigilance*, pp. 75–93.

24. Allan Brandt, *No Magic Bullet: A Social History of Venereal Disease in the United States since 1880* (New York: Oxford University Press, 1985), pp. 9–10, 40.
25. Buenos Aires Municipality, *Actas,* March 4, 1864, p. 54.
26. Ibid., pp. 53–55. The council's assertion that no philanthropic societies existed was untrue and probably reflected its reluctance to permit the women's Sociedad de Beneficencia to assume full responsibility for this problem. See chapter 3.
27. Carlos Gallarani, "Reglamentación de la prostitución: Fundamentos de esta importante medida de hijiene pública. Proyecto adaptable a la ciudad del Rosario (República Arjentina)," *Revista Médico-quirúrgica* 6 (1869–70): 271; Luis Tamini, "Reglamentación de las casas de prostitución," *Revista Médico-quirúrgica* 6, 8 (1869): 132–39.
28. Tamini, "Reglamentación," p. 133.
29. Ibid., pp. 135–39.
30. Buenos Aires Municipality, *Actas,* October 25, 1870, p. 351.
31. Ibid., January 5, 1875, pp. 317–23.
32. In Sweden, for example, all women suspected of prostitution were given gynecological examinations and, if unemployed and unmarried, forced into workhouses or bordellos. Johansson, "Life-Chances." See also Harsin, *Policing Prostitution in Nineteenth-Century Paris,* and Gibson, *Prostitution and the State in Italy.*
33. Francisco Romay, *Historia de la policía federal argentina,* vol. 5 (Buenos Aires: Biblioteca Policial, 1966), pp. 281–83.
34. Numerous petitions and police actions can be found in the Salud Pública section of the Archivo Histórico

de la Municipalidad de Buenos Aires (hereafter AHMBA).
35. Buenos Aires Municipality, *Memoria,* 1876, pp. 104–5.
36. Buenos Aires Municipality, *Actas,* October 15, 1874, p. 249.
37. Ibid., October 30, 1875, pp. 443–45.
38. Ibid., July 7, 1880, pp. 66–67; Buenos Aires Municipality, *Memoria,* 1903, p. 69.
39. Buenos Aires Municipality, *Memoria,* 1876, pp. 104–5.
40. Ibid., 1880, p. 206.
41. James R. Scobie, *Buenos Aires: Plaza to Suburb, 1870–1910* (New York: Oxford University Press, 1974), pp. 109–13 recounts Alvear's efforts to beautify the city.
42. José Manuel Irizar, "Servicio sanitario de la prostitución," *Anales del Departamento Nacional de Higiene,* 1904, pp. 108–9.
43. Buenos Aires Municipality, *Actas,* January 29, 1881, pp. 17–18.
44. See the refusal of the municipal council to finance workhouses and educational training for destitute women and youths; ibid., November 9, 1883, p. 368.
45. Buenos Aires Municipality, *Memoria,* 1893–94, p. 161; Buenos Aires Municipality, *Actas,* September 10, 1888, pp. 263–65.
46. Letter from the sección higiene of the municipal council to president of the municipality, June 1, 1881. Signed by Drs. Coni, Ramos Mejía, and Domingo Parodi; AHMBA, Salud Pública, 1881, Legajo 25.
47. Buenos Aires Municipality, *Dictámenes de la asesoría municipal 1878–1894,* 3 vols. (Buenos Aires: Imprenta de la Lotería Nacional, 1896), 3:89–90.
48. The sequence of events began with a petition from neighbors on June 30,

1885, AHMBA, Salud Pública, 1885, legajo 42. Then the police confirmed what neighbors said in a letter to the intendente, September 11, 1885, AHMBA, Salud Pública, legajo 42. After the women were arrested they filed a complaint that included data on the houses. Petition of September 19, 1885, AHMBA, Salud Pública, legajo 42. The judgment of the asesor municipal can be found in Buenos Aires Municipality, *Dictámenes de la asesoría municipal*, 3:99–100.

49. Petition of Candida Buschini, July 22, 1886, AHMBA, Salud Pública, 1886, legajo 99; note from the asesor to the intendente regarding his order to evict people from Talcahuano Street, October 2, 1886, AHMBA, Salud Pública, 1886, legajo 99.

50. Decision of L. Beláustegui, September 10, 1880, in Buenos Aires Municipality, *Dictámenes de la asesoría municipal*, 3:11.

51. Letter of police to intendente, October 2, 1886, AHMBA, Salud Pública, 1886, legajo 99.

52. See, for example, the report of the arrest and fine levied on Ramona Risso for clandestine prostitution, October 15, 1887, AHMBA, Salud Pública, 1887, legajo 130.

53. Municipality of Buenos Aires, *Actas*, September 10, 1888, pp. 263–66.

54. Emilio R. Coni, *Código de higiene y medicina legal de la República Argentina*, 2 vols. (Buenos Aires: Juan Etchepareborda, 1891), 1:216–21; 372–73.

55. Ernest A. Crider, "Modernization and Human Welfare: The Asistencia Publica and Buenos Aires, 1883–1910," Ph.D. diss., Ohio State University, 1976, pp. 145–46; Buenos Aires Municipality, *Anuario*

estadístico de la ciudad de Buenos Aires, 1891, p. 225. The number 2,007 differs slightly from the 1,959 reported by Jacinte Fernández to the League of Nations, "Part of reply by Jacinte Fernández, Judge of the Political Division, Buenos Aires Police, to League of Nations," August 27, 1924, NVA Minutes, box 111.

56. Crider, "Modernization and Human Welfare," pp. 145–47; *La Nación*, November 4, 1892; Buenos Aires Municipality, *Actas*, August 24, 1892, pp. 395–99.

57. Buenos Aires Municipality, *Actas*, March 10, 1891, pp. 210–11.

58. Ibid., comments of Dr. Torino, p. 212.

59. Ibid., June 2, 1891, pp. 439–41; October 20, p. 659.

60. Ibid., November 7, 1894, pp. 628–30.

61. Pareja, *Prostitución en Buenos Aires*, pp. 184–85; Asociación Nacional Argentina contra la Trata de Blancas, *Memoria*, 1902–3, p. 14; Buenos Aires Municipality, *Actas*, July 27, 1904, pp. 316–17.

62. Irizar, "Servicio sanitario de la prostitución," pp. 120–22; ordinance, articles 1–17.

63. Ibid., pp. 122–23, articles 18–30.

64. Ibid., pp. 123–24, articles 31–43.

65. Asociación Nacional Argentina contra la Trata de Blancas, *Memoria*, 1902–3, p. 14; Buenos Aires Municipality, *Actas*, July 27, 1904.

66. The number of legal bordellos between 1897 and 1903 can be found in Irizar, "Servicio sanitario de la prostitución," p. 116.

67. José Penna and Horacio Madero, *La administración sanitaria y asistencia pública en la ciudad de Buenos Aires*, 2 vols. (Buenos Aires: Guillermo Kraft, 1910), 1:397–98.

68. *El País*, April 4, 1908; April 20, 1908.

69. Buenos Aires Municipality, *Actas*, September 16, 1913, p. 486; December 9, 1913, p. 642; the exemptions for bordellos were given on September 16, p. 486, and December 26, pp. 816–17.

70. Buenos Aires Municipality, *Memoria*, 1878, pp. 98–101.

71. Ibid.

72. Walkowitz, *Prostitution and Victorian Society*, p. 250.

73. Clipping from *La Tribuna*, May 7, 1880, found in AHMBA, Salud Pública, 1880, legajo 26.

74. Municipality of Buenos Aires, *Dictámenes de la asesoría municipal*, 3:208–10.

75. Buenos Aires Municipality, *Actas*, December 16, 1895, p. 919.

76. Buenos Aires Municipality, *Memoria*, 1893–94, p. 163.

77. James R. Scobie, *Revolution on the Pampas: A Social History of Argentine Wheat, 1860–1910* (Austin: University of Texas Press, 1964), for the modernization of Argentine wheat production; Slatta, *Gauchos and the Vanishing Frontier*, chap. 4, discusses the relation of women and their work to the cattle economy of Buenos Aires. Juan Bialet-Massé's classic investigation of working conditions in the Argentine interior documented the status of female laborers outside Buenos Aires in the first decade of the twentieth century. See Juan Bialet-Massé, *El estado de las clases obreras argentinas a comienzos del siglo* (Córdoba: Universidad Nacional de Córdoba, 1968), especially chap. 28. For a comparison of women's work in Buenos Aires city and several Argentine provinces see Guy, "Women, Peonage and Industrialization."

78. Scobie, *Buenos Aires: Plaza to Suburb*, pp. 137–38.

79. Buenos Aires Municipality, *Censo general*, 1887, 2:304–5.

80. Adrián Patroni, *Los trabajadores en Argentina* (Buenos Aires, 1897), pp. 99–100.

81. Buenos Aires Municipality, *Memoria*, 1894, p. 173.

82. Quoted in Scobie, *Buenos Aires: Plaza to Suburb*, pp. 140–41.

83. Crider, "Modernization and Human Welfare," pp. 147–48; Municipality of Buenos Aires, *Actas*, April 1, 1910, pp. 163–65; April 12, 174.

84. Argentine Republic, *Segundo censo*, 3:364–65; *Tercer censo*, 8:211, 216. The 1895 figures on commercial employment differ from previous statistics I have presented because earlier tables identified women by profession rather than place of employment. Hence women could have worked as domestic servants, cooks, and laundresses for commercial establishments, but would not have been identified with the commercial sector. Guy, "Women, Peonage and Industrialization," p. 78.

85. Emilio R. Coni, *Higiene pública: El servicio sanitario de la ciudad de Buenos Aires* (Buenos Aires: Pablo E. Coni, 1880), p. 12; Juan Lazarte, *Sociología de la prostitución* (Buenos Aires: Kier, 1945), pp. 132–33; Enrique Revilla, "El ejercicio de la prostitución en Buenos Aires: Proyecto de ordenanza elevado a la intendencia municipal," *Archivos de Psiquiatría, Criminología y Ciencias Afines*, 2, 1 (January 1903): 77; Buenos Aires Municipality, *Anuario estadístico de la ciudad de Buenos Aires*, 1915–23, p. 133.

86. Suriano, *La huelga de inquilinos de 1907*, pp. 61–82.

87. Argentine Republic, *Tercer censo,* 3:21, 4:201–13; Guy, "Women, Peonage and Industrialization," p. 66.

88. See *La Vanguardia,* January 9, 1904, p. 4; May 14, 1904, p. 3; November 12, 1904; January 13, 1908, p. 1; March 1, 1908, p. 2, for strikes and labor organizations involving women. See also Guy, "Lower-Class Families, Women and the Law in Nineteenth-Century Argentina," p. 328.

89. These figures come from a study of factories that employed more than one hundred people. Argentine Republic, Departamento Nacional del Trabajo, División de Estadística, *Industria textil* (Buenos Aires, 1939), p. 24; Guy, "Women, Peonage and Industrialization," p. 83.

90. Donna J. Guy, "Emilio and Gabriela Coni: Reformers, Public Health, and Working Women," in *The Human Tradition in Latin America: The Nineteenth Century,* ed. Judith Ewell and William H. Beezley (Wilmington, Del.: Scholarly Resources, 1989), pp. 233–48. Articles 17 and 18 in Gabriela Laperrière de Coni, *Proyecto de ley de protección del trabajo de la mujer y del niño en las fábricas presentado a la intendencia municipal* (Buenos Aires: Liga Argentina contra la Tuberculosis, 1902), p. 4.

91. Coni, *Proyecto de ley de protección,* p. 16; Guy, "Women, Peonage and Industrialization," p. 83.

92. Alejandro M. Unsain, "El trabajo a domicilio en Buenos Aires," *Boletín del Departamento Nacional del Trabajo* 25 (December 31, 1913): pp. 877–78, 887–90.

93. Ibid., p. 892.

94. Carolina Muzilli, *El trabajo femenino* (Buenos Aires: L. J. Rosso, 1916).

95. Buenos Aires Municipality, *Memoria,* 1909, pp. 95–96; Buenos Aires Municipality, *Memoria de la Dirección General de la Administración Pública correspondiente al año 1910* (Buenos Aires: La Semana Médica, 1911), p. 160. The practice of Europeans' entering Argentina as Uruguayans was a long-standing custom noted by the League of Nations' 1927 report on white slavery. It presents a problem similar to that of women's changing their names to appear French, since French prostitutes were considered more glamorous and cultured. Thus the numbers of Frenchwomen are also suspect.

96. Buenos Aires Municipality, *Memoria de la Dirección General de la Administración Pública correspondiente al año 1910,* pp. 161–65.

97. Ibid., p. 164.

98. Buenos Aires Municipality, *Memoria,* 1912, pp. 190–92.

99. For data on Tandil houses see Slatta, *Gauchos and the Vanishing Frontier,* pp. 66–67; La Plata statistics can be found in Buenos Aires Province, *Censo general de la ciudad de La Plata, capital de la provincia* (La Plata: "La Popular," 1910), p. 115.

100. Coni, *Código de higiene y medicina legal,* 2:270–72; Roberto A. Ferrero, "La marginalia cordobesa," *Todo Es Historia* 184 (September 1982): 87–89.

101. Coni, *Código de higiene y medicina legal,* 2:153–56; Zinni, *Rosario de satanás,* pp. 103–7. Rosario de Santa Fe, *Segundo censo municipal de la ciudad de Santa Fe* (Rosario: Tipografía de La Capital, 1908), pp. 376–77; Report of Luis A. Vila, in Rosario Municipality, *Memoria del consejo ejecutor municipal presen-*

tada al consejo deliberante en diciembre 1881 (Rosario: El Independiente, 1882), pp. 68–69.

102. Coni, *Código de higiene y medicina legal*, 2:193–98.

103. Antonio B. Pont, in Dr. Emilio R. Coni, *Higiene aplicada a la provincia de Corrientes* (Buenos Aires: Pablo E. Coni, 1898), pp. 343–45.

CHAPTER 3

1. One of the few studies of the class-based assumptions of Argentine public health reforms can be found in José Pedro Barran et al., *Sectores populares y vida urbana* (Buenos Aires: CLACSO, 1984); Donna J. Guy, "Public Health, Gender and Private Morality: Paid Labor and the Formation of the Body Politic in Buenos Aires," *Gender and History*, 2, 3 (Autumn 1990): 297–317.

2. Quoted in Diego Abad de Santillán, *Gran enciclopedia argentina* (Buenos Aires: Ediar, 1956–64), 4:48. See also Vicente Osvaldo Cutolo, *Nuevo diccionario biográfico argentino*, 7 vols. (Buenos Aires: Elche, 1968–), 6:70–73. The law creating the Departamento Nacional de Higiene can be found in AGN, Ministerio del Interior, 1980, legajo 1.

3. Crider, "Modernization and Human Welfare," pp. 35–36; Ismael Bucich Escobar, *Buenos Aires ciudad* (Buenos Aires: El Ateneo, 1930), p. 372.

4. Parentheses appeared in the text. Emilio R. Coni, *Memorias de un médico higienista* (Buenos Aires: A. Flaiban, 1918), p. 189.

5. Emilio R. Coni, "Algunos datos relativos a la mortalidad de la ciudad de Buenos Aires durante el año 1876," *Revista Médico-quirúrgica* 14, 12 (September 1877): 271–72.

6. Emilio R. Coni, *Progrès de l'Hygiène dans le République Argentine* (Paris: J.-B. Ballière, 1887), pp. 227–28.

7. Coni, *Higiene pública*, p. 6. See the 1880 petition of Coni, Pirovano, and Ramos Mejía to have the municipal council terminate the 15,000 peso license fee and spend 15,000 pesos to set up a municipal prostitute inspection system until a prostitutes' registry could be established. AHMBA, Salud Pública, 1880, Legajo 26.

8. Ibid.; Foucault, *Birth of the Clinic*, p. 33.

9. Coni, *Higiene pública*, p. 7.

10. Benjamin Dupont, *Pornografía de Buenos Aires: De la necesidad imprescindible de un dispensario de salubridad y de una oficina de costumbres para reglamentar y reprimir la prostitución* (Buenos Aires: Pablo E. Coni, 1879), pp. 12–13. Biographical data on Dupont can be found in Cutolo, *Nuevo diccionario biográfico argentino*, 2:612–13. Coni had an explanatory section praising Dupont's work. See Coni, *Higiene pública*, pp. 4, 12. For philosophical statements in the de Parras Castañeda work, see Juan de Parras Castañeda, *Prostitución: Estudio de proyecto para su reglamentación* (Buenos Aires: Martínez, 1884), pp. 16–18.

11. Coni, *Memorias de un médico higienista*, p. 183. Letter of resignation to Minister of the Interior del Viso, January 8, 1881, AGN, Ministerio del Interior, 1881, legajo 2.

12. Susini petition and response can be found in AHMBA, Salud Pública, 1881, legajo 25.

13. Coni, *Código de higiene y medicina legal*, 1:83–86.

14. Penna and Madero, *Administración sanitaria y asistencia pública en la ciudad de Buenos Aires*, 1:392.

15. Crider, "Modernization and Human Welfare," p. 37.
16. Cynthia Jeffress Little, "The Society of Beneficence in Buenos Aires, 1823–1900," Ph.D. diss., Temple University, 1980; Sáenz Quesada, *Estado rebelde*, pp. 336–40. For the state of the Sociedad de Beneficencia in 1879–80 see the letter and accompanying diagram from the society to the minister of the interior. Letter dated December 31, 1880, AGN, Ministerio del Interior, 1881 expedientes, legajo 1.
17. Letter from S. Molina, Médico de Entradas, Hospital de Mujeres, to Sociedad de Beneficencia president Angela V. de Lahitte, October 11, 1880; Letter from the secretary, Sociedad de Beneficencia to the Sección Higiene de la Comisión Municipal, October 12, 1880, AHMBA, Salud Pública, 1880, legajo 26. Little, "Society of Beneficence in Buenos Aires," p. 204.
18. Sáenz Quesada, *Estado rebelde*, pp. 336–39.
19. Brito Foresti, "Profilaxis de las enfermedades venéreas y reglamentación de la prostitución," *La Semana Médica* 26 (April 1919): 16–20. The philosophy of incarceration within the British lock hospitals is discussed in Walkowitz, *Prostitution and Victorian Society*, p. 59.
20. Coni, *Código de higiene y medicina legal*, 1:354.
21. Ibid., Reglamento interno del Dispensario de Salubridad, articles 13 and 23, 1:218–19.
22. Decisions of July 16, 1889, and July 31, 1893, Buenos Aires Municipality, *Dictámenes de la asesoría municipal*, 3:175, 286–87.
23. Francisco de Veyga, "Inversión sexual adquirida: Tipo profesional," *Archivos de Psiquiatría, Criminología y Ciencias Afines* 4, 3 (April 1903): 195.
24. Ibid., pp. 193–99.
25. Francisco de Veyga, "La inversión sexual adquerida: Tipo profesional, un invertido comerciante," *Archivos de Psiquiatría, Criminología y Ciencias Afines* 2, 8 (August 1903): 492–96.
26. Francisco de Veyga, "Los auxiliares del vicio y del delito," *Archivos de Psiquiatría, Criminología y Ciencias Afines* 3 (May–June 1904): 289–313.
27. Eusebio Gómez, "La mala vida en *Archivos de Psiquiatría, Criminología y Ciencias Afines* 6 (1907): 434–35; *La mala vida en Buenos Aires* (Buenos Aires: Juan Roldan, 1908); See also Dr. Looyer, *Los grandes misterios de la mala vida en Buenos Aires comparada con la de los grandes capitales europeos* (Buenos Aires: Rafael Palumbo, 1911).
28. Municipality of Buenos Aires, *Actas*, October 26, 1894, p. 559.
29. Ibid., p. 600.
30. Ibid.
31. Ibid., pp. 600–605.
32. Ibid., p. 603.
33. Emilio R. Coni, "Casas de sanidad para prostitutas," *Anales de Higiene Pública y Medicina Legal* 3, 1 (March 1893): 3–4; idem, *El estado actual de la lucha antivenérea en América* (Buenos Aires: A. de Martino, 1921), p. 9.
34. Coni, *Memorias de un médico higienista*, pp. 640–41.
35. Silvestre Oliva, "Proyecto de la ordenanza reglamentaria de la prostitución," *Proceedings of the Second Pan American Scientific Congress*, 9, 8, part 1 (Washington, D.C.: Government Printing Office, 1917), p. 522.
36. Enrique Rosas Lacoigne, *La verdad sobre la prostitución en la ciudad de*

Buenos Aires (Buenos Aires, 1924), pp. 4–19.

37. José Manuel Irizar, "Reglamento de la prostitución," *Anales del Departamento Nacional de Higiene*, 4, 15 (December 1902): 782.

38. Enrique Prins, "Sobre la prostitución en Buenos Aires," *Archivos de Psiquiatría, Criminología y Ciencias Afines* 2, 12 (December 1903): 722–30.

39. José María Ramos Mejía, *Las multitudes argentinas: Estudio de psicología colectiva para servir de introducción al libro "Rosas y su tiempo,"* revised edition with an introduction by A. Bonilla and San Martín (Buenos Aires: J. Lajouane, 1912).

40. Sergio Bagú, *Vida de José Ingenieros* (Buenos Aires: EUDEBA, 1963), p. 33. Cutolo, *Nuevo diccionario biográfico argentino*, 6:49. For the role of Ingenieros and the Socialist party in the prostitution debate in Argentina see Guy, "White Slavery, Public Health and the Socialist Position on Legalized Prostitution in Argentina."

41. José Ingenieros, *El delito y la pena ante la filosofía biológica* (Buenos Aires: Penitenciaría Nacional, 1910), p. 14.

42. José Ingenieros, *Sistema penitenciario* (Buenos Aires: Penitenciaría Nacional, 1911), pp. 17–18.

43. Fermín Rodríguez, "Influencia del estado civil sobre el suicidio," *Archivos de Psiquiatría y Criminología y Ciencias Afines* 4 (July–August 1905): 387–97.

44. Pauline Tarnowsky, *Etude anthropométrique sur les prostitués et les voleuses* (Paris, 1869); Caesar Lombroso and William Ferrero, *The Female Offender* (London: T. Fisher Unwin, 1895); Berta Perelstein, *Positivismo y antipositivismo en la Argentina* (Buenos Aires: Procyon, 1952), p. 126. Osvaldo Loudet, *Figuras próximas y lejanas al margen de la historia* (Buenos Aires: Academia Argentina de Letras, 1970), pp. 194–95.

45. Gómez, *La mala vida en Buenos Aires*, pp. 128–29, 182.

46. José Ingenieros, prologue to Gómez, *La mala vida en Buenos Aires*, pp. 7–15. Ingenieros did not mention specific crimes or illnesses, but he did equate the boundaries of mental illness and criminality to definitions imposed by the social system.

47. José Ingenieros, *Obras completas revisadas y anotadas por Aníbal Ponce*, vol. 23, *Tratado del amor* (Buenos Aires: L. J. Rosso, 1940, p. 149.

48. Leopoldo Zea, *The Latin American Mind*, trans. James H. Abbott and Lowell Dunham (Norman: University of Oklahoma Press, 1963), p. 213; Solomon Lipp, *Three Argentine Thinkers*, (New York: Philosophical Library, 1969), pp. 16–19.

49. *Women in a Changing World*, pp. 241–42; Lily Sosa de Newton, *Diccionario biográfico de mujeres argentinas* (Buenos Aires, 1972), pp. 164–65; Asunción Lavrin, "The Ideology of Feminism in the Southern Cone, 1900–1940," Wilson Center Working Paper no. 169 (Washington, D.C., 1986), provides a general overview of feminist ideology.

50. Sosa de Newton, *Diccionario biográfico de mujeres argentinas*, pp. 193–94, 67–68; María del Carmen Feijó, "Las luchas feministas," *Todo Es Historia* 128 (January 1978): 10.

51. *Primer congreso femenino internacional de la República Argentina* (Buenos Aires: A. Ceppi, 1911), p. 298.

52. Ibid., pp. 299–301; Paul McHugh, *Prostitution and Victorian Social Re-*

form, (London: Croom Helm, 1980) p. 167.

53. Sosa de Newton, *Diccionario biográfico de mujeres argentinas*, p. 125; Letter from Petrona Eyle to president, National Vigilance Society, June 23, 1917, NVA, CO1B, box 111; Letter from Mrs. Lighton Robinson to Mr. F. A. R. Sempkins, May 2, 1928, NVA CO1, Correspondence, box 111.

54. Nicolás Cuello, *Acción femenina* (Buenos Aires, 1939).

55. Alicia Moreau de Justo, "The White Slave Trade in South America," *Proceedings of the International Conference of Women Physicians*, vol. 6 (New York: Women's Press, 1920), p. 75.

56. Paulina Luisi, *Bases y propósitos de la Federación Abolicionista Internacional*, Palabras pronunciadas en la asamblea de la sección argentina, verificada el día 27 de febrero de 1919 (Buenos Aires: Talleres Gráficos "Juan Perroti," 1919).

57. Moreau de Justo, "White Slave Trade in South America," pp. 89–90.

58. Alicia Moreau de Justo, on September 7, 1935. Reprinted in the Liga Argentina de Profilaxis Social, *Por la salud de la raza* (Buenos Aires: Gráfico Argentino, 1936), p. 30.

59. Paulina Luisi, *El problema de la prostitución: Abolicionismo o reglamentarismo* (Montevideo: La Industrial, 1921), pp. 71–74.

60. For a complete list of officers in the Liga Argentina de Profilaxis Social see Abad de Santillán, *Gran enciclopedia argentina*, 6:530.

61. Alfredo Fernández Verano, "Acción de la Liga Argentina de Profilaxis Social," in *Para una patria grande, un pueblo sano*, 2d ed. (Buenos Aires: Fabril Financiera, 1939), pp. 180–81.

62. The Blackwelder and Johnson study of crime in Buenos Aires focuses almost exclusively on males, since the number of female felons was statistically unimportant. Julia Kirk Blackwelder and Lyman Johnson, "Changing Criminal Patterns in Buenos Aires, 1890–1914," *Journal of Latin American Studies* 14, 2 (1982): 359–80; Donna J. Guy, "Prostitution and Female Criminality in Buenos Aires, 1875–1937," in *The Problem of Order in Changing Societies: Essays on Crime and Policing in Argentina and Uruguay, 1750–1940*, ed. Lyman L. Johnson (Albuquerque: University of New Mexico Press, 1990), pp. 99–102.

63. Buenos Aires Police, *Memoria*, 1881, pp. 260–61; 1882, pp. 262–63; 1883, pp. 118–19; 1893, pp. 63–65.

64. Buenos Aires Police, *Memoria*, 1881, pp. 184–89; 230–31.

65. Letter of Pedro A. Costa to Police Chief Enrique García Mérou, September 13, 1884, Buenos Aires Police, *Memoria*, 1884–85, pp. 20–23; misdemeanor statistics by sex, p. 252.

66. C. y A., *La prostitución en Buenos Aires* (Buenos Aires: "Courrier de la Plata," 1885), p. iv.

67. Ibid., pp. 2–12.

68. Batiz, *Buenos Aires, la ribera y los prostíbulos en 1880*, p. 89.

69. Buenos Aires Municipality, *Statistical Yearbook for the City of Buenos Aires*, 1913, p. 254. Unfortunately this information was not analyzed from the perspective of gender.

70. Laurentino C. Mejías, *La policía por dentro: Mis cuentos* (Barcelona: Imprenta Viuda de Luis Tasso, 1913), pp. 78–79.

71. Julio L. Alsogaray, *Trilogía de la trata de blancas: Rufianes—policía—*

municipalidad, 2d ed. (Buenos Aires: Tor, n.d.).

72. Pareja, *Prostitución en Buenos Aires.*

CHAPTER 4

1. Sofer, "From Pale to Pampa," pp. 112–15, 132, 134, 137.
2. Argentine Republic, Cámara de Diputados, *Diario de Sesiones*, June 20, 1917, pp. 138–50.
3. Ibid.
4. Angel M. Giménez, *Contra la reglamentación de la prostitución. Abolición de las ordenanzas municipales y profilaxis de las enfermedades venéreas. Proyectos y discursos pronunciados en el Consejo Deliberante de Buenos Aires en las sesiones del 7 de enero, 16, 19, y 21 de mayo de 1919* (Buenos Aires: Sociedad Luz, n.d.), pp. 3, 25–26, 68–69.
5. Ibid., pp. 113–20.
6. League of Nations, *Report of the Special Body of Experts on Traffic in Women and Children*, 2:12.
7. Ibid., p. 18.
8. Quoted in Alsogaray, *Triología de la trata de blancas*, pp. 43–44.
9. Ibid., pp. 43–44, 110.
10. Ricardo C. Nuñez, *Derecho penal argentino*, vol. 4 (Buenos Aires: Biblioteca Omeba, 1964), pp. 336–37, 377.
11. Buenos Aires Municipality, *Actas*, March 20, 1923, pp. 173–75.
12. Ibid., May 11, 1923, p. 591; June 1, 1923, p. 740.
13. Decree of December 30, 1925, quoted in letter of Mrs. Lighton Robinson to Mr. Sempkins, March 7, 1928, NVA Correspondence, CO1E, box 112.
14. Mirelman, "Jews in Argentina (1890–1930)," p. 13.
15. *Vigilance Record*, April 1920, p. 45.
16. Ibid., March 1923, p. 19.

17. Executive Minutes of the International Bureau, February 25, 1927, NVA, box 192, International Bureau, volume 2; undated clipping attached to letter from Mrs. Lighton Robinson to Mr. Sempkins, January 28, 1931, NVA Correspondence, CO1, box 111; Obituary of Mrs. Lighton Robinson, published September 12, 1939, NVA Correspondence, CO1A, box 112.
18. *Vigilance Record*, May, 1921, p. 38.
19. "Extent of the Enquiry," in League of Nations, *Report of the Special Body of Experts on Traffic in Women and Children*, 1:6.
20. Ibid., p. 11.
21. League of Nations, *Report of the Special Body of Experts on the Traffic in Women and Children*, 2:69–71.
22. Ibid., pp. 107–9.
23. Ibid., p. 15.
24. H. Wilson Harris, *Human Merchandise: A Study of the International Traffic in Women* (London: Ernest Benn, 1928), pp. 18–19, 215, 223.
25. L. L. Hyams, *Lettre ouverte addressé par un homme aux jeunes filles* (Bordeaux: Edition du "Rélévement Social," [1929]), pp. 7–8; NVA, file 27B, box 115.
26. League of Nations, *Report of the Special Body of Experts on Traffic in Women and Children*, part 2 (Geneva, 1927), p. 19; Buenos Aires Police, *Memoria*, 1915–16, pp. 28, 388–89.
27. Korn, *Buenos Aires: Los huéspedes del 20*, p. 142n.
28. Buenos Aires Police, *Memoria*, 1916, pp. 388–89; 1919–20, p. 38; 1923, pp. 43–46; 1924, pp. 9–10; 1926, pp. 9–10.
29. Quoted in Mirelman, "Jews in Argentina (1890–1930)," pp. 89–90.
30. JAPGW, *Annual Report*, 1924, pp. 24–25, 28.

31. Ibid., 1926, pp. 32–35.
32. Bra, *Organización negra*, pp. 25, 52–53.
33. Ibid., p. 89.
34. Quoted in League of Nations, *Report of the Special Body of Experts in Traffic in Women and Children*, 2:173.
35. Newspaper clipping enclosed in letter of Mrs. Lighton Robinson, July 10, 1928, NVA Correspondence, COIA, box 111.
36. Extract from letter of Mrs. Lighton Robinson, December 3, 1928, NVA Correspondence, COIA, box 111.
37. Héctor Nicolás Zinni, *La Mafia en Argentina* (Rosario: Centro Editorial, 1975).
38. Bra, *Organización negra*, pp. 91–114.
39. Alsogaray, *Trilogía de la trata de blancas*, pp. 123, 126.
40. Londres, *Road to Buenos Ayres*, pp. 167–68.
41. Ibid., pp. 175, 177, 179.
42. Ibid., pp. 79, 134, 136.
43. Victorio Luis Bessero, *Los tratantes de blancas en Buenos Aires: El escándalo de la pseuda sociedad "Varsovia" o "Migdal"* (Buenos Aires, 1930).
44. Pareja, *La prostitución en Buenos Aires*, pp. 61–62.
45. Letter from Mrs. Lighton Robinson, November 16, 1929, NVA Correspondence, COI, box 111.
46. This report was published in League of Nations, Advisory Committee on Social Questions, *Enquiry into Measures of Rehabilitation of Adult Prostitutes: Conclusions and Recommendations*, 4 parts (Geneva, 1939), 1:124–25.
47. See chapter 5.
48. Lazarte, *Sociología de la prostitución*, p. 132.
49. Pareja, *Prostitución en Buenos Aires*.
50. Unpaginated diagram found after p. 224 in Pareja, "Estado de la prosti-

tución reglamentada el día 31 de diciembre de 1934," in *Prostitución en Buenos Aires*. Clipping from *La Prensa*, July 25, 1929, NVA Correspondence, COI, box 111; Korn, *Buenos Aires: Los huéspedes del 20*, p. 142.
51. Asociación Nacional Argentina contra la Trata de Blancas, *Memoria*, 1917, p. 9; 1918, p. 4.
52. Letter from Mrs. Lighton Robinson to Mr. F. A. R. Sempkins, May 2, 1928, complained that the Argentine committee was closed down and had done little because Dr. Petrona Eyle had refused to join Lighton Robinson in port work; NVA Correspondence, COI, box 111.
53. *Report of the Sixth International Congress for the Suppression of Traffic in Women and Children held in Graz (Austria) on September 18, 19, and 20th, 1924* (Geneva, 1924), Summary, May 11, 1925, pp. 1–2.
54. *Gaceta del Foro*, November 2, 1930, 89:13.
55. Ibid., p. 16.
56. Ibid., pp. 17–18; Bristow, *Prostitution and Prejudice*, p. 122.
57. Retold in Korn, *Buenos Aires: Los huéspedes del 20*, pp. 84–88.
58. Ibid., p. 98.
59. Alsogaray, *Trilogía de la trata de blancas*, p. 125n.
60. Clippings from the *Buenos Aires Herald*, May 6, 23, 1930; May 31, 1930; NVA, COIJ, box 112; *Standard*, January 23, 1931, NVA Correspondence, COI, box 112.
61. Buenos Aires Municipality, Decreto derogando la ordenanza sobre la reglamentación de la prostitución, December 24, 1930, AGN, Ministerio del Interior, 1931 Expedientes, legajo 8, no. 6.362-M.

62. See the debates in Buenos Aires Municipality, *Actas*, April 15, 1932, pp. 681–82; October 3, 1933, pp. 2184–86; May 25, 1933, pp. 758–59; September 18, 1934, pp. 2137–38, 2150–52; November 20, 1934, pp. 2897–2901, December 7, 1934, p. 3368; December 18, 1934, pp. 3712–14.

63. Ordinances and decrees reprinted in Buenos Aires Police, *Memoria*, 1934, pp. 242–45.

64. Buenos Aires Police, *Memoria*, 1935, p. l; 1936, p. l.

65. Ibid., 1935, p. 26.

66. Letter from N. Bronson William, May 19, 1932, NA, RG 59, 835.1151, 1930–39, box 5876; League of Nations, Traffic in Women and Children Committee, *Abolition of Licensed Houses* (Geneva, 1935), annex 2, page 7.

67. Decree of Provisional Government of Argentina, March 27, 1931, AGN, Ministerio del Interior, 1931, legajo 8, expediente 6.362-M.

68. Argentine Republic, Cámara de Diputados, *Diario de Sesiones*, September 15, 1933, pp. 411–14.

69. Ibid., June 12, 1935, pp. 333–34.

70. The deputies' debates can be found in ibid., September 26, 1935, pp. 552–68; December 9, 1936, pp. 939–49; the Senate debates are in Argentine Republic, Cámara de Senadores, *Diario de Sesiones*, September 18, 1936, pp. 261–84; December 17, 1936, pp. 303–11.

71. These conclusions are based on statistics compiled by the Argentine Departamento Nacional del Trabajo and quoted in Nancy Caro Hollander, "Women in the Political Economy of Argentina," Ph.D. diss., University of California, Los Angeles, 1974, pp. 115–16.

72. These figures come from a study of factories that employed more than one hundred people. Argentine Republic, Departamento Nacional del Trabajo, División de Estadística, *Industria textil* (Buenos Aires, 1939), p. 24.

73. Law 11.317, Argentine Republic, Cámara de Diputados, *Diario de Sesiones*, 1924 7:327–29.

74. Guy, "Lower-Class Families, Women, and the Law in Nineteenth-Century Argentina," p. 328.

75. Buenos Aires Municipality, *Actas*, May 13, 1921, pp. 640–41; August 19, pp. 1751–53.

76. Ibid., April 6, 1923, p. 236.

77. Carlos Silvestre, "Interpretación de la ley 12.331: Prestación de servicios gratuitos de profilaxis venérea. Su obligación en los establicimientos fabriles," *Gaceta Textil*, June 1939, p. 11.

78. Sandra McGee Deutsch, *Counter Revolution in Argentina, 1900–1932: The Argentine Patriotic League* (Lincoln: University of Nebraska Press, 1986), pp. 210–12; Instituto Alejandro E. Bunge, *Soluciones argentinas a los problemas económicas y sociales del presente* (Buenos Aires: Kraft, 1945), pp. 162–64.

CHAPTER 5

1. Angel Rama, *La ciudad letrada* (Hanover, N.H.: Ediciones del Norte, 1984), p. 143.

2. Julie M. Taylor, "Tango: Theme of Class and Nation," *Ethnomusicology* 20, 2 (May 1976): 281–82.

3. Matamoro, *Ciudad del tango*, p. 51.

4. *La Pampa*, December 15, 1881, p. 1.

5. José Gobello, "Orígines de la letra de tango," in Pampín, *Historia del tango*, 1:101–2. See Andrés M. Carretero,

El compadrito y el tango (Buenos Aires: Pampa y Cielo, 1964), p. 49.

6. Buenos Aires Municipality, *Actas,* November 23, 1915, p. 650.
7. Ernesto Eiris, "Los certificados de salud de las mujeres contratadas en las cabarets de Rosario," *Publicaciones Médicas* 3, 1 (March 1937): 4.
8. León Benarós, "El tango y los lugares y casas de baile," in Pampín, *Historia del tango,* 2:227.
9. These conclusions are based upon an analysis of early tango lyrics published in Pampin, *Historia del tango.*
10. Ibid., 198, 201.
11. For a glimpse into the life and work of one such lyricist, see Puccia, *Buenos Aires de Angel G. Villoldo.*
12. Simon Collier, *The Life, Times, and Music of Carlos Gardel* (Pittsburgh: University of Pittsburgh Press, 1986), p. 57.
13. Luis Adolfo Sierra, "La escuela decareana," in Pampín, *Historia del tango,* 7: 1010–11; Osvaldo D. Zucchi, "El bandoneón en el tango," in ibid., 5:661–70.
14. Lewis A. Erenberg, *Steppin' Out: New York Nightlife and the Transformation of American Culture, 1890–1930* (Chicago: University of Chicago Press, 1981), p. 164. The Castles wrote a book on modern dancing in 1914.
15. Ibid., p. 163.
16. Domingo F. Casadevall, *Buenos Aires: Arrabal, sainete, tango* (Buenos Aires: Fabril, 1968), p. 145; Collier, *Life, Music, and Times of Carlos Gardel,* p. 57; Tomás de Lara and Inés Leonilda Roncetti de Panti, *El tema del tango en la literatura argentina* (Buenos Aires: Ediciones Culturales Argentinas, 1961), pp. 134–35, traces the movement of the cabaret from the working-class southern

neighborhoods to the downtown area of Buenos Aires.

17. *Caras y Caretas* 3 (August 27, 1910).
18. "El tango en Europa," ibid., 6 (1913): 787; see also "El entusiasmo por el tango en Europa," ibid., 5 (1913): 780, and "La tangomanía en Europa," ibid., 1 (1914): 796; Casadevall, *Buenos Aires: Arrabal, sainete, tango,* p. 151.
19. José María a Salaverría, "El tango caricaturizado," *Caras y Caretas* 1 (January 31, 1914).
20. "Nostalgia," music by Arturo de Bassi, lyrics by L. González Calderón, ibid., 7 (November 9, 1912).
21. Collier, *Life, Times, and Music of Carlos Gardel,* pp. 60–61.
22. Ibid., pp. 35–36.
23. National Vigilance Association, *Congress of the White Slave Traffic,* p. 71.
24. Cohen, *Report of the Secretary on His Visit to South America in 1913,* pp. 33, 12–13.
25. *Vigilance Record* 7 (July, 1914), p. 50.
26. *Report of the Seventh International Congress for the Suppression of Traffic in Women and Children,* June 29, 1927, pp. 36–37.
27. Domingo F. Casadevall, *El tema de la mala vida en el teatro nacional* (Buenos Aires: Guillermo Kraft, 1957), pp. 167–68.
28. Darío Cantón, *Gardel: ¿A quién le cantás?* (Buenos Aires: La Flor, 1972), p. 199.
29. Copy of letter, Great Britain, PRO, FO 371/4477/310.
30. "White Slave Traffic in South America," May 25, 1920, FO 371/4477/307; *Vigilance Record* 1 (January 1928): 4.
31. Julio Mafud, *Sociología del tango* (Buenos Aires: Américalee, 1966), pp. 31–33.

32. Maxine Molyneux, "No God, No Boss, No Husband: Anarchist Feminism in Nineteenth-Century Argentina," *Latin American Perspectives* 13, 1 (Winter 1986): 119–45; Iaacov Oved, *El anarquismo y el movimiento obrero en Argentina* (Mexico City: Siglo XXI, 1978), pp. 73–74, 100.

33. Cantón, *Gardel, ¿A quién le cantás?* pp. 24–26. See also David Foster's insightful work on narrative rights in the tango. David William Foster, "'Narrative Rights' in the Argentine Tango," *Symposium* 37 (1983–84): 261–71.

34. Translated from lyrics published in Pampín, *Historia del tango*, 6:823; Idea Vilariño, *Las letras del tango* (Buenos Aires: Schapire, 1965), pp. 136, 139, 142.

35. Translated from Cantón, *Gardel: ¿A quién le cantás?* p. 153.

36. Ibid., pp. 140, 197.

37. Ibid., p. 107.

38. Mafud, *Sociología del tango*, pp. 15, 20, 31–33. Mafud dates the onset of this new phase to 1910. Beatriz Sarlo has examined the ways literature confronted the impact of modernization on gender roles. Beatriz Sarlo, *Una modernidad periférica: Buenos Aires 1920 y 1930* (Buenos Aires: Nueva Visión, 1988).

39. Ezequiel Martínez Estrada, *X-ray of the Pampa*, trans. Alain Swietlicki (Austin: University of Texas Press, 1971), pp. 254–55.

40. Ibid., pp. 257–58.

41. Ibid., p. 256.

42. Ibid., pp. 258–60.

43. Cantón, *Gardel: ¿A quién le cantás?* pp. 218–19.

44. Quoted in Norberto Galasso, *Escritos inéditos de Enrique Santos Discépolo* (Buenos Aires: Ediciones de Pensamiento Nacional, 1981), p. 29.

45. Collier, *Life, Times, and Music of Carlos Gardel*, p. 68; Estela Dos Santos, *Las mujeres del tango* (Buenos Aires: Centro Editor de América Latina, 1972), p. 16.

46. Dos Santos, *Mujeres del tango*, p. 21.

47. Ibid., pp. 14, 18; Cantón, *Gardel: ¿A quién le cantás?* pp. 125–26.

48. Dos Santos, *Mujeres del tango*, p. 14.

49. Blas Raúl Gallo, *Historia del sainete nacional* (Buenos Aires: Buenos Aires Leyendo, 1970), pp. 86–88.

50. Casadevall, *Buenos Aires: Arrabal, sainete, tango*, p. 47.

51. Miguel Ocampo, *Otra revista* (Buenos Aires: La Industria, 1891), p. 19.

52. Angela Blanco Amores de Pagella, *Motivaciones del teatro argentino en el siglo XX* (Buenos Aires: Ediciones Culturales Argentinas, 1973), pp. 13, 38–39; 40–41.

53. Casadevall, *Buenos Aires: Arrabal, sainete, tango*, pp. 74–75, 159; Gallo, *Historia del sainete nacional*, pp. 187–88.

54. José González Castillo, *Los invertidos* (Buenos Aires: Argentores Ediciones del Carro de Tespis, 1957).

55. Casadevall, *Buenos Aires: Arrabal, sainete, tango*, p. 123.

56. Buenos Aires Municipality, *Censo, 1910*, 2:357–59.

57. Casadevall, *Buenos Aires: Arrabal, sainete, tango*, pp. 149, 161.

58. Ibid., pp. 155–56.

59. Blanco Amores de Pagella, *Motivaciones del teatro argentino en el siglo XX*, p. 22.

60. Stasys Gostautas, *Buenos Aires y Arlt (Dostoievsky, Martínez Estrada y Scalabrini Ortiz)* (Madrid: Insula, 1977), p. 26; Myron Lichtblau, "The Argentine Novel in the Nineteenth Century," Ph.D. diss., Columbia University, 1957), pp. 284–87.

61. Eduardo López Bagó, *Carne importada (costumbres de Buenos Aires): Novela médico-social* (Buenos Aires, n.d.). I have determined that the novel was written after 1890 because of its reference to a club of Jewish pimps that dates to the late 1880s.

62. Abad de Santillán, *Gran enciclopedia argentina*, 7:539. Francisco A. Sicardi, *Libro extraño* (Buenos Aires, 1904).

63. Sicardi, *Libro extraño*, pp. 451–620.

64. Ibid., pp. 500–501.

65. Ibid., p. 538.

66. José Ingenieros, *"Hacia la justicia": La piedad homicida* (Buenos Aires: Pablo Ingegnieros, n.d.), pp. 5–6.

67. Ibid., pp. 27–31.

68. Oved, *Anarquismo y el movimiento obrero en Argentina*, p. 246.

69. Mabel Susana Agresti, "Manuel Gálvez y la novela realista," *Todo Es Historia* 16, 187 (December 1982): 81–82.

70. Gálvez, *Recuerdos de la vida literaria*, 2:309; idem, *Trata de blancas*; Manuel Gálvez, *La inseguridad de la vida obrera* (Buenos Aires: Alsina, 1913).

71. Gálvez, *Trata de blancas*, pp. 28–43, 87.

72. Manuel Gálvez, *Nacha Regules* (Buenos Aires: Centro Editor de América Latina, 1968).

73. Ibid., pp. 5–7.

74. Manuel Gálvez, *Historia de arrabal* (Buenos Aires: Deucalion, 1956).

75. Gálvez, *Recuerdos de la vida literaria*, 108–9.

76. See Myron Lichtblau, *Manuel Gálvez* (New York: Twayne, 1972), p. 42, for another opinion.

77. Gálvez, *Nacha Regules*, p. 28.

78. Gálvez, *Recuerdos de la vida literaria*, 2:123, 125.

79. Gálvez, *Nacha Regules*, p. 40.

80. Gálvez, *Recuerdos de la vida literaria*, 2:120.

81. Muzilli, *Trabajo femenino*, p. 20.

82. Gálvez, *Nacha Regules*, p. 32.

83. Ibid., p. 193.

84. Ibid., p. 204.

85. Roberto Arlt, *The Seven Madmen*, trans. Naomi Lindstrom (Boston: David R. Godine, 1984); idem, *Los siete locos; Los lanzallamas* (Caracas: Biblioteca Ayacucho, 1978).

86. Daniel C. Scroggins, *Las aguafuertes porteñas de Roberto Arlt* (Buenos Aires: Ediciones Culturales Argentinas, 1981), p. 82.

87. Roberto Arlt, *Los lanzallamas*, in *Los siete locos; Los lanzallamas*, pp. 192–93.

88. Ibid, p. 199.

89. Kathleen Elizabeth Newman, "The Argentine Political Novel: Determinations in Discourse," Ph.D. diss., Stanford University, 1983, pp. 99–100.

90. Clara Beter, *Versos de una . . .* (Buenos Aires: Claridad, n.d.), p. 45.

91. Elías Castelnuovo [pseud. Ronald Chaves], in ibid., pp. 12–13; For details on Castelnuovo, see Christopher Towne Leland, *The Last Happy Men: The Generation of 1922, Fiction, and the Argentine Reality* (Syracuse: Syracuse University Press, 1986), pp. 57–59.

92. César Tiempo, *Clara Beter y otras fatamorganas* (Buenos Aires: Peña Lillo, 1974), pp. 17–24.

93. Nicholas Fraser and Marysa Navarro, *Eva Perón* (New York: W. W. Norton, 1985), p. 46.

94. Joseph A. Page, *Perón: A Biography* (New York: Random House, 1983), pp. 79, 145, 291, 335. Robert Crassweller, *Perón and the Enigmas of Argentina* (New York: W. W. Norton, 1987), pp. 274–75; Carlos H. Wais-

man, *Reversal of Development in Argentina: Postwar Counterrevolutionary Policies and Their Structural Consequences* (Princeton: Princeton University Press, 1987), pp. 242–50.

CHAPTER 6

1. *La Prensa*, December 28, 1954, p. 6; December 29, pp. 3–4; December 30, pp. 4, 7; London *Times*, December 31, 1954.
2. *La Prensa*, December 31, 1954, p. 3.
3. Ibid., p. 3; London *Times*, December 31, 1954, p. 5.
4. *New York Times*, December 31, 1954, p. 4.
5. Tulio Carella, *Picaresca porteña* (Buenos Aires: Siglo XX, 1966), p. 35.
6. Paulina Luisi, *A propósito de los proyectos sobre moralidad*, palabras pronunciadas en la asamblea verificada por la Federación Abolicionista en la Sociedad Científica Argentina el día 24 de abril de 1919 (Buenos Aires: "J. Perrotti," 1919); Luisi, *Bases y propósitos de la Federación Abolicionista Internacional*, p. 24.
7. Speech of January 19, 1919, to the Buenos Aires municipal council. Giménez, *Contra la reglamentación de la prostitución*, pp. 94–95.
8. *Vigilance Record* 1 (January 1924): 6.
9. Angel Gímenez, statement of January 19, 1919, in Buenos Aires Municipality, *Actas*, April 24, 1925, pp. 268–70. The citation was quoted in Martín Aberg Cobo, *Contralor de la moralidad pública* (Buenos Aires: Francisco A. Colombo, 1941), p. 70–72.
10. The three songs were "Que vachaché" (What Can I Do about It?), "Chorra" (Thief), and "Esta noche me emborracho" (Tonight I'm Going to Get Drunk). Norberto Galasso,

Discépolo y su época (Buenos Aires: Jorge Alvarez, 1967), p. 60.
11. Isidro Satanowsky, *La obra cinematográfica frente al derecho*, 4 vols. (Buenos Aires: Ediar, 1955), 4:301.
12. Ibid., 4:303–4.
13. Aberg Cobo, *Contralor municipal de la moralidad pública*, pp. 83–84.
14. Tallon, *Tango en sus etapas de música prohibida*, pp. 28–29.
15. Donald Castro, "Popular Culture as a Source for the Historian: The Tango under Perón, 1943–1955," paper presented at the Latin American Studies Association, Boston, October 1986, pp. 4–5, 8–9.
16. Enrique R. Aftalión, "Prostitución, proxenetismo y delito," *Revista de Policía y Criminalística de Buenos Aires* 4, 19 (April–June, 1940): 6, 11, 18.
17. Pedro L. Baliña, José C. Belbey, and Alberto Zwanck, "La lucha antivenérea: Planteo del problema, directivas para su solución," *La Semana Médica* 42, 36 (September 5, 1935): 670.
18. Ibid., p. 671.
19. Carlos Eduardo Lucena, "Un factor de propagación venérea: La mujer de dancing. Resultado del exámen médico sistemático," *Revista Médica de Rosario* 28, 9 (1938): 984.
20. "Resultado de la ley en los años que lleva de aplicación," in *Administración sanitaria y asistencia social en Rosario: La ley 12.331. Resultados de su aplicación en Rosario* (Rosario, 1942).
21. Carella, *Picaresca porteña*, pp. 40–42.
22. Juan José Sebreli, *Buenos Aires: Vida cotidiana y alienación*, 15th ed. (Buenos Aires: Siglo XX, 1979), pp. 71–72.
23. Ernesto J. J. Bott, *Las condiciones de la lucha contra la trata de blancas* (Buenos Aires: Oceana, 1916), p. 12.

24. Roberto Arlt, "Ayer ví ganar a los argentinos," in Jean Cau et al., *El fútbol* (Buenos Aires: Jorge Alvarez, 1967), pp. 29–40. Martínez Estrada, *X-ray of the Pampa*, p. 277.

25. Ibid., p. 382. For a history of psychoanalysis in Argentina see Jorge Balán, *Profesión y identidad en una sociedad dividida: La medicina y el origen del psicoanálisis en la Argentina* (Buenos Aires: CEDES, 1988), p. 11.

26. Marcelo Mario Suárez-Orozco, "A Study of Argentine Soccer: The Dynamics of Its Fans and Their Folklore," *Journal of Psychoanalytic Anthropology* 3, 1 (Winter 1982): 7–28. A less Freudian and more anthropological view of soccer can be found in Eduardo Archetti, "Fútbol, violencia, y afirmación masculina," *Debates en la Sociedad y Cultura* 1 (April–May 1985): 38–44; and idem, "El fútbol y el otro machismo," *Palabra Suelta* 1 (1987): 12–16. The quotation is from Archetti, "Fútbol, violencia, y afirmación masculina," p. 40.

27. Juan José Sebreli, *Fútbol y masas* (Buenos Aires: Galerna, 1981), pp. 96–97.

28. Ibid., p. 163.

29. This decree has been reprinted in many documents. One example is *Boletín Administrativo de la Secretaría de Salud Pública de la Nación* 1, 3 (November–December 1946), p. 100. The origin of the decree seems to have been a draft of revisions to the Law of Social Profilaxis drawn up in 1943 by Drs. Miguel Palant and Elías García del Rey, Archivo del Ministerio de Salud Pública de la Nación.

30. Prudencio Plaza, Jefe de Sanidad para la Armada, "Proyecto de ley de creación de dispensarios para la profilaxis y tratamiento de las enfermedades venéreas y reglamentación de la prostitución," in Argentine Republic, Ministerio del Interior, Departamento Nacional de Higiene, *Conferencia sanitaria nacional: Buenos Aires, 1923* (Buenos Aires: Talleres Gráficos Editorial Argentina de Ciencias Políticas, 1923), pp. 276–80.

31. Carlos Luis Jauregui, *La homosexual en la Argentina* (Buenos Aires: Tarso, 1987), pp. 162–63.

32. Ibid., p. 163.

33. Castro, "Popular Culture as a Source for the Historian," pp. 10–11.

34. Satanowsky, *Obra cinematográfica frente al derecho*, 4:243.

35. Ibid., 4:249–52.

36. Ibid., 4:254–57, 306–8.

37. David Tamarin, *The Argentine Labor Movement, 1930–1945: A Study of the Origins of Peronism* (Albuquerque: University of New Mexico Press, 1985), chap. 7.

38. "Los dividendos del deporte," *Primera Plana*, September 6, 1966, p. 40.

39. "Fútbol y boxeo," *Primera Plana*, September 13, 1966, pp. 40–45.

40. Mentioned in Ramón Carrillo's speech of June 1, 1946, inaugurating the Secretariat of Public Health. Reprinted in Ramón Carrillo, *Política sanitaria argentina*, 2 vols. (Buenos Aires: Ministerio de Salud Pública de la Nación, 1949) 1:11–14; Rodolfo Alzugaray, "Ramón Carrillo y la salud pública," *Todo Es Historia* 1, 117 (February 1977): pp. 6–27.

41. Decreto 9.863, September 9, 1946, signed by Perón, Ramón Carrillo, and A. G. Borlenghi, carpeta 155, Archivo del Ministerio de Salud Pública de la Nación.

42. Ibid., article 8, p. 2.

43. Argentine Republic, Ministerio de Salud Pública de la Nación, *Perón habla a los médicos* (Buenos Aires: Ministerio de Salud Pública, 1950), p. 31.

44. Alejandro Dicovsky, "Plan de saneamiento venéreo: Capítulo inicial," *Archivos de la Secretaría de Salud Pública* 1, 2 (January 1947): 39.

45. Ibid., pp. 40–41.

46. Many of these reforms were already in place by 1948 when Dr. Oscar L. Camaño, director of social hygiene, wrote a letter describing these facilities to Julio G. Nougues, director of the código sanitario (sanitary code). Letter of September 14, 1948, Archivo del Ministerio de Salud Pública de la Nación.

47. "El abolicionismo no excluye la policía sanitaria," *Archivos de la Secretaría de Salud Pública* 4, 5 (November 1948): 387.

48. Ibid., p. 392.

49. "El problema de la prostitución," ibid., p. 421.

50. Nicolás V. Greco, "La ley 12.331 de profilaxis de las enfermedades venéreas debe reformarse," ibid., p. 450.

51. Ibid., p. 451.

52. Ibid., p. 355.

53. Argentine Republic, Secretaría de Salud Pública de la Nación, *Plan analítico de salud pública*, 2 vols. (Buenos Aires, 1947), 2:982–83.

54. Ibid., 2:985–89.

55. Ibid., 2:990–91.

56. Ibid., 2:992.

57. Ibid., 2:1011–12.

58. Ibid., 2:1018–19.

59. Argentine Republic, Cámara de Diputados, *Diario de Sesiones*, November 20 and 21, 1946, pp. 4–6.

60. Ibid., September 26, 1947, pp. 340–42.

61. Ibid., July 19–20, 1951, pp. 1131–32.

62. Guillermo F. Frugoni Rey, "Nuevamente en torno a la ley de profilaxis," *Criterio* 23, 1117 (June 1950): 389–90.

63. Luis María Baliña, "Orientación social, la verdadera profilaxis venerea," *Criterio* 25, 1165 (June 1952): 405–6.

64. Carrillo's press conferences as well as transcriptions of critical articles regarding the penicillin factory can be found in Carrillo, *Política sanitaria Argentina*, 1:119–31. He also gave the factory's inaugural address on May 19, 1949, ibid., 2:512–31.

65. Ernesto Goldar, *Buenos Aires: Vida cotidiana en la década del 50* (Buenos Aires: Plus Ultra, 1980), pp. 202–3.

66. "Antecedentes locales de la ley 12.331," in *Enciclopedia jurídica Omeba*, vol. 23 (Buenos Aires: Biblioteca Omeba, 1967), p. 663.

CONCLUSION

1. Francisco Ciccotti, *La trata de las blanquísimas* (Buenos Aires: Biblioteca "PAM," 1932), pp. 23, 97–101.

Bibliography

ARCHIVAL SOURCES
Archivo del Ministerio de Salud Pública de la Nación
Archivo General de la Nación Argentina (AGN)
Archivo Histórico de la Municipalidad de Buenos Aires (AHMBA)
Fawcett Library, City of London Polytechnic
    International Committee for the Suppression of White Slavery
National Vigilance Association International Bureau, National Vigilance
    Association Executive Minutes
National Vigilance Association Correspondence
National Archives of the United States of America
    Record Group 85
    Record Group 59
Public Record Office, Great Britain (PRO)

PERIODICALS
Actas del Consejo Municipal de la Ciudad de Buenos Aires
Anuario Estadístico de la Ciudad de Buenos Aires
Archivos de la Secretaría de Salud Pública
Boletín Administrativa de la Secretaría de Salud Pública de la Nación
Buenos Aires Herald
Le Bulletin Continental
Caras y Caretas
Criterio
El Diario
Gaceta del Foro

Gaceta Textil
La Nación
New York Times
El País
La Patria Argentina
La Prensa
Primera Plana
El Puente de los Suspiros
La República
Standard
Times (London)
Todo es Historia
La Tribuna
La Vanguardia
Vida Femenina
Vigilance Record

SECONDARY SOURCES

Abad de Santillán, Diego. *Gran encyclopedia argentina*. 9 vols. Buenos
   Aires: Ediar, 1956–64.

Aberg Cobo, Martín. *Contralor de la moralidad pública*. Buenos Aires:
   Francisco A. Colombo, 1941.

Aftalión, Enrique R. "Prostitución, proxenetismo y delito." *Revista de
   Policía y Criminalística de Buenos Aires* 4, 19 (April–June 1940): 4–20.

Agresti, Mabel Susana. "Manuel Gálvez y la novela realista." *Todo es
   Historia* 16, 187 (December 1982): 81–91.

Alberdi, Juan Bautista. *Obras completas*. 8 vols. Buenos Aires: Imprenta de
   la Tribuna Nacional, 1887.

Alsogaray, Julio L. *Trilogía de la trata de blancas: Rufianes—policía—
   municipalidad*. 2d ed. Buenos Aires: Tor, n.d.

Anderson, Benedict R. O. *Imagined Communities: Reflections on the Origin
   and Spread of Nationalism*. London: Verso, 1983.

Alzugaray, Rodolfo. "Ramón Carrillo y la salud pública." *Todo Es Historia*
   1, 117 (February 1977): 6–27.

Archetti, Eduardo. "El fútbol y el otro machismo." *Palabra Suelta* 1
   (1987): 12–16.

_____. "Fútbol, violencia, y afirmación masculina." *Debates en la Sociedad y
   la Cultura* 1 (April–May 1985): 38–44.

Argentine Republic. *Boletín Oficial.* 1913–55.

_____. *Código civil.* Buenos Aires: Pablo E. Coni, 1874.

_____. *Ordenanzas generales de la policía de Buenos Aires, 1880–1907.* Buenos Aires, 1907.

_____. *Primer censo de la República Argentina verificado en los días 15, 16 y 17 de septiembre de 1869.* Buenos Aires: Imprenta del Porvenir, 1872.

Argentine Republic, Cámara de Diputados. *Diario de Sesiones.* 1907–54.

Argentine Republic, Cámara de Senadores. *Diario de Sesiones.* 1907–54.

Argentine Republic, Comisión Directiva del Censo. *Segundo censo de la República Argentina.* 3 vols. Buenos Aires: Taller Tipográfico de la Penitenciaria Nacional, 1898.

_____. *Tercer Censo nacional de la República Argentina.* 10 vols. Buenos Aires: L. J. Rosso, 1917–19.

Argentine Republic, Departamento Nacional del Trabajo, División de Estadística. *Industria textil.* Buenos Aires, 1939.

Argentine Republic, Ministerio del Interior, Departamento Nacional de Higiene. *Conferencia sanitaria nacional: Buenos Aires, 1923.* Buenos Aires: Editorial Argentina de Ciencias Políticas, 1923.

Argentine Republic, Ministerio de Salud Pública de la Nación. *Perón habla a los médicos.* Buenos Aires: Ministerio de Salud Pública, 1950.

_____. *Personal directivo del Ministerio de Salud Pública: Asignación de funciones.* Buenos Aires: Ministerio de Salud Pública de la Nación, 1949.

Argentine Republic, Secretaría de Salud Pública de la Nación. *Plan analítico de salud pública.* 2 vols. Buenos Aires, 1947.

Arlt, Roberto. *The Seven Madmen.* Trans. Naomi Lindstrom. Boston: David R. Godine, 1984.

_____. *Los siete locos; Los lanzallamas.* Caracas: Biblioteca Ayacucho, 1978.

Asociación Nacional Argentina contra la Trata de Blancas. *Memoria,* 1902–8.

Avedaño, L. "Reglamentación de la prostitución." *La Crónica Médica* 9, 98 (February 29, 1892): 29–30.

Avni, Haim. *Argentina y la historia de la inmigración judía 1810–1850.* Jerusalem: Universitaria Magnes, Universidad Hebrea de Jerusalem, 1983.

Bagú, Sergio. *Vida de José Ingenieros.* Buenos Aires: EUDEBA, 1963.

Balán, Jorge. *Profesión y identidad en una sociedad dividida: La medicina y el origen del psicoanálisis en la Argentina.* Buenos Aires: CEDES, 1988.

Balestra, Juan. *El noventa: Una evolución política argentina.* Buenos Aires: Luis Fariña, 1971.

Baliña, Luis María. "Orientación social, la verdadera profilaxis venérea." *Criterio* 25, 1165 (June 1952): 405–6.

Baliña, Pedro L. "El problema de la prostitución." *Archivos de la Secretaría de Salud Pública* 4, 5 (November 1948): 415–39.

_____. "'Enfermedades secretas': Concepto y expresión que no deben subsistir." *Revista Argentina de Dermatosifilogía* 15 (1931): 137.

Baliña, Pedro L., José C. Belbey, and Alberto Zwanck. "La lucha antivenérea." *La Semana Médica* 42, 36 (September 5, 1935): 669–81.

Barran, José Pedro, Benjamín Nahum, Diego Armus, María Elena Langdon, Jorge E. Hardoy, Pancho Liernur, Olga Paterlini de Koch, Juan Rial, Graciela M. Viñuales, Vicente E. Espinoza, Juan Suriano, Leandro Gutiérrez, Ricardo González, and María Angélica Illanes Oliva. *Sectores populares y vida urbana.* Buenos Aires: CLACSO, 1984.

Barry, Kathleen. *Female Sexual Slavery.* New York: Avon, 1979.

Batiz, Adolfo. *Buenos Aires, la ribera y los prostíbulos en 1880.* Buenos Aires: AGA-TAURA, n.d.

Bermann, Gregorio. "Sobre una 'prostituta nata.'" *Primera Conferencia Latino-Americana de Neurología, Psiquiatría y Medicina Legal* 2 (1928): 711.

Bermann, Gregorio, and J. A. Herrera. "Forma nueva y peligrosa de tráfico venéreo." *Revista Argentina de Dermatosifilogía* 19 (1935): 311.

Bernaqui Jaureguy, Carlos Alberto. *Estudio dogmático-crítico sobre la Ley de Profilaxis Antivenérea (12.331).* 2 vols. Buenos Aires: PROCMO, 1950.

Bessero, Victorio Luis. *Los tratantes de blancas en Buenos Aires: El escándalo de la pseuda sociedad "Varsovia" o "Migdal."* Buenos Aires, 1930.

Beter, Clara. *Versos de una . . .* Buenos Aires: Claridad, n.d.

Bialet-Massé, Juan. *El estado de las clases obreras argentinas a comienzos del siglo.* Córdoba: Universidad Nacional de Córdoba, 1968.

Billington-Grieg, Teresa. "The Truth about White Slavery." *English Review,* June 1913.

Blackwelder, Julia Kirk, and Lyman Johnson. "Changing Criminal Patterns in Buenos Aires, 1890–1914." *Journal of Latin American Studies* 14, 2 (1982): 359–80.

Blanco Amores de Pagella, Angela. *Motivaciones del teatro argentino en el siglo XX.* Buenos Aires: Ediciones Culturales Argentina, 1973.

Bott, Ernesto J. J. *Las condiciones de la lucha contra la trata de blancas.* Buenos Aires: Oceana, 1916.

Bra, Gerardo. *La organización negra: La increíble historia de la Zwi Migdal.* Buenos Aires: Corregidor, 1982.

Brandt, Allan. *No Magic Bullet: A Social History of Venereal Disease in the United States since 1880.* New York: Oxford University Press, 1985.

Brantlinger, Patrick. *Bread and Circuses: Theories of Mass Culture as Social Decay.* Ithaca: Cornell University Press, 1983.

Bristow, Edward J. *Prostitution and Prejudice: The Jewish Fight against White Slavery, 1870–1939.* Oxford: Clarendon Press, 1982.

———. *Vice and Vigilance: Purity Movements in Britain since 1700.* Dublin: Gill and Macmillan, 1977.

Bucich Escobar, Ismael. *Buenos Aires ciudad.* Buenos Aires: El Ateneo, 1930.

Buenos Aires Municipality. *Anuario estadístico de la ciudad de Buenos Aires.* 1889–1923.

———. *Censo general de población, edificación, comercio e industrias de la ciudad de Buenos Aires.* 2 vols. Buenos Aires: Cía. Sud-Americana de Billetes de Banco, 1889.

———. *Censo general de población, edificación, comercio e industrias de la ciudad de Buenos Aires.* 3 vols. Buenos Aires: Sud-Americana de Billetes de Banco, 1910.

———. *Dictámenes de la asesoría municipal, 1878–1894.* 3 vols. Buenos Aires: Imprenta de la Lotería Nacional, 1896.

———. *Memoria de la Dirección General de la Administración Pública correspondiente al año 1910.* Buenos Aires: La Semana Médica, 1911.

———. *Sentencias y resoluciones judiciales en asuntos de carácter municipal.* 3 vols. Buenos Aires: Imprenta de la Lotería Nacional, 1895.

———. *Memorias de la Dirección General de la Administración Sanitaria y Asistencia Pública correspondientes a los años 1906, 1907, 1908 y 1909 por Dres. José Penna y Horacio Madero.* Buenos Aires: La Semana Médica, 1910.

———. *Memorias de la Municipalidad.* 1859–1955.

———. *Statistical Yearbook for the City of Buenos Aires.* Buenos Aires, 1913.

Buenos Aires Municipality, Comisión Municipal de la Ciudad de Buenos Aires. *Actas de la Comisión Municipal de la Ciudad de Buenos Aires,* 1864–1936.

Buenos Aires Municipality, Dirección General de Administración Sanitaria y Asistencia Pública. *Resumen de la memoria de la Administración Sanitaria y Asistencia Pública correspondiente al año 1926.* Buenos Aires: Talleres Gráficos Tuduri, 1927.

Buenos Aires Municipality, Dirección General de Estadística Municipal. *Boletín Mensual de la Municipalidad de Buenos Aires,* 1886–.

Buenos Aires Police. *Memoria de la Policía de Buenos Aires.* 1906–9.

Buenos Aires Province. *Censo general de la ciudad de La Plata, capital de la provincia.* La Plata: "La Popular," 1910.

Bullough, Vern L., and James Brundage, eds. *Sexual Practices and the Medieval Church.* Buffalo, N.Y.: Prometheus Books, 1982.

Bullough, Vern L., and Bonnie Bullough. *Women and Prostitution: A Social History.* Buffalo, N.Y.: Prometheus Books, 1987.

Bullrich, Rafael Augusto. *Francisco A. Sicardi.* Buenos Aires: Talleres Gráficos de Anicto López, 1944.

C. y A. *La prostitución en Buenos Aires.* Buenos Aires: Courrier de la Plata, 1885.

Cacopardo, María. *Argentina: Aspectos demográficos de la población económicamente activa en el período 1869–1895.* Santiago: Celade, 1969.

Camaño, Oscar A. L. "Prostitución." *El Día Médico* 21, 30 (June 13, 1949): 1161–66.

Cantón, Darío. *Gardel: ¿A quién le cantás?* Buenos Aires: Ediciones de la Flor, 1972.

Carella, Tulio. *Picaresca porteña.* Buenos Aires: Siglo XX, 1966.

Carluci, Francisco (Jefe Dispensario 16). "El problema de las enfermedades venéreas en nuestra Capital Federal." *Revista de la Asociación Argentina de Venereología y Profilaxis Social* 10, 10 (December 1946): 37–44.

Carrera, José Luis, and Benon Reinecke. "Estadística de infecciones venéreas durante los diez primeras meses de vigencia de la ordenanza sobre moralidad." *Archivos de la Asociación de Médicos del Hospital Salaberry* 11, 5 (December 1935): 235–37.

Carretero, Andrés M. *El compadrito y el tango.* Buenos Aires: Pampa y Cielo, 1964.

Carrillo, Ramón. *Política sanitaria argentina.* 2 vols. Buenos Aires: Ministerio de Salud Pública de la Nación, 1949.

Casadevall, Domingo F. *Buenos Aires: Arrabal, sainete, tango.* Buenos Aires: Fabril, 1968.

_____. *El tema de la mala vida en el teatro nacional.* Buenos Aires: Guillermo Kraft, 1957.

Castro, Donald. "Popular Culture as a Source for the Historian: The Tango under Perón, 1943–1955." Paper presented at the Latin American Studies Association, Boston, October 1986.

Cau, Jean, et al. *El fútbol*. Buenos Aires: Jorge Alvarez, 1967.

Ciccotti, Francisco. *La trata de las blanquísimas*. Buenos Aires: Biblioteca "PAM," 1932.

Cohen, Samuel. *Report of the Secretary on His Visit to South America, 1913*. Oxford: Jewish Association for the Protection of Girls and Women, 1913.

Collier, Simon. *The Life, Times, and Music of Carlos Gardel*. Pittsburgh: University of Pittsburgh Press, 1986.

Coni, Emilio. "Algunos datos relativos a la mortalidad de la ciudad de Buenos Aires durante el año 1876." *Revista Médico-quirúrgica* 14, 12 (September 1877): 271–72.

———. "Casas de sanidad para prostitutas." *Anales de Higiene Pública y Medicina Legal* 3, 1 (March 1893): 3.

———. *Causes de la morbidité et de la mortalité de la première enfance à Buénos Ayres*. Buenos Aires: Paul-Emile Coni, 1886.

———. *Código de higiene y medicina legal de la República Argentina*. 2 vols. Buenos Aires: Juan Etchepareborda, 1891.

———. *Cómo combatir las enfermedades venéreas en mi ciudad*. Buenos Aires, 1924.

———. *El estado actual de la lucha antivenérea en América*. Buenos Aires: A. de Martino, 1921.

———. *Higiene aplicada a la provincia de Corrientes*. Buenos Aires: Pablo E. Coni, 1898.

———. *Higiene pública: El servicio sanitario de la ciudad de Buenos Aires*. Buenos Aires: Pablo E. Coni, 1880.

———. *Memorias de un médico higienista*. Buenos Aires: A. Flaiban, 1918.

———. *Progrès de l'hygiène dans le République Argentine*. Paris: J.-B. Ballière, 1887.

———. *Reseña estadística y descriptiva de La Plata*. Buenos Aires: Establecimiento Tipográfico de La República.

Coni, Gabriela Laperrière de. *Proyecto de ley de protección del trabajo de la mujer y del niño en las fábricas presentado a la intendencia municipal*. Buenos Aires: Liga Argentina contra la Tuberculosis, 1902.

Coote, William A. *A Romance of Philanthropy*. London: National Vigilance Association, 1916.

Crassweller, Robert. *Perón and the Enigmas of Argentina*. New York: W. W. Norton, 1987.

Crider, Ernest A. "Modernization and Human Welfare: The Asistencia

Publica and Buenos Aires, 1883–1910." Ph.D. diss., Ohio State University, 1976.

Cuello, Nicolás. *Acción femenina*. Buenos Aires, 1939.

Cuneo, Carlos, and Abel González. *La delincuencia*. No. 54. *La historia popular*. Buenos Aires: Centro Editor, 1971.

Cutolo, Vicente Osvaldo. *Nuevo diccionario biográfico argentino*. 7 vols. Buenos Aires: Elche, 1968–.

Dávalos y Lissón, Pedro. *La prostitución en la ciudad de Lima*. Lima: Imprenta La Industria, 1909.

De Cires, E. "La criminalidad en Buenos Aires (carta abierta)." *Revista Argentina de Ciencias Políticas* 2, 22 (July 1912): 493–501.

De Lara, Tomás, and Inés Leonilda Roncetti de Panti. *El tema del tango en la literatura argentina*. Buenos Aires: Ediciones Culturales Argentinas, 1961.

Deutsch, Sandra McGee. *Counter Revolution in Argentina, 1990–1932: The Argentine Patriotic League*. Lincoln: University of Nebraska Press, 1986.

De Veyga, Francisco. "Inversión sexual adquerida: Tipo profesional." *Archivos de Psiquiatría, Criminología y Ciencias Afines* 4, 3 (April 1903): 193–208.

———. "El amor en los invertidos sexuales." *Archivos de Psiquiatría, Criminología y Ciencias Afines* 2, 6 (May 1903): 333–41.

———. "La inversión sexual adquerida: Tipo profesional, un invertido comerciante." *Archivos de Psiquiatría, Criminología y Ciencias Afines* 2, 8 (August 1903): 492–96.

———. "Los auxiliares del vicio y del delito." *Archivos de Psiquiatría, Criminología y Ciencias Afines* 3 (May–June 1904): 289–313.

Dicovsky, Alejandro. "Plan de saneamiento venéreo: Capítulo inicial." *Archivos de la Secretaría de Salud Pública* 1, 2 (January 1947): 39–45.

[La Dirección]. "El abolicionismo no excluye la policía sanitaria." *Archivos de la Secretaría de Salud Pública* 4, 5 (November 1948): 387–92.

Dis, Emilio. *Código lunfardo*. Buenos Aires: Editorial Caburé, 1976.

Domínguez, Silverio [Ceferino de la Calle]. *Palomas y gavilanes*. Buenos Aires: Libraire Générale, 1888.

Donzelot, Jacques. *The Policing of Families*. Trans. Robert Hurley. New York: Pantheon Books, 1977.

Dos Santos, Esta. *Las mujeres del tango*. Buenos Aires: Centro Editor de América Latina, 1972.

Dupont, Benjamín. *Pornografía de Buenos Aires: De la necesidad imprescindible de un dispensario de salubridad y de una oficina de costumbres para reglamentar y reprimir la prostitución.* Buenos Aires: Pablo E. Coni, 1879.

Ehrenberg, Lewis A. *Steppin' Out: New York Nightlife and the Transformation of American Culture, 1890–1930.* Chicago: University of Chicago Press, 1981.

Eiris, Ernesto. "Los certificados de salud de las mujeres contratadas en las cabarets de Rosario." *Publicaciones Médicas* 3, 11 (March 1937): 1–11.

———. *Para una patria grande, un pueblo sano.* 2d ed. Buenos Aires: Fabril Financiera, 1939.

———. *Trece años de acción profiláctica.* Buenos Aires: La Gráfica, 1931.

Enciclopedia jurídica Omeba. Buenos Aires: Biblioteca Omeba, 1967.

Evans, Richard J. "Prostitution, State and Society in Imperial Germany." *Past and Present* 70 (1976): 106–29.

Fédération Abolitionniste Internationale. *Dixième Congrès tenu à Genève, le 7–11 septembre 1908.* Geneva: Secrétariat Général de la Fédération, 1909.

Feijó, María del Carmen. "Las luchas feministas." *Todo Es Historia* 128 (January 1978): 6–23.

Fernández, José M. M. "La experiencia abolicionista de Rosario." *Revista Médica del Rosario* 24, 8 (August 1934): 750–59.

Fernández Verano, Alfredo. "Acción de la Liga Argentina de Profilaxis Social." In *Para una patria grande, un pueblo sano.* 2d ed. Buenos Aires: Fabril Financiera, 1939.

———. "Lucha antivenérea en la Argentina: Acción desarrollada por la Liga Argentina de Profilaxis Social." *La Semana Médica* 31 (1924): 513–16.

Ferrer, Horacio. *El libro de tango: Arte popular de Buenos Aires.* Buenos Aires, 1980.

Ferrero, Roberto A. "La marginalia cordobesa." *Todo es Historia* 184 (September 1982): 68–91.

The Fifth International Congress for the Suppression of the White Slave Traffic. London: National Vigilance Association, 1913.

Foresti, Brito. "Profilaxis de las enfermedades venéreas y reglamentación de la prostitución." *La Semana Médica* 26 (April 1919): 16–20.

Foster, David. *Currents in the Contemporary Argentine Novel.* Columbia: University of Missouri Press, 1975.

_____. "'Narrative Rights' in the Argentine Tango." *Symposium* 37 (1983–84): 261–71.

Foucault, Michel. *The Birth of the Clinic: An Archeology of Medical Perception.* Trans. A. M. Sheridan Smith. New York: Vintage Books, 1975.

_____. *Discipline and Punish: The Birth of the Prison.* Trans. Alan Sheridan. New York: Random House, 1979.

_____. *The History of Sexuality.* Vol. 1. An Introduction. Trans. Robert Hurley. New York: Pantheon Books, 1978.

_____. *Madness and Civilization: A History of Insanity in the Age of Reason.* Trans. Richard Howard. New York: Vintage Books, 1973.

Fraser, Nicholas, and Marysa Navarro. *Eva Perón.* New York: W. W. Norton, 1985.

Freire, Gilberto. *Ordem e progresso.* 2 vols. Rio de Janeiro: José Olympio, 1959.

Freundlich de Seefeld, Ruth. "La integración social de extranjeros en Buenos Aires: Según sus pautas matrimoniales, ¿Pluralismo cultural o crisol de razas? (1860–1923)." *Estudios Migratorios Latinoamericanos* 1, 2 (April 1986): 203–11.

Frugoni Rey, Guillermo F. "Nuevamente en torno a la ley de profilaxis." *Criterio* 23, 1117 (June 1950): 389–90.

Galasso, Norberto. *Discépolo y su época.* Buenos Aires: Jorge Alvarez, 1967.

_____. *Escritos inéditos de Enrique Santos Discépolo.* Buenos Aires: Ediciones de Pensamiento Nacional, 1981.

Gallarani, Carlos. "Reglamentación de la prostitución: Fundamentos de esta importante medida de hijiene pública. Proyecto adaptable a la ciudad del Rosario (República Arjentina)." *Revista Médico-quirúrgica* 6 (1869–70).

Gallo, Blas Raúl. *Historia del sainete nacional.* Buenos Aires: Buenos Aires Leyendo, 1970.

Gálvez, Manuel. *Historia de arrabal.* Buenos Aires: Deucalion, 1956.

_____. *La inseguridad de la vida obrera.* Buenos Aires: Alsina, 1913.

_____. *Nacha Regules.* Buenos Aires: Centro Editor de América Latina, 1968.

_____. *Recuerdos de la vida literaria.* 4 vols. Buenos Aires: Hachette, 1961.

_____. *La trata de blancas: Tesis para optar al grado de doctor en jurisprudencia.* Buenos Aires: José Tragant, 1905.

Garzon, Rafael, Jr., Albino Pierini, and Luis E. Rodríguez. "Reglamentarismo y abolicionismo en la República Argentina." *Acta Médica de Córdoba* 12, 2 (1967): 94–97.

Gibson, Mary. *Prostitution and the State in Italy, 1860–1915.* New Brunswick: Rutgers University Press, 1986.

Gilman, Sander L. *Jewish Self-Hatred: Anti-Semitism and the Hidden Language of the Jews.* Baltimore: Johns Hopkins University Press, 1986.

Giménez, Angel M. *Contra la reglamentación de la prostitución. Abolición de las ordenanzas municipales y profilaxis de las enfermedades venéreas. Proyectos y discursos pronunciados en el Consejo Deliberante de Buenos Aires en las sesiones del 7 de enero, 16, 19 y 21 de mayo de 1919.* Buenos Aires: Sociedad Luz, n.d.

———. *El problema sexual: La reglamentación de la prostitución y la represión de la trata de blancas ante la justicia penal.* Buenos Aires: Sociedad Luz, 1930.

———. *La reglamentación de la prostitución y la represión de la trata de blancas ante la justicia penal: Proyecto de ley presentado a la Cámara de Diputados en la sesión del 20 de junio de 1917.* Buenos Aires: La Semana Médica, 1918.

Goldar, Ernesto. *Buenos Aires: Vida cotidiana an la década del 50.* Buenos Aires: Plus Ultra, 1980.

———. *La "mala vida."* Buenos Aires: Centro Editor de América Latina, 1971.

———. *Proceso a Roberto Arlt.* Buenos Aires: Editorial Plus Ultra, 1985.

Gómez, Eusebio. "La mala vida." *Archivos de Psiquiatría, Criminología y Ciencias Afines* 6 (1907): 434–35.

———. *La mala vida en Buenos Aires.* Introduction by José Ingenieros. Buenos Aires: Juan Roldan, 1908.

González Castillo, José. *Los invertidos.* Buenos Aires: Argentores Ediciones del Carro de Tespis, 1957.

Gostautas, Stasys. *Buenos Aires y Arlt (Dostoievsky, Martínez Estrada y Scalabrini Ortiz).* Madrid: Insula, 1977.

Guy, Donna J. "Emilio and Gabriela Coni: Reformers, Public Health, and Working Women." In *The Human Tradition in Latin America: The Nineteenth Century,* ed. Judith Ewell and William Beezley. Wilmington, Del.: Scholarly Resources, 1989.

———. "Lower-Class Families, Women and the Law in Nineteenth-

Century Argentina." *Journal of Family History* 10, 3 (Fall 1985): 318–31.

———. "Prostitution and Female Criminality in Buenos Aires, 1875–1937." In *The Problem of Order in Changing Societies: Essays on Crime and Policing in Argentina and Uruguay, 1750–1940,* ed. Lyman L. Johnson. Albuquerque: University of New Mexico Press, 1990.

———. "Public Health, Gender and Private Morality: Paid Labor and the Formation of the Body Politic in Buenos Aires." *Gender and History* 2, 3 (Autumn 1990): 297–317.

———. "White Slavery, Public Health and the Socialist Position on Legalized Prostitution in Argentina, 1913–1936." *Latin American Research Review* 23, 3 (1988): 60–80.

———. "Women, Peonage and Industrialization: Argentina, 1810–1914." *Latin American Research Review* 16, 3 (Fall 1981): 65–89.

Harris, H. Wilson. *Human Merchandise: A Study of the International Traffic in Women.* London: Ernest Benn, 1928.

Harsin, Jill. *Policing Prostitution in Nineteenth-Century Paris.* Princeton: Princeton University Press, 1985.

Hollander, Nancy Caro. "Women in the Political Economy of Argentina." Ph.D. diss., University of California, Los Angeles, 1974.

Hyams, L. L. *Lettre ouverte addressé par un homme aux jeunes filles.* Bordeaux: Edition du "Rélévement Social," [1929].

Ingenieros, José. *La criminología.* Buenos Aires: Penitenciaria Nacional, 1911.

———. *Criminología.* Madrid: Daniel Jorre, 1913.

———. *El delito y la pena ante la filosofía biológica.* Buenos Aires: Penitenciaría Nacional, 1910.

———. *"Hacia la justicia": La piedad homicida.* Buenos Aires: Pablo Ingegnieros, n.d.

———. *La législation du travail dans la République Argentina: Essai critique sur le projet du ministre Gonzalez.* Trans. Charles Barthez. Paris: Edouard Cornély, 1906.

———. *Obras completas revisadas y anotadas por Anibal Ponce.* Vol. 23. *Tratado del amor.* Buenos Aires: L. F. Rosso, 1940.

———. *Sistema penitenciario.* Buenos Aires: Penitenciaria Nacional, 1911.

Instituto Alejandro E. Bunge. *Soluciones argentinas a los problemas económicas y sociales del presente.* Buenos Aires: Kraft, 1945.

International Abolitionist Federation. *Caractère de la fédération.* Geneva, 1899.

_____. *Cinquième congrès international tenu du 10 au 13 septembre 1889 à Genève: Compte rendu officiel des travaux de congrès.* Geneva, 1890.

In the Grip of the White Slave Trader. [By the author of *The White Slave Traffic*]. London: MAP, n.d.

Irizar, José Manuel. "Reglamento de la prostitución." *Anales del Departamento Nacional de Higiene* 4, 15 (December 1902): 775–90.

_____. "Servicio sanitario de la prostitución." *Anales del Departamento Nacional de Higiene*, 1904, p. 107.

Jauregui, Carlos Luis. *La homosexual en la Argentina.* Buenos Aires: Tarso, 1987.

Jewish Association for the Protection of Girls and Women [JAPGW]. *Annual Reports.* 1904–32.

_____. *Official Report of the Jewish International Conference on the Suppression of the Traffic in Girls and Women: Private and Confidential Report.* London: JAPGW, 1910.

Johansson, Gunilla. "Life Chances: Prostitutes in the Swedish Reglamentation System, 1850–1915." Paper presented at the seventh Berkshire Conference on the History of Women, Wellesley College, June 20, 1987.

Kaplan, Marion A. *The Jewish Feminist Movement in Germany: The Campaigns of the Judischer Frauenbund, 1904–1938.* Westport, Conn.: Greenwood Press, 1979.

Klemensiewicz, Rolf. "El problema de la lucha antivenérea en el Chaco Santafesino." *La Semana Médica* 36, 1 (January 3, 1929): 27–35.

Klimpel, Felicitas. *La mujer, el delito, y la sociedad.* Buenos Aires: El Ateneo, 1945.

Korn, Frances. *Buenos Aires: Los huéspedes del 20.* Buenos Aires: Editorial Sudamericana, 1974.

Lafuente Machain, R. de. *Buenos Aires en el siglo XVII.* Buenos Aires: EMECE, 1944.

Lancelotti, M. A. "La criminalidad en Buenos Aires, 1885–1910." *Revista Argentina de Ciencias Políticas* 2, 21 (June 1912): 346–42.

Lanteri, Julieta. "La prostitución." In *Primero congreso femenino internacional de la república Argentina.* Buenos Aires: A. Ceppi, 1911.

Lavrin, Asunción. "The Ideology of Feminism in the Southern Cone, 1900–1940." Wilson Center Working Paper no. 169. Washington, D.C., 1986.

Lazarte, Juan. *Sociedad y prostitución.* Rosario: Argus, 1935.

_____. *Sociología de la prostitución.* Buenos Aires: Kier, 1945.

League of Nations. *Nationality and Status of Women: Statements Presented by International Women's Organizations.* Geneva, 1935.

_____. *Report of the Special Body of Experts on Traffic in Women and Children.* 2 parts. Geneva, 1927.

League of Nations, Advisory Committee on Social Questions. *Enquiry into Measures of Rehabilitation of Prostitutes: Conclusions and Recommendations.* 4 parts. Geneva, 1939.

League of Nations, Traffic in Women and Children Committee. *Abolition of Licensed Houses.* Geneva, 1935.

Leland, Christopher Towne. *The Last Happy Men: The Generation of 1922, Fiction and the Argentine Reality.* Syracuse: Syracuse University Press, 1986.

Lichtblau, Myron. "The Argentine Novel in the Nineteenth Century." Ph.D. diss., Columbia University, 1957.

_____. *Manuel Gálvez.* New York: Twayne, 1972.

Liga Argentina de Profilaxis Social. *Por la salud de la raza.* Buenos Aires: Gráfico Argentino, 1936.

_____. *Volantes.*

Lipp, Solomon. *Three Argentine Thinkers.* New York: Philosophical Library, 1969.

Little, Cynthia Jeffress. "The Society of Beneficence in Buenos Aires, 1823–1900." Ph.D. diss., Temple University, 1980.

Lombroso, Caesar, and William Ferrero. *The Female Offender.* London: T. Fisher Unwin, 1895.

Londres, Albert. *The Road to Buenos Ayres.* Trans. Eric Sutton. New York: Blue Ribbon Books, 1928.

Looyer, Dr. *Los grandes misterios de la mala vida en Buenos Aires comparada con la de las grandes capitales europeos.* Buenos Aires: Rafael Palumbo, 1911.

López Bagó, Eduardo. *Carne importada (costumbres de Buenos Aires): Novela médico-social.* Buenos Aires, n.d.

Loudet, Osvaldo. *Figuras próximas y lejanas al margen de la historia.* Buenos Aires: Academia Argentina de Letras, 1970.

_____. *Médicos argentinos.* Buenos Aires: Huemul, 1966.

Lucena, Carlos Eduardo. "Un factor de propagación venérea: La mujer de dancing. Resultado del exámen médico sistemático." *Revista Médica de Rosario* 28, 9 (September 1938): 983–87.

Luisi, Paulina. "Algunas consideraciones sobre prostitución y enfermedades venéreas." *Congreso Médico del Centenario 5 a 12 de octubre de 1930*. Vol. 4. Montevideo: A. Monteverde, 1930.

_____. *Bases y propósitos de la Federación Abolicionista Internacional*. Buenos Aires: "Juan Perrotti," 1919.

_____. *El problema de la prostitución: Abolicionismo o reglamentarismo*. Montevideo: La Industrial, 1921.

_____. *A propósito de los proyectos sobre moralidad*. Palabras pronunciadas en la asamblea verificada por la Federación Abolicionista en la Sociedad Científica Argentina el día 24 de abril de 1919. Buenos Aires: "J. Perrotti," 1919.

_____. *Una vergüenza social. La reglamentación de la prostitución. Conferencia dada en la Asociación Cristiana de Jóvenes de Buenos Aires, sept. 1918*. Buenos Aires: J. Perrotti, 1919.

Macías, Anna. *Against All Odds: The Feminist Movement in Mexico to 1940*. Westport, Conn.: Greenwood Press, 1982.

McCreery, David. "Una vida de miseria y verguenza: Prostitución femenina en la ciudad de Guatemala, 1880–1920." *Mesoamérica* 7, 11 (June 1986): 35–59.

McHugh, Paul. *Prostitution and Victorian Social Reform*. London: Croom Helm, 1980.

Mafud, Julio. *Sociología del tango*. Buenos Aires: Américalee, 1966.

Martínez, Alberto B. *Censo general de la población, edificación, comercio e industrias de la ciudad de Buenos Aires*. 3 vols. Buenos Aires: Cía. Sud-Americana de Billetes de Banco, 1910.

Martínez Estrada, Ezequiel. *X-ray of the Pampa*. Trans. Alain Swietlicki. Austin: University of Texas Press, 1971.

Matamoro, Blas. *La ciudad del tango: Tango histórico y sociedad*. 2d ed. Buenos Aires: Galerna, 1982.

Mejías, Laurentino C. *La policía por dentro: Mis cuentos*. Barcelona: Viuda de Luis Tasso, 1913.

Méndez Avellaneda, Juan María. "El motín de la 'Lady Shore.'" *Todo Es Historia* 265 (July 1989): 6–27.

Merkel, Felipe. *Reglamentación de la prostitución en Lima*. Lima: Gil, 1908.

Mirelman, Victor A. "The Jews in Argentina (1890–1930): Assimilation and Particularism." Ph.D. diss., Columbia University, 1973.

Molyneux, Maxine. "No God, No Boss, No Husband: Anarchist Feminism in Nineteenth-Century Argentina." *Latin American Perspectives* 13, 1 (Winter 1986): 119–45.

Montero, Belisario. "La profilaxia internacional de la sífilis: Comunicación oficial." *Archivos de Psiquiatría, Criminología y Ciencias Afines* 2, 12 (December 1903): 715–21.

_____. [Consul general de la Argentina en Bélgica]. "Trata de blancas y moralidad pública." *Archivos de Psiquiatría, Criminología y Ciencias Afines* 2, 12 (December 1903): 722–30.

_____. "The White Slave Trade in South America." *Proceedings of the International Conference of Women Physicians.* Vol. 6. New York: Women's Press, 1920.

Mosse, George. *Nationalism and Sexuality: Respectability and Abnormal Sexuality in Modern Europe.* New York: Howard Fertig, 1985.

Muzilli, Carolina. *El trabajo femenino.* Buenos Aires: L. J. Rosso, 1916.

National Vigilance Association. *Congress of the White Slave Traffic.* London: National Vigilance Association, 1899.

_____. *Fourth Annual Report of the Executive Committee, November 26, 1889.* London, 1889.

_____. *Fifth Annual Report of the Executive Committee, November 26, 1890.* London, 1890.

Newman, Kathleen Elizabeth. "The Argentine Political Novel: Determinations in Discourse." Ph.D. diss., Stanford University, 1983.

Nuñez, Ricardo C. *Derecho penal argentino.* Vol. 4. Buenos Aires: Biblioteca Omeba, 1964.

Ocampo, Miguel. *Otra revista.* Buenos Aires: La Industria, 1891.

Oliva, Silvestre. "Proyecto de la ordenanza reglamentaria de la prostitución." In *Proceedings of the Second Pan American Scientific Conference,* vol. 9, sec. 8, part 1. Washington, D.C.: Government Printing Office, 1917.

Onselen, Charles van. *Studies in the Social and Economic History of the Witwatersrand, 1886–1914.* Vol. 1. *New Babylon.* New York: Longman, 1982.

Otis, Leah Lydia. *Prostitution in Medieval Society: The History of an Urban Institution in Languedoc.* Chicago: University of Chicago Press, 1985.

Oved, Iaacov. *El anarquismo y el movimiento obrero en Argentina.* Mexico City: Siglo XXI, 1978.

Pagano, José León, Jr. *Criminalidad argentina.* Buenos Aires: Depalma, 1964.

Page, Joseph A. *Perón: A Biography.* New York: Random House, 1983.

Palacios, Alfredo. *La defensa del valor humano: Legislación social argentina.* Buenos Aires: Claridad, 1939.

Pampín, Manuel, ed. *La historia del tango*. Vol. 1. *Sus orígines*. Buenos
Aires: Corregidor, 1976.

_____. *La historia del tango*. Vol. 2. *Primera época*. Buenos Aires:
Corregidor, 1977.

_____. *La historia del tango*. Vol. 6. *Los años veinte*. Buenos Aires:
Corregidor, 1977.

Pareja, Ernesto M. *La prostitución en Buenos Aires*. Buenos Aires: Tor,
1936.

Parras Castañeda, Juan de. *Prostitución: Estudio de proyecto para su
reglamentación*. Buenos Aires: Martínez, 1884.

Patroni, Adrián. *Los trabajadores en Argentina*. Buenos Aires, 1897.

Perelstein, Berta. *Positivismo y antipositivismo en la Argentina*. Buenos
Aires: Procyon, 1952.

Penna, José, and Horacio Madero. *La administración sanitaria y asistencia
pública en la ciudad de Buenos Aires*. 2 vols. Buenos Aires: Guillermo
Kraft, 1910.

Primer congreso femenino internacional de la república Argentina. Buenos
Aires: A. Ceppi, 1911.

Prins, Enrique. "Sobre la prostitución en Buenos Aires." *Archivos de
Psiquiatría, Criminología y Ciencias Afines* 2, 12 (December 1903):
722–30.

"El problema de la prostitución." *Archivos de la Secretaría de Salud Pública*
4, 5 (November 1948): 415–21.

Puccia, Enrique Horacio. *El Buenos Aires de Angel G. Villoldo (1860 . . .
1919)*. Buenos Aires, 1976.

Puente, José J. *El Día Médico* 5, 4 (1932): 97.

Quinta Conferencia Sanitaria Internacional Americana. *Higiene y asistencia
pública en Chile*. Santiago: Barcelona, 1911.

Rama, Angel. *La ciudad letrada*. Hanover, N.H.: Ediciones del Norte,
1984.

Ramos Mejía, José María. *Las multitudes argentina: Estudio de psicología
colectiva para servir de introducción al libro "Rosas y su tiempo."* Revised
edition with an introduction by A. Bonilla y San Martin. Buenos
Aires: J. Lajouane, 1912.

Repetto, Nicolás. *Mi paso por la política: De Roca a Yrigoyen*. Buenos
Aires: Santiago Rueda, 1956.

*Report of the Seventh International Congress for the Suppression of Traffic in
Women and Children, June 29, 1927*.

Report of the Sixth International Congress for the Suppression of Traffic in Women and Children Held in Graz (Austria) on September 18, 19, and 20, 1924. Geneva, 1924.

"Resultado de la ley en los años que lleva de aplicación." In *Administración sanitaria y asistencia social en Rosario: La ley 12.331. Resultados de su aplicación en Rosario.* Rosario, 1942.

Revilla, Enrique. "El ejercicio de la prostitución en Buenos Aires: Proyecto de Ordenanza elevado a la intendencia municipal." *Archivos de Psiquiatría, Criminología y Ciencias Afines* 2, 1 (January 1903): 74–80.

Rock, David. *Politics in Argentina, 1890–1930: The Rise and Fall of Radicalism.* London: Cambridge University Press, 1975.

Rodríguez, Fermín. "Influencia del estado civil sobre el suicidio." *Archivos de Psiquiatría, Criminología y Ciencias Afines* 4 (July–August 1905): 385–404.

Romay, Francisco L. *Historia de la policía federal argentina.* Vol. 5. Buenos Aires: Biblioteca Policial, 1966.

Rosario de Santa Fe. *Anuario estadístico de la provincia de Santa Fe.* Rosario, 1912.

――――. "La Ley 12.331: Resultados de su aplicación en Rosario." *Administración Sanitaria y Asistencia Social de Rosario.* Rosario, [1942].

――――. *Segundo censo municipal de la ciudad del Rosario de Santa Fe.* Rosario: La Capital, 1908.

――――. *Tercer censo municipal del Rosario de Santa Fe levantado el 26 de abril de 1910.* Rosario: República, 1910.

Rosario Municipality. *Memoria del consejo ejecutor municipal presentada al consejo deliberante en diciembre 1881.* Rosario: El Independiente, 1882.

Rosen, Ruth. *The Lost Sisterhood: Prostitution in America, 1900–1918.* Baltimore: Johns Hopkins University Press, 1982.

Rosés Lacoigne, Enrique. *La verdad sobre la prostitución en la ciudad de Buenos Aires.* Buenos Aires, 1924.

Rossiaud, Jacques. *Medieval Prostitution.* Trans. Lydia G. Cochrane. London: Basil Blackwell, 1988.

Sáenz Quesada, María. *El estado rebelde: Buenos Aires entre 1850/1860.* Buenos Aires: Belgrano, 1982.

Sampay, Arturo Enrique, comp. *Las constituciones de la Argentina (1810–1972).* Buenos Aires: EUDEBA, 1975.

Sarlo, Beatriz. *El imperio de los sentimientos: Narraciones de circulación periódica en Argentina (1917–1927).* Buenos Aires: Catálogos, 1985.

_____. *Una modernidad periférica: Buenos Aires 1920 y 1930*. Buenos Aires: Nueva Visión, 1988.

Satanowsky, Isidro. *La obra cinematográfica frente al derecho*. 4 vols. Buenos Aires: Ediar, 1955.

Scobie, James R. *Buenos Aires: Plaza to Suburb, 1870–1910*. New York: Oxford University Press, 1974.

_____. *Revolution on the Pampas: A Social History of Argentine Wheat, 1860–1910*. Austin: University of Texas Press, 1964.

Scott, Joan W. "Gender: A Useful Category of Historical Analysis." *American Historical Review* 91, 5 (December 1986): 1053–75.

Scroggins, Daniel C. *Las aguafuertes porteñas de Roberto Arlt*. Buenos Aires: Ediciones Culturales Argentinas, 1981.

Sebreli, Juan José. *Buenos Aires: Vida cotidiana y alienación*. 15th ed. Buenos Aires: Siglo XX, 1979.

_____. *Fútbol y masas*. Buenos Aires: Galerna, 1981.

Sicardi, Francisco A. *Horas de evolución: La República Argentina y su desenvolvimiento*. Buenos Aires: Jesús Menéndez, 1938.

_____. *Libro extraño*. Buenos Aires, 1904.

_____. "La vida del delito y de la prostitución: Impresiones médico-literarias." *Archivos de Psiquiatría, Criminología y Ciencias Afines* 2, 1 (January 1903): 11–21.

Signorelli, Vicente M. "La mujer y la prostitución." *Revista de Policía y Criminalística* 2, 12–13 (1938): 52–53.

Silvestre, Carlos. "Interpretación de la ley 12.331: Prestación de servicios gratuitos de profilaxis venérea. Su obligación en los establecimientos fabriles." *Gaceta Textil*, June 1939, p. 11.

Slatta, Richard W. *Gauchos and the Vanishing Frontier*. Lincoln: University of Nebraska Press, 1983.

Smith-Rosenberg, Carroll. *Disorderly Conduct: Visions of Gender in Victorian America*. New York: Alfred A. Knopf, 1985.

Sofer, Eugene Franklin. "From Pale to Pampa: Eastern European Jewish Social Mobility in Gran Buenos Aires, 1890–1945." Ph.D. diss., University of California, Los Angeles, 1976.

Solari, Enrique Félix. "Lucha antivenérea." *La Semana Médica* 34, 48 (December 1, 1927): 1531–36.

Solari, Juan Antonio. *José Ingenieros en las jornadas fundadoras del partido Socialista*. Buenos Aires: La Vanguardia, 1976.

Soler, Ricaurte. *El positivismo argentino*. Buenos Aires: Paidós, 1968.

Sormani, J. "De la profilaxis de las enfermedades venéreas y especialmente de la sífilis." *Revista Médico-quirúrgica* 20 (1883–84): 95–99, 148–52, 160–85.

Sosa de Newton, Lily. *Las argentinas de ayer a hoy.* Buenos Aires: L. V. Zanetti, 1967.

———. *Diccionario biográfico de mujeres argentinas.* Buenos Aires, 1972.

Sternbach, Nancy. "The Death of a Beautiful Woman: The Femme Fatale in the Spanish-American *Modernista Novel.*" Ph.D. diss., University of Arizona, 1984.

Suárez-Orozco, Marcelo Mario. "A Study of Argentine Soccer: The Dynamics of Its Fans and Their Folklore." *Journal of Psychoanalytic Anthropology* 3, 1 (Winter 1982): 7–28.

Suriano, Juan. *La huelga de inquilinos de 1907.* Buenos Aires: Centro Editor de América Latina, 1983.

Susini, Telémaco. "La nueva ordenanza sobre prostitución." *Anales del Departamento Nacional de Higiene* 11, 1 (January 1904): 6–15, 55–72, 106–21, 150–61.

Symanski, Richard. *The Immoral Landscape: Female Prostitution in Western Societies.* Toronto: Butterworths, 1981.

Szuchman, Mark D. "Continuity and Conflict in Buenos Aires: Comments on the Historical City." In *Buenos Aires: Four Hundred Years,* ed. Stanley R. Ross and Thomas F. McGann. Austin: University of Texas Press, 1982.

———. "Disorder and Social Control in Buenos Aires, 1810–1860." *Journal of Interdisciplinary History* 15, 1 (Summer 1984): 83–110.

Tallon, José Sebastian. *El tango en sus etapas de música prohibida.* 2d ed. Buenos Aires: Instituto Amigos del Libro Argentino, 1964.

Tamarin, David. *The Argentine Labor Movement, 1930–1945: A Study of the Origins of Peronism.* Albuquerque: University of New Mexico Press, 1985.

Tamini, Luis. "Reglamentación de las casas de prostitución." *Revista Médico-quirúrgica* 6, 8 (1869): 132–39.

Tarnowsky, Pauline. *Etude anthropométrique sur les prostitués et les voleuses.* Paris, 1869.

Taylor, Julie M. "Tango: Theme of Class and Nation." *Ethnomusicology* 20, 2 (May 1976): 273–92.

Tiempo, César. *Clara Beter y otras fatamorganas.* Buenos Aires: Peña Lillo, 1974.

Unsain, Alejandro. "El trabajo a domicilio en Buenos Aires." *Boletín del Departamento Nacional del Trabajo* 25 (December 31, 1913): 896–917.

Vazeilles, José. *Los Socialistas.* Buenos Aires: Jorge Alvarez, 1967.

Vezzetti, Hugo. *La locura en la Argentina.* Buenos Aires: Folios, 1983.

Vilariño, Idea. *Las letras del tango.* Buenos Aires: Schapire, 1965.

Villarroel, Luis F. *Tango, folklore de Buenos Aires.* Buenos Aires: IDEAGRAF, 1957.

Wainerman, Catalina H., and Marysa Navarro. *El trabajo de la mujer en la Argentina: Un análisis preliminar de las ideas dominantes en las primeras décadas del siglo XX.* Cuadernos del CENEP 7. Buenos Aires: CENEP, 1979.

Waisman, Carlos H. *Reversal of Development in Argentina: Postwar Counterrevolutionary Policies and Their Structural Consequences.* Princeton: Princeton University Press, 1987.

Walkowitz, Judith R. *Prostitution and Victorian Society: Women, Class and the State.* Cambridge: Cambridge University Press, 1980.

Walter, Richard J. *The Socialist Party of Argentina, 1890–1930.* Austin: University of Texas Press, 1977.

Weeks, Jeffrey. *Sex, Politics and Society: The Regulation of Sexuality since 1800.* New York: Longman Group, 1981.

Women in a Changing World: The Dynamic Story of the International Council of Women since 1888. London: Routledge and Kegan Paul, 1966.

Yuval-Davies, Nira, and Flora Anthias. *Woman—Nation—State.* London: Macmillan, 1989.

Zea, Leopoldo. *The Latin American Mind.* Trans. James H. Abbott and Lowell Dunham. Norman: University of Oklahoma Press, 1963.

Zinni, Héctor Nicolás. *La Mafia en Argentina.* Rosario: Centro Editorial, 1975.

_____. *El Rosario de las satanás: Historia triste de la mala vida.* Rosario: Centauro, 1980.

Index

Printed in the United States
66547LVS00003B/142